BELLA CHAGALL

First
Encounter

ILLUSTRATIONS BY
MARC CHAGALL

TRANSLATED BY
BARBARA BRAY

SCHOCKEN BOOKS
NEW YORK

First published by Schocken Books 1983
10 9 8 7 6 5 4 3 2 1   83 84 85 86

Jacket illustration copyright © 1973 by Marc Chagall

Burning Lights
Original Yiddish text copyright © 1945 by Ida Chagall
English translation copyright © 1983 by Ida Chagall
Illustrations copyright © 1945–1973 by Marc Chagall

First Encounter
Original Yiddish text and German version copyright © 1947 by Ida Chagall
English translation copyright © 1983 by Ida Chagall
Illustrations copyright © 1945–1973 by Marc Chagall

Translated from the French *Lumières Allumées* copyright © Ida Chagall
and Editions Gallimard 1973 for the French translation

Library of Congress Cataloging in Publication Data

Chagall, Bella, 1895–1944.
First encounter.
Translation of Lumières allumées, which was itself
a translation from the Yiddish Brenendike licht.
1. Chagall, Bella, 1895–1944. 2. Jews—
Byelorussian S.S.R.—Vitebsk—Biography. 3. Jews—
Byelorussian S.S.R.—Vitebsk—Social life and customs.
4. Vitebsk (Byelorussian S.S.R.)—Biography.
5. Chagall, Marc, 1887–   . 6. Artists—France—
Biography. 7. Wives—Byelorussian S.S.R.—Vitebsk—
Biography. I. Title.
DS135.R95C4713   1983   947'.656 [B]   80–6189

Manufactured in the United States of America
ISBN 0–8052–3768–2

CONTENTS

Burning Lights

First Encounter

From My Notebooks

BURNING LIGHTS

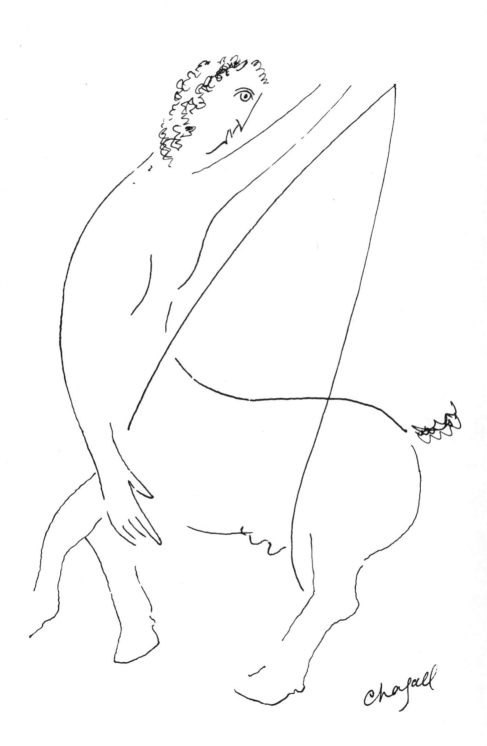

Heritage

Strange, but I suddenly want to write. And to write in my faltering mother tongue, which I've hardly used since I left my parents' house.

Far away as my childhood has drifted, it now comes back closer and closer, till I can almost feel its breath.

I can see myself quite clearly: a plump little thing, rushing through the house from room to room, hiding on the broad windowsills, knees drawn up, curled in a ball like some small animal.

Father, Mother, the two grandmothers, my handsome grandfather, our own family and others, weddings and funerals, rich and poor, our streets, our gardens—they all float before my eyes like the deep waters of our river, the Dvina.

My parents' house no longer exists. Everything, everyone is dead or gone.

My father—may he intercede in heaven for us all!—is dead. My mother—God only knows if she's still alive—is in a profane city among strangers. The children are scattered in this world and the next. But each carries with him, as a part of our lost heritage, like a piece of our father's shroud, the breath of home.

I unfold my portion of the legacy, and there at once are the smells of the old house. My ears start to ring with the din of the shop, with the lilting chant of the rabbi on holy days. From every corner comes a shade which, as soon as I touch it, draws me into a dance with other shades. They circle around me, brush my shoulders, snatch at my hands and feet, then all swoop down at once like a swarm of flies on a summer's day. I can't escape.

And I want to save from the darkness one day, one hour, one moment of the old home.

But much as I long to rescue my memories and not let them be blotted out forever, with me, how can one bring such moments back, how conjure a scrap of life out of withered remains?

Then I remember how you, dear friend, often used to ask me to tell you about my life before you knew me.

So I write for you. Our town is even dearer to you than to me, and you with your great heart will understand what I haven't been able to say.

The one thing that worries me is whether my little girl, who spent only the first year of her life in my parents' house, will understand. I dare to hope so.

Saint-Dié, France, 1939

The Courtyard

After the midday meal the house was deserted. Everyone was out. A great big house and nobody in it. You could easily have let in the goat from the yard or the chickens from the hen run.

Only from the kitchen came the clatter of dishes.

"Have you swept the dining room?"

The voice propelled Sasha out of the kitchen, bearing a long-handled broom.

"What are you doing in here?"

"Nothing," said I.

"Well, clear out. I have to sweep up."

"Who's stopping you? Sweep!"

She swept the floor, and together with the crumbs cleared away the last warm echoes of voices. The dining room grew chill.

The walls looked suddenly old, the wallpaper faded. The empty table stood useless in the middle of the room. I felt useless too.

Where could I go?

I wandered around the house and came to the bedroom. My parents' narrow beds looked forbidding. But who wanted to lie down in broad daylight anyway?

The glittering metal seemed to threaten; the big brass knobs and the bars at head and foot stood like sentries. I went nearer, and the brass discharged a volley of brightness. When I looked into the knobs, my face was all twisted, my nose squashed flat. I fled, and bumped into a closed door.

I'd completely forgotten there was a parlor. The door was always shut. I was rather scared of the place. When my brother got married, the old Viennese chairs had been replaced—to please his in-laws—with new upholstered ones, and the room had become as strange as if it were no longer part of the house.

It was dark in there. A thick moss of green plush covered the sofa. As soon as anyone—even the cat—sat on it, the springs groaned as if they were ill and couldn't bear to be touched. The carpet was lawn green, and the pattern of roses in the middle warned you not to set even the shadow of a foot on the grass. Even the tall, narrow mirror was green from reflecting the green furniture day and night.

An old palm withered away with melancholy alone in the green gloom. With the windows always shut and the curtains drawn, it never saw the sun. Instead it basked in the reflections of two bronze candlesticks on tall stands, their branches holding short white candles that were never lit.

From the ceiling hung a chandelier, also of bronze, alive only in the quivering of its little crystal drops. At night the palm must have thought the lamp was a planet and the crystal drops stars, all shining for it. The palm must have been stronger than bronze itself to hold out day after day, month after month, year after year.

No one stayed in the parlor for long. They hurried through as if it were a bridge from one room to another. Only Father use to pray there in the morning with his prayer shawl and phylacteries. He probably felt as if he were praying out in a field. When he went in there during the day to look up some religious text, he didn't even glance around.

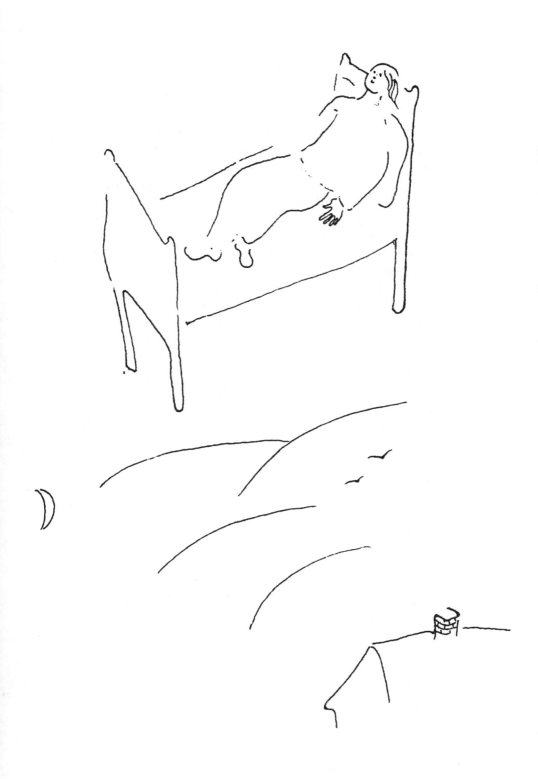

The bookcase was the only old piece of furniture left in the parlor. It had always been there, in a corner by the door. It was probably too heavy to move. There it stood, absorbed in its books, with no connection between it and the bustle of the rest of the house.

I went up to it as to some elderly aunt. When I touched it the short legs groaned, as if it was all they could do to bear its weight.

I peered through the glass doors: one row of shelves above the other, each a little synagogue in itself. There, wedged together with their backs to the glass, stood long rows of Talmud volumes, thin and tall in their hard black covers, like old Jews lined up by a wall to recite the Prayer of Benedictions. On another shelf were fat Bibles and prayer books for the yearly cycle of services. And on others again were piles of prayer books for women—in Yiddish, not Hebrew—so many that you could almost hear the murmur. As I looked I could tell they were angry with me.

I ran away, and as I did they called after me just as my grandfather used to scold my mother. Why was I being taught Russian? Why didn't they get someone to teach me Yiddish instead?

Oh, that reminded me: my little rebbe would soon be here. I used to fall asleep as he tried to teach me the alphabet. I must hide.

"Bashenka!"

Sasha tried to stop me.

"Where are you tearing off to?"

"None of your business! Nowhere!"

The back landing was metal, the strips so thin and wide apart my heels got caught in the spaces.

The house was tall, and in the courtyard flights of steps led up and down, handrails like chains holding them up. The top flight led to an attic with a skylight where the photographer lived. The bottom flight ended almost in the middle of the yard.

Under the lowest steps was my own special corner. Here I had my shop. Here my mudpies were set out to dry. Here stood my old sardine cans full of flour and oats and pebbles and bits of broken china and colored glass—all the scraps I picked up in the yard and saved from being trodden underfoot.

The yard was small and square, cramped between the high walls, but it held a whole world. The sun never reached right down into it, but a patch of sky gleamed overhead and sometimes the walls sent down jets of light. All around were the doors and windows of the Hotel Brozi. Every window belonged to a separate room, and from each a different head popped out every day. Whenever new guests arrived, they would draw the curtains.

"See, miss? Some new people have come."

The baker, who'd come out into the yard to cool off, pointed at a pair of curtains.

"They're probably just off the train and needing a rest. So mind you don't make any noise." He took a quick gulp of fresh air and hurried back to his lair.

Me, make noise?

I'd have liked to ask some questions, but he was gone. Perhaps he could have told me why the people were tired. It was the train that had done the traveling.

The old baker knew I was scared of him, with his floury face and apron and tall white cap.

Me, make a noise? Wasn't I just sitting quietly on the steps? There was plenty of noise in the yard without me. The hotel staff kept running in and out like mice. As fast as one came, another went; as fast as one emptied something, another filled it up. Old women came in off the street to sell eggs and chickens and cream. Pandemonium.

The hens cackled, the cat got under people's feet, the dog rushed up with tongue lolling out and tail wagging, and a cock, terrified, tried to struggle from its owner's grasp. The cat fled into a corner. The dog pranced all around the yard sniffing at everything like a steward making an inspection. The various servants fell over one another and cursed.

"Buy this fine cockerel!" cried an old peasant woman.

"To the devil with you and your rooster! It's older than Abraham's father!"

"What? May my hands and feet drop off if I tell a lie!"

"Be off, you old witch! Do you hear? Out!"

Both the little old woman and her cockerel fell silent. She waited. Perhaps the man's anger would pass. Look, now he was going on at someone else.

"What the hell are you doing? You've rolled the barrel right in the mud!"

"Eh? What? You must be drunk! Loudmouth! Picking on everybody like that! Just you wait . . ."

"Hey, Piotr, Stepan!" someone yelled from the kitchen. "The devil take the pair of you! Have you peeled the spuds? The cook's waiting . . ."

The two boys rushed back indoors, the old woman at their heels.

"Piotr, take the cock and show it to them in the kitchen. Just roast it and you'll see—you'll be licking your fingers!"

No one listened. In vain she begged her heart out. Sadly she bowed her head and put the bird back in its basket.

"Gla-a-sha, where are you?" A cry from a window, long drawn out like a whistle. "Gla-a-sha! Hurry, the lady in Number One's ringing for you."

Only the hotel laundresses, ironing by the open window, didn't bicker. They sang as if the steam from the irons warmed their hearts. Sometimes it sounded as though they were sobbing. Their sad strain stretched out endlessly, like the piles of linen awaiting them.

Now the landlord's two daughters ran out into the yard, squealing with laughter. I started to run toward them but drew back: their mouths seemed to be dripping with gore. But no, they were only munching boiled crayfish.

"What are you doing? Ugh!" It looked as if they were eating live mice.

"Ivan," they both shouted toward the stable door, "bring the horses. We're going out."

Two great horses whinnied from within by way of answer.

Their sturdy black cruppers gleamed; little tears of sweat ran down their necks. They steamed, tossed their manes, and blindly sought the bag of oats the coachman had hung on the wall. Then they buried their muzzles in it and seemed to go to sleep. Only their long necks quivered.

The coachman's hair and boots were as well oiled as his horses, as he stood and stroked them.

"Ivan," I asked, "haven't you just come back from town?"

"Work's one thing and play's another. Isn't that right, boy?" He gave one of the horses a rap on the flank.

Both beasts raised an eye out of the nosebag and glared at him. Why couldn't they be left to eat in peace? They vented their wrath on the flies, swishing their tails.

They were heated with motion and found it hard to keep still. They bent and stretched their knees; they pawed the ground. Not long ago they'd been driving through the town with flashing eyes and twinkling hooves, leaving street after street behind them. And here in the stable their every movement jangled the heavy iron chains that tied them to the beams.

"Prrrh!" They whinnied as they ate, and from her byre the cow replied.

I felt I had to rush over to her. The stable was open and the horses had fresh air. But the cow was shut up like a thief in jail.

A fine red cow, and people were ashamed of her! Her stall was dark and dirty, tucked away in a corner of the yard by the garbage cans. The walls were so thin the wind blew through, and the rain came in through the cracks. A large hole in the door was all the cow had for a window, and it was through this I gazed at her.

She lay there wearily, buried in dirty straw, tormented by flies but unmoving, as if she herself were only a heap of garbage. Was she really so lazy? She heard the flies buzzing, and from time to time sleepily flicked her long, thin, mud-stiffened tail and drove them off. Only her head seemed alive. Now she would prick up one ear, now let the other flop down. She heard every sound in the yard, and quietly, sadly, chewed over each one. Her mouth slavered. Tears trickled from the corners of her eyes and along her nostrils.

I couldn't bear to meet her glance. It weighed on my heart like a stone, as if it were I who'd shut her away.

"Moo," I called through the hole.

"Moo," she answered slowly but with a cheerful look, glad I had remembered her.

But she knew I couldn't open the door and set her free.

Sadly she let her head droop again, and lay there till milking time. Then, as soon as she scented the bran and hot water, she slowly heaved herself up—belly, legs, and udder—and moved over to the door. There she waited, listening to every sound, hearing Sasha throw big chunks of long-leafed beets, potatoes, and cooked carrots into the trough, then adding hot water and stirring the mixture so that it wouldn't scald. Her tongue hung out, she butted her horns against the door, and as soon as Sasha opened the shed she made a rush, stamping her hooves and scattering bits of dried mud from her sides. Through the yard she charged, head down, looking at no one, angry with the whole world. As she passed the carriage in the middle of the yard, she gave it a thump. Perhaps she was getting her own back on the horses for being made more fuss over than she was.

She plunged her head in the trough up to the neck, drinking the water and chewing the vegetables. Food ran from her muzzle as her jaws worked, and her belly swelled up like a bellows. At last, still hungry, she licked avidly around the empty trough.

Then Sasha came up and gave her a smack on the belly. The warm touch surprised her, and she let herself be milked.

"Wait, Bashenka," called Sasha," you're supposed to have a glass of fresh milk."

Sasha knew I couldn't bear the sound of the teats squirting foaming milk into the pail. And it always seemed to me to smell of sweat.

"No, Sasha, I haven't got time! The teacher's coming for my lesson—"

"Just a mouthful . . ."

"Tomorrow!"

And I laughed and ran away.

The Bath

The Sabbath began for me on Thursday evening.

Mother would hurry out of the shop as if tearing herself away by force from the noise of the week. A voice would call, "Bashenka, where are you? We're going to the bath. Sasha, are the clothes ready? Quick, I haven't much time!"

The maid wrapped the clothes up so tight that they almost burst out of the paper, got me into my coat and galoshes, and fastened my hood so that I could hardly breathe.

"Don't cry, silly," she said, drying my tears. "It's freezing outside, and all I need is for you to catch cold, God forbid."

Mother and I slipped furtively out the front door as if it were Saturday already and the shop were closed. Mother would have been embarrassed to go through the shop with the clothes under her arm, even though they were wrapped up in a parcel. There were still a lot of men in the shop, and who knows, someone might have kept her talking. We had to hurry; she'd already waited till the last minute.

The sleigh that was to take us to the bath was waiting out in the street. The driver—always the same one, from the rank opposite the house—knew Mother went to the bathhouse at the same time every Thursday evening.

As soon as we got outside, the cold, snowy evening enveloped us in a damp shawl. In the sleigh, under the worn fur rugs, I could feel from the hand Mother held me with—God forbid I should fall out!—that she'd already forgotten the noise and bustle of the shop and was flying along with the sleigh toward another, purer air. She seemed astir already with the prayers that would, God willing, be recited this Sabbath eve.

We hadn't far to go. The driver took us by a short cut to the dark bank of a little river, the Vitba, where the Jewish bathhouse stood. The sleigh cut through the tingling air. Lights blinked down at us from the higher bank on the other side— the lights of Padlo, the little market square.

I knew the market well. I knew the stall-holders, the stalls, and best of all the dairy in the cellar. Before going down the stone steps into it you had to pray to God, the stairs were so wet and slippery. It was as cold as a tomb. The gray walls oozed water. One tiny lamp with a smoky glass lit the whole place, its feeble rays scarcely reaching the blocks of yellow butter and the big bowl of cream, still less the corner from which the hard Gomel cheeses, like babies' heads, emerged.

Only the tall scales were clearly visible. They hung like a throne in the middle of the cellar, their chains swinging like long, dark tresses and the two copper pans bearing up some poor bits of food as solemnly as if they were weighing out Justice itself.

The dairywomen hastened to and fro in their long, rough, greasy skirts. With mittened fingers they snatched off lumps of butter, filled jugs with milk, and tossed one another bits of white cheese like snowballs. And all the time they shrieked as if they were being cudgeled. Probably they did it to keep warm. Every so often an insult would sound through the clammy room, and oaths would fly like fiery darts from one counter to another.

"The plague take you! Your goods stink!"

"Curses on my head if I lie!"

The women squealed like mice in their holes, their rough words making them glow with anger like the cauldrons outside, around which other women wrapped in long shawls sat selling roasted beans.

They abused each other with such verve it was almost exhilarating.

All these cries came to us in the distance as we drove to the bath. One curse drifted to us on the wind, hung in the air, was borne down and buried by the snow. We had arrived.

"Come back for us, God willing, in a couple of hours," said Mother to the driver, though he'd known the routine for years.

At the entrance sat the woman who sold tickets, all muffled up like a bale of cloth. At first she didn't move; the end of her nose and her fingertips were all we could see of her. On the table by the tickets lay some frozen apples and pears. A drop of blue kvass, no doubt blue with cold, sparkled in a bottle.

Slowly, as if our breath were thawing her, the ticket-seller opened her icy lips and gave us a chilly smile.

"You get frozen stiff sitting still all day," she said, melting gradually. "The wind's blowing in all directions. You could petrify waiting here for a human being to come along."

Mother gave her a friendly smile and bought me an apple.

We went through a little door into the bathhouse. The sound of the latch roused two or three women lying naked on the benches, covered by their shawls. They buzzed around like flies.

"Good evening, Alteshka, good evening. You're late. How are you, Alta? All the children well? And how are you, Bashenka?" They prodded me from all sides.

"Really—no evil eye!—you're shooting up like a loaf in front of the fire."

They were pleased not to have waited in vain. Their dark shawls fell away from them like wings, and I was dazzled by their white bodies. Everything grew brighter, clearer.

In this warm anteroom where the muggy air mixed with the cold draft from outside, I scarcely recognized the bath attendants, although they were always the same. Every Thursday they seemed older and uglier.

16

The youngest of them, who still smelled of her musty shawl, grabbed me in her bony hands.

"Cold, isn't it? So undo your dress quickly and into the box with it. Do you have another with you? Come on, best foot forward!" She talked to me as if I were a horse.

Before I could look around, my boots were off and flying with my rolled-up stockings into the black chest I'd been perched on. I was lifted up and down with the lid so fast I couldn't see what went on in the dark pit in which my clothes were flung.

The wind blew through the chinks in the frost-flowered, snow-silted windows. My teeth chattered, and the woman wrapped me up in a towel.

"It won't be long before you're nice and warm. Now for the bath."

I was dazed. She dragged me to the door like a hen due for slaughter, her hands like iron pincers.

"Mind you don't fall, Bashenka. It's slippery."

As soon as I got through the door I found I was unable to breathe. Half-fainting, I just let myself be hauled along. I could hardly see a thing through the hot steam. A tin lamp hung from a hook over the door, its tiny glass loose in the frame so that it rattled and flickered every time the door opened or shut.

I stood still, too frightened to move. The floor was wet and slithery. Water dripped down my legs and down from the ceiling and walls. The whole room was sweating.

The woman sluiced the bench with a bucket of water for me to sit down. She hadn't time to talk. Her thin, glistening spine twisted and turned like a cat's tail.

Not far off, buckets of boiling water breathed their scalding mist into my face.

But the warmth of the bench was reassuring, and I sat and dangled my feet in a tub of tepid water. The woman approached. Her breasts hung before my eyes like deflated balloons, her drumlike belly squashed my nose. There I was, trapped between the buckets and the woman, unable even to turn around.

Rough fingers seized my long hair. The woman grabbed a

bar of soap and began to scrub my head, rubbing the soap back and forth as if she were ironing. The wet locks fell all around me. I was dizzy, but I swallowed my tears and saved my energy to wipe away the lather stinging my eyes. It went into my ears and mouth as well. Blindly I dipped my fingers into a nearby tub of cold water and wiped the soap away as best I could, but I didn't really regain consciousness until my hair was rinsed. Then soft, clear water ran soothingly into my eyes, and I breathed, straightened up, and looked about me.

I heard the door creak, and there on the threshold stood Mother, white and naked.

She was swallowed up at once in a cloud of warm steam. Two women attended her, one on either side. Drops of sweat hung from their sagging breasts and bellies. Little streams of water trickled from the hair tucked behind their ears.

Mother stood shy and silent by the door. The two attendants rushed over to the buckets, turned the taps full on, and scoured the bench appointed for her to sit on.

Mother sat meekly down, her ample body occupying the whole seat. I was so exhausted with all the washing and rubbing I could scarcely see her, but she felt embarrassed in my presence and cast down her eyes, even though I was only looking at her hair. Instead of the usual thick, curly wig, I could see her own thin locks. Stifled for years under the heavy wig, unable to breathe, they had gradually dwindled. I felt sad, all the strength suddenly drained out of me, and I offered no resistance when the washing started up again.

It was as if the attendant laid hold of my soul at the same time as my body. She set me down on the bench like a lump of dough and began kneading and pinching. I turned over onto my stomach, and she gave me such a slap on the behind I almost jumped up.

"What do you say, Bashenka? It's doing you good, eh?"

She'd suddenly found her tongue.

"Look how red you are! It's a real pleasure to pinch you."

It was torture, but I could only wait for her to finish. Then suddenly came a shock. A torrent descended over my shoulders. I vanished beneath it, then felt myself borne up

and swept along as if by a river. It was the woman dousing me, and now I felt warm and cozy and melting like wax.

"Phew," the woman sighed with relief and wiped her nose with her wet hand. "You're shining like a diamond now, Bashenka, bless you."

She gazed at me out of glassy, washed-out eyes, then briskly wrapped me up in a warm towel. She'd probably have liked to dry herself a bit. Instead she slowly encircled me with both arms, as if I were her white Sabbath candles and she were blessing them.

I looked across to see what was happening to Mother. Of course she'd been soaped and rubbed too, and no doubt had enjoyed the warm shower as much as I had. But she didn't get let off so lightly.

When the ablutions were over, the oldest attendant brought a low stool and sat at Mother's feet. She put a brass candlestick on a little box, lit the candle, fanned the flame, and started to tell Mother about her hard life. Her back was bowed, her head bent toward Mother's feet, weighed down by all her woes.

"May the Lord pity us and deliver us from all evil," she said, looking upward. "Amen."

Then as if to forget her sorrows she addressed herself to Mother's toenails. With every prayer she murmured before she trimmed another, the candle flame seemed to burn brighter and drive away some of the darkness from her heart. Mother watched what she did to her feet, and listened patiently to what she said. There beyond the candle they both seemed isolated in a bright halo from the gloom of the rest of the room. Their two white faces shone out, as if purified for sacrifice.

When Mother's toes were all nice and shiny, the old woman raised her head and said in a low voice, "Now the ritual bath, Alta."

Mother caught her breath as though the old woman had told her a secret. Slowly both of them stood, straightened up, and inhaled deeply, as if about to enter the holy of holies. Their pale forms vanished into the darkness.

I was afraid to follow them. You had to go through a hot room where tortured spirits lay suffering on long benches, scourged with birch twigs, glistening with water, and groaning as if roasting on red-hot coals. The heat went in through my mouth and gripped my heart.

"It must be a hell for people who've committed a great many sins," I thought. And with that I rushed after Mother anyway.

I found myself in a room as dark as a jail.

The old woman stood on a little jetty holding a candle and a linen bath sheet. Mother—I was so afraid for her—went calmly down the slippery steps and into the water up to her neck.

As the old woman uttered a blessing, Mother flinched like a condemned man, shut her eyes, held her nose, and ducked right under as if, God forbid, forever.

"Ko-o-osher!" cried the old woman in prophetic tones.

I jumped as if thunderstruck, trembled, and waited. Surely a flash of lighting would descend from the black ceiling and slay us all. Or a flood pour from the stone walls and drown us.

'Ko-o-osher!" cried the old woman again.

Where was Mother? There was no sign of her.

Then suddenly the water seemed to open, and out came her head. She shook off the wet as if she'd just risen from the seabed. Three times the old woman shouted, and three times Mother sank into the black water. I could hardly wait for the old woman to stop calling out and for Mother to stop having to go under. She was tired, and water was coming from her mouth and ears. But now she was smiling. Delight streamed the length of her body. She emerged from the water—as if from a flame—clean and purified.

"Good health and long life, Alta!"

The old woman was smiling. She held the linen sheet up in her thin hands. Mother wrapped herself up as if in white wings, and she too smiled like an angel.

Dressed now, but still steaming from the heat, I waited for Mother and chewed at my apple, which by now had thawed.

No sooner had Mother rejoined me than she started to hurry me, as if she'd suddenly remembered it was a weekday

and the shop was still open. The sanctity and warmth of the bath fell away from her. She wanted to be off.

The women told her their latest troubles as they handed her her clothes, ending with her shoes. It was as if they were afraid she might leave them with their hearts only half unburdened till the following Thursday. With trembling hands they tied our discarded clothes up in a parcel; and they wrapped me up like a parcel too.

I was so bloated with the heat I could hardly move. Mother handed out tips and listened to the lengthy benedictions that followed us on our way.

"May it be a blessing to you, Alta. Goodbye till next Thursday, God willing. Get home safely! Keep well, Bashenka!"

Each vied with the other. They all huddled into their shawls.

The door seemed to open of its own accord, and we stood on the threshold for a moment. Heavens, it was cold! Snow was falling out of the somber sky. The flakes shone like stars. Was it day or night? I saw only glimmering white. I felt only cold.

The driver and his horse had turned into a mound of snow. Were they frozen?

"Good health!" grinned the man. His lips broke through his icy mustache, bits of snow dropped from his bushy brows. His little horse whinnied, eager to be off again.

"Get home safely!" came the cry from the bathhouse.

The sleigh set off.

"Hup! Hup!" cried the driver, flourishing the whip over his lean old nag.

When we got home, Mother rushed in even faster than she'd rushed out, and put down the parcel of clothes. The smells of the house and shop rose up to meet us.

"God knows what's been happening while I've been away!"

As if guilty of some neglect, she hastily rinsed her flushed face and hurried into the shop.

Now I was sorry the warm bath had ended so soon.

Sabbath

Right from the start, Friday was different from all other days.

Waffles and pastries were laid out for breakfast on the broad windowsill, together with a pyramid of tsibulnikis.

No cooked lunch was provided on Friday. Instead, everyone was given a tsibulnik. Like an oven full of red-hot coals, a tsibulnik was stuffed with fried onions. It was so big you could scarcely get your hand around it; when you bit into it, your jaws stuck. And the pastry needed a glass of cold milk to wash it down.

"Never mind," said Sasha, the maid. "You eat it. Plenty of time to get hungry between now and dinner."

The house was busy all day on the eve of the Sabbath. Early in the morning the onions had to be peeled and chopped. The kitchen was a hive of activity. Oven and stove were lit. Chaya cooked, baked, plucked chickens. The soft down stuck to her apron, clung to her hair, fluttered around her like so many tiny chicks. She grated a pile of onions on a little board until they were reduced to pulp. Her eyes streamed with tears, and

it seemed to me we all reeked of onions. The whole house was filled with different smells, each more piquant than the last.

A big fat fish flopped about in a bucket of water, gasping desperately through open gills. In a last spurt of energy it lashed out with its tail, overturned the pail, sent the water flying, then lay, jaws agape, on the floor. I was fascinated by its sharp fins. It was as if not just one fish but a whole catch had jumped out of the bucket, and they were all trying to snap at our feet.

Chaya stood over the outstretched carp like an executioner. Its scales glittered wetly. She got hold of it by the tail, then lifted it onto the chopping board. She took a knife and plunged it into the round belly. Blood spurted out, the fish burst open. Chaya ruthlessly cut it up in pieces and tore off the skin. Chopped onion and soaked bread filled it as with new blood. Each portion seemed almost alive, and jumped into the copper pan of its own volition. As they simmered, they turned first yellow, then reddish. The aroma wafted up my nostrils, bringing the first scent of the Sabbath.

Everyone was astir. My young brothers hurried with the rebbe, their teacher, to the bath. Sasha went to and fro in the dining room, scolding one of the boys for dawdling.

"Come on, you've had enough tea! I've got to polish the samovar—it'll soon be Sabbath."

"She won't let me have one more glass! Look at the female rabbi!"

Sasha, a Russian who'd worked in our house for years, was very strict about the dietary laws and watched over the Sabbath as if it were her own Sunday. Without more ado, she got hold of the heavy urn, picked up the tray and drip-bowl from the table, snatched the sugar bowl and spoon from my brother's grasp, and turned her back on him. Laden like an ass, she bore the whole lot off to the kitchen to be polished until they shone.

Chaya lumbered to meet her on her fat legs, carrying a board sprinkled with flour, and so long it looked like a plank from the floor. Two or three great golden hallahs, or Sabbath loaves, sat on it like queens, surrounded by smaller ones of nicely browned, braided dough. At the edge was a miniature loaf that Chaya had made for me out of a scrap of dough left over. All the loaves were fresh from the oven and glowed as if sunburned.

A sight to gladden Chaya's heart. She could hardly bear to part with them.

"God be praised and thanked! The Sabbath loaves have come out all right." She smiled happily.

Carefully she slid her works of art onto a towel spread out on the windowsill. She covered them up with another, as if to protect them from the evil eye. Having first been bloated by the heat, they now stifled in their own steam before finally cooling down.

Suddenly Father came into the room. He took out a pocketknife—what was Father doing with a pocketknife?—and spread out a sheet of paper. Then he sat down, put his hands on the table, and slowly began to trim his nails, producing crescent-shaped clippings. You could hear them falling on the paper. When he'd finished, he wrapped them up into a little parcel and dropped them into the stove, murmuring a prayer. After watching the parcel burn for a moment, he went back into the shop.

"Chaya, give me a bit of bread!" An old Jewish woman had appeared at the kitchen door. She was dressed in rags, with a tattered shawl over her head and another over her shoulders. Her wizened face was as crumpled as her clothes. From beneath the shawl that almost covered her low forehead hung tangled gray wisps, like dusty flocks of wool. Only her eyes sparkled out of all that dimness, the last glow in a heap of ashes.

The beggarwoman stood there in the doorway, blocking the light from outside. She knew she was late, and was afraid of the cook. I could hear her apprehensive breathing.

Chaya, busy around the oven, suddenly sniffed: she'd caught a whiff of the sharp, musty smell emanating from the beggar.

"Oh, there you are, are you? Woken up at last, eh?" she cried. "My God, another of you! How's anyone to cope with you all? What's today, then—the New Year? All the poor in the town come here."

27

The beggarwoman stood with her head guiltily bowed.

But already Chaya sounded a bit more friendly.

"Couldn't you have come earlier? It'll soon be time to bless the candles. . . . Oh, well! Here, catch! It'll be stale before the third meal of the Sabbath anyway. . . ."

Grumbling, Chaya stuffed half a loaf into the beggar's dress.

"You know," I whispered to the old woman surreptitiously, "one of our assistants is giving out alms at the door of the shop."

She gave me a sharp look. She'd probably been there already. She visited us every Friday. She slipped silently away.

Sasha snatched up a pail of water as if the floor must be washed after the old woman had stood on it. First she went into the dining room and kicked off her worn slippers, then she came and stood barefoot in the middle of the kitchen. A glance this way and that, and she hitched up her petticoats one after another, propping them on her stomach. Then she grabbed the wet cloth and attacked the boards. Water slopped out of the pail and streamed from the cloth, and Sasha's white feet were flecked with wet dust.

"Sasha, wait! It's like a river. Let me climb on your back and be ferried across!"

"Are you mad?" cried Sasha. "Get off at once! Careful, you'll make it all dirty again. Now stop it or I'll smack your bottom. Ow, don't tickle—you're scratching me, you little cat!"

All of a sudden she straightened up and I fell off her back onto the wet floor.

"Serves you right! Come along now and help me set the table. It'll soon be dark."

We opened up the big table and put in the extra leaves. That made it so long you couldn't reach both ends even with arms outstretched. A glossy white damask cloth was spread rustling over it. The table legs disappeared under the folds, which fell to the ground like a train.

Sasha chased me out, then called me back. "Bashenka, come and put the napkins out."

". . . There are still some left. What shall I do with them?"

"Put one where your father sits."

I went to my father's place and laid a napkin over the Sabbath loaf like someone veiling a bride.

Mother's five-branched silver candlestick already stood at the other end of the table. Two extra candles had been set out beside it, no doubt to make a lucky number. Each of the seven holders held a tall white candle. Compared with Mother's, my own silver candle-holder was small and insignificant. Father had given it to me. It was chased in a fine spider's-web pattern, and had a little cup to catch the drops of wax.

The table stood like a white dream palace, so still it seemed to be waiting for something. Suddenly the edges of the cloth began to stir. I could hear a sound in the distance: the iron shutter of the shop was being rolled down; the bolts grated in the sockets. Thank goodness, they were shutting at last! You could hear the voices of the assistants, anxious to get home.

"Don't stop to do any more or you'll miss the tram." Mother was hurrying the cashier. She lived on the other side of town but always lingered on after the others.

Now Father came home, and I greeted him as if he were a guest.

"Bashka, do you know where I can find a clean collar and cuffs?"

"Here, Father, on the dressing table."

He went over, but turned away after catching sight of himself in the mirror.

"What's this? They've used so much starch the studs won't go through the holes."

Father was getting hot and bothered over his clean collar.

"Shall I go and ask Sasha for another one?" I offered.

"There isn't time. We have to go to the synagogue."

Sasha brought the samovar into the dining room and lit the lamp. The shining urn steamed and hissed like a locomotive. The overhead light shed a circle of brightness and warmth. Father sat down at the table and calmly drank some tea sweetened with jam.

Mother was the last to leave the shop; she stayed to make sure everything was properly locked up. I could hear her quick step. Now she was shutting the steel door. Now I could hear the rustle of her dress. Now her soft shoes were approaching the dining room. For a moment she stood still in the doorway, as if dazzled by the white tablecloth and the silver candlesticks. Then she quickly washed her face and hands and put on the freshly washed lace collar she always wore on Friday evening.

It was a completely new Mother who now came over and lit the candles one after the other with a match. All seven flared up, lighting her face from beneath while she looked down, hypnotized. Slowly, three times, she encircled the flames with her hands as if embracing her own heart. The troubles of the week melted with the candles.

Mother covered her face with her hands and blessed the lights, her whispered benediction seeping through her fingers and lending added strength to the yellow flames. Her hands shone in the candlelight like the Tablets of the Law in the holy ark.

I went up close, to be near those hands and that blessing, and tried to look into her eyes. But they were hidden behind her fingers.

Now I lit my own little candle, and like Mother put my hands over my face and murmured blessings on the light as if through a screen. No sooner was the candle lit than it started to melt. I tried to hold back its tears with my hand.

I could hear Mother including names in her prayers: Father, the children, her own father and mother. Then my own name was spoken into the flame. I could feel the heat.

"The Almighty bless them all!" Mother dropped her hands at last.

"Amen," said I in a stifled voice through my fingers.

"Good Sabbath!" cried Mother. Her face looked purified, as if it had absorbed the brightness of the Sabbath lights.

"Good Sabbath," answered Father from the other end of the table, and stood up to leave for the synagogue.

"Good Sabbath," called the cook from the kitchen. Chaya had taken her two brass candlesticks down from the shelf, stuck a couple of short candles in them, and spread a little white cloth over the newly scrubbed table. The workaday

kitchen seemed to have vanished. The white cloth and the little candles had brought it peace and quiet.

Everything was cleared away or hanging in its proper place. The oven was closed with a sheet of iron; the pots and pans had gone. The walls looked whiter, with the drops of moisture wiped off. All was swept and garnished for the Sabbath.

Chaya sat at the table, not knowing what to do with her idle hands. Suddenly she grew sad. She wanted to be alone, so that for a little while she too might feel like the mistress of a household.

"Take yourself off for a bit, Sasha," she said, nodding toward the door.

Once on her own, she lit the candles. Though brought up and living for years among strangers, she remembered she too had had a father and mother and a home of her own.

"God hasn't blessed me with a family of my own, blessed be His name. Perhaps I have sinned." A tear trickled down her cheek as the candles began to melt. "But thank God I live among good people, I live as a Jewish woman in a Jewish house.... Now, I've got a prayer book somewhere. Where did I put it? ... Day and night all alone with the maid, without a word of religion, I could easily turn into a heathen."

She found her greasy prayer book, leafed through it, then lifted up her voice and blessed the lights.

They'd all gone to the synagogue, and Mother and I were left at home. The candles burned for us alone. It was as if they'd warmed the sky too; it shone comfortably in on us through the window.

Mother was praying silently beneath the flickering chandelier. I could hear her murmuring. Now and then a candle would sigh too. Mine was almost burned out. I went as close to the wall as I could and recited the Prayer of Benedictions.

The wall breathed like something living. I'd have liked to grow into it, but dared not even touch it with my prayer book.

Then there were voices in the hall. My brothers were back from the synagogue, pushing and shoving and shouting.

"What did you think of the cantor? He gabbled as if the place was on fire."

"Did you say all the Prayer of Benedictions?"

"I was standing next to Uncle Beril and he spat all over me."

"Israel! Don't be so rude! Help me with this sleeve, the lining's as crooked as a Turkish pretzel."

"Get away, it's you that's crooked!"

And they threw their coats at one another.

Mendel stood to one side. "What shall I do if I'm asked to read from the Torah tomorrow?"

"Shake like a leaf!" said Abrashka.

"Quiet!" said their teacher, who'd just come in. "Don't you know better than to make fun of everybody? Wish people a good Sabbath, you rascals."

He spoke quietly and calmly, without his weekday excitability.

Why were my brothers always so rowdy when they came home from the synagogue? They always had to be forced to go, yet when they came back you couldn't hear yourself speak for their laughter, and they brought enough stories home to last the whole week. So what happened at the synagogue?

And why did Father stay there so long? He was always the last to come home. Probably he was put off by the other men praying loudly, and didn't begin the Prayer of Benedictions until everyone else was starting to leave. Even on Friday he stayed late in the synagogue. When all the rest had gone, it was quiet. Only a few flies buzzed around the lamps.

Father, alone in his place by the eastern wall, swayed to and fro like the tree in the yard that could be glimpsed through the window. He prayed quietly, eyes closed, completely rapt. The verses seemed to hover and flutter around him. The beadle watched from a distance, a thin little man, thinner than the two large books on the table beside him.

The beadle had stopped praying long ago; he always finished first so that the congregation wouldn't have to wait for him. He just sat by the wall and waited for Father. When Father swayed, the beadle swayed in his corner; when Father sighed, so did he. When he heard Father's footsteps, he straightened up; when Father left the eastern wall, he leaped off the bench.

"Good Sabbath, good Sabbath, Reb Shmuel Noah!" he cried, glad that he could soon go home.

"Good Sabbath," answered Father, as if waking from a dream. The beadle helped him into his coat.

"Reb Shmuel Noah," he murmured, "there are a couple of soldiers out in the yard. They're strangers here. They come from respectable homes. . . ."

"What?" Father had already turned back. "Go and tell them to stay. I'll invite them home with me. God forbid a child of Jewish parents should go without supper on the Sabbath!"

"Good Sabbath!"

Father was embarrassed at being so late.

"Alta, here are two nice Jewish boys. Ask them to eat with us," he said to Mother, pointing to the two soldiers still standing shyly in the doorway.

My brothers, quiet now, looked at the guests. Abrashka bounded up and went over to them. He was fascinated by the bright buttons on their uniforms and had to touch them.

"Can I try your belt on? Where's your gun?"

The boys hustled the visitors over to the table.

Father washed his hands, pouring water from the heavy copper jug three times over each, then slowly drying them finger by finger. My brothers followed, vying with each other for the last drop left in the jug, and all snatching at the towel.

Chairs were pulled out, then scraped in to the table again as everyone took his rightful place.

"Quiet!" said Father. "All this noise on the Sabbath! You ought to be ashamed, in front of guests. Now that'll do—it's time to bless the wine. Kiddush!" He pointed to the brimming cup.

Everyone stood up. Silence fell. Chaya the cook looked on from the doorway. Father waited a moment, gathering his strength. The silver cup, engraved with little black flowers, swung in his hands like a miniature bucket. Some wine spilled over his fingers and onto the tablecloth. He

34

grasped the cup more firmly, with all five fingers, then began to sway from side to side, eyes closed, murmuring the blessing. It was as if the prayer were drawn up out of the cup. His high forehead was furrowed, his words turned into singing, and the melody seemed steeped in wine. The wine appeared to glow a deeper red, and all of us were cradled by the music.

"Amen." Father, his eyes still lowered, raised the cup to his lips and drank.

"Amen!" we all cried.

"Amen," said Chaya from the door, then hurried back to the kitchen.

Mother drank a few drops of wine, murmuring, "Thanks be to God it is given us to celebrate the Sabbath in good health. Bashenka, say the blessing." And she passed what was left in the cup to me.

The wine tickled my tongue. I sat in my usual place between Father and Mother and could feel their breath on my face. Now and then Father's beard brushed my shoulder. There was a red drop of wine on his mustache, as if he'd pressed the cup to his lips so fervently he'd made them bleed.

"Would you like to say the kiddush?" Father asked the elder of the two soldiers. And the drop of wine fell from his mustache onto me.

"No, thank you," said the soldier, blushing and clearing his throat.

"All right. Now, let's bless the bread." And Father said the prayer and cut up the Sabbath loaf.

Hands stretched out toward him from all over the table. Then everyone turned toward the door. Sasha had appeared there, and the room was filled with the smell of onions and pepper. Blushing, because all eyes were on her, Sasha slowly carried the fish over to Mother, the long dish bobbing in her hands like a boat.

The pieces of fish were so tightly packed together it was hard to separate them. Each clung to the next, all frozen in the pool of aspic.

"Mother, can I have the bit at the end?"

Mother prised the pieces out of the jelly and laid them one after the other on our plates. Everyone began to eat, heads bent, all around the table. Bones were already piled at the sides of several plates, and Mother was still serving.

Father wiped his mouth and spoke to the soldiers.

"Where are you from? Are your parents still alive? What do they do for a living?"

The soldiers, who'd been leaning forward dealing with the fish bones, looked up startled, as if caught in some misdeed, and stammered their answers with their mouths full.

Then my brothers began.

"What do you have to do in the army? Are the officers decent, or do they beat you? Where do you sleep? Can you fire a gun?"

The two soldiers, attacked from all sides, pushed away their plates in perplexity. Should they answer? If so, which question first? Or ought they to go on eating so as not to keep everyone waiting?

"Boys, leave the guests alone," said Father. "With all your questions, we'll be sitting here till midnight."

Then the soup tureen was brought in, full of golden chicken broth with grains of rice and reddish streaks of saffron floating in it. On the bottom of the dish lay two white boiled chickens. They looked alive.

"Mother, can I have the gizzard?" said Abrashka, eager to be first.

Mother gave him a look. "Always thinking of yourself!"

She turned to me. "Here's a leg," she said, "and a few vegetables. You like these, don't you?"

Some bright red carrots smiled up at me from my plate. "And who wants a wing?"

Two of them flew like whole birds from Mother's hands. She went on carving.

"The neck? A piece of breast?" She hardly had time to serve herself.

We were all exhausted. Our eyelids drooped. The tablecloth was covered with stains. Dinner was ending with the candles.

Next day, the Sabbath itself, the whole house rested after the midday meal. Only Chaya the cook stayed awake. All week she waited for the Sabbath, and when it came she couldn't believe it would ever end. She would rummage among her things, proudly bring out the treasures she'd been given as presents, and get herself up to go out for one of her long walks.

She'd open her wardrobe and lose herself in contemplation of its contents, airing and beating them and going through a whole heap of clothes as if they were the accumulated years.

"See, this was given to me for Passover a couple of years ago. And this hat belonged to my mistress at that time. And this . . ."

"That'll do!" laughed Sasha. "Everyone else has started out long ago."

"But I can't go out like this! What shall I wear?"

Decked out as if for a wedding, three times as bulky as usual, Chaya could hardly stand. Her new shoes pinched. But she swaggered as if every eye in the street would be glued on her in envy.

"What do you say, Sasha? No one would think I was a servant, would they?"

She twisted and turned in front of her cheap little mirror. "Look—real silk!"

She smoothed herself down, adjusted her flower-trimmed hat, and stalked to the door. As soon as she crossed the threshold, she was in another world.

The whole street was bound to stare, to turn around to look at her dress and her hat. And who knows? Perhaps today, this very Saturday, she might meet the man who was fated for her. . . .

As she went, she said to the maid in a mistresslike voice: "Don't forget—take them some tea when they wake up."

An hour or two later she would come home, more exhausted than with all the work of the week. The house would be full of men come for the Sabbath talk, discussing what the rabbi had said.

"What did that verse mean? One interpretation is . . ."

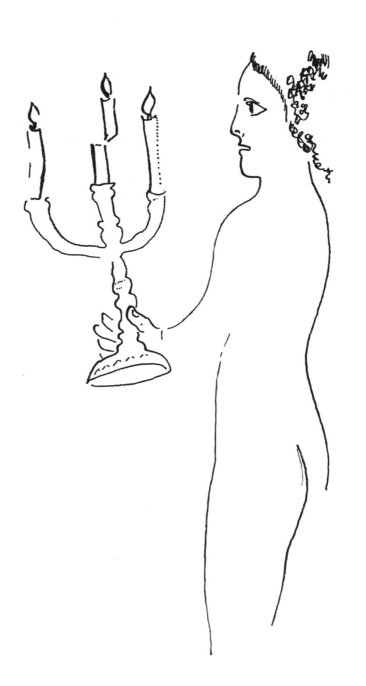

It sounded as though they were quarreling, but they quieted down when the cold fish was brought in.

Evening came. Father looked out of the window and saw the first star, risen in the blue sky at the same time as the crescent moon. He went outside, looking suddenly small in the majestic moonlight. I followed.

"Aren't you going to make Havdalah?" I asked.

Indoors again, I held the braided candle, like a chain twisted and heavy with the weight of the coming week. Even the flame was thick and opulent. Father quenched the candle with the remains of the wine he'd just drunk.

"A good week!"

"A good week," Mother answered pensively. "May it be a good week."

Already her face was dimmed by the light of weekday.

The Teacher

The old rebbe who came to give us lessons scurried through the yard like a shadow. My heart missed a beat.

Small and squat, he hugged the walls as though afraid of brushing against anyone. His threadbare, rusty-black coat was tight across his narrow shoulders, and his straggly goatee hung down sadly.

"Well, Bashenka?" He forced a smile. "Have you learned your alphabet? Call Abramele, will you? We're going to work hard today, aren't we?"

I ran through the house shouting, "Abrashka, Abrashka, the rebbe's here!"

But my brother had seen that for himself. From the little room where he always hid when it was time for lessons, he whispered to me, "Give him a glass of tea and some jam!"

"But aren't you coming?" I whispered back through the keyhole. "I can't stay with him all the time on my own."

"Go on, I'll come soon. Tell him I've got a stomach ache."

The teacher sat at the table, sighed, wiped his glasses, blew

his nose, and took a pinch of snuff. Then he leafed through the prayer book he always carried with him.

"Where have you got to, then, children?" He looked around, still keeping his place with his finger.

"Here I am, " I said. "Would you like a glass of tea?" I put the hot tea and jam down by his prayer book.

A little cloud of steam rose from the glass and misted his eyeglasses; the smell of the cherry jam tickled his nostrils. He sipped a few drops, felt warmer, and didn't put the glass down until it was empty.

"Would you like some more?" Without waiting for an answer, I snatched up the glass and ran off.

"But where's Abramele? Isn't he at home?" The old man told me not to bring any more tea.

"Yes, rebbe," I said. "He's here. I'll go and call him. He said he wouldn't be long."

"Abrashka!" I knocked at the door. "The teacher's waiting. Come on."

"Have you given him some tea? And some jam?"

"Yes, several glasses of tea. And he's getting sick from all the jam. I'm scared. Do come out for a minute."

"I can't. I've really got a stomach ache now."

I knew he was lying. He hadn't got a pain. He was just trying to duck out of the lesson.

Back I went to the teacher, sitting disconsolate by his empty glass.

"Rebbe, some more tea? They've just heated up the samovar again." And before he could say anything, I grabbed the glass.

I was ashamed to put the tea down in front of him, ashamed to look him in the eye. The hot tea was making his face red, and he was starting to blink.

I was suddenly afraid. Perhaps he was going to faint from the heat? He looked so weak sitting there with his eyes shut and his head bent.

I looked at him, but scarcely recognized him. He'd suddenly grown so old. His body was hidden by the table; all that was visible was his little head and beard. Only now did I notice how worn his face was, how withered his neck. He was yellower than the pages of the old prayer book open on the table in front of him. Even his mustache and fingertips were yellow, from the snuff he took.

Was he really so old? His coat smelled of age too.

"Perhaps," I thought, "he's too weak to go home on his own. Perhaps we ought to send for one of his family to come and fetch him. But where does he live? Has he got any children? And are they as difficult as he is?"

It struck me that he had no one. He was alone in the world, solitary as a stone.

And I was glad he was asleep, and hadn't seen me blushing. It seemed to me he had fallen asleep not because of the hot tea but from grief, because we were such bad pupils. He was not ambitious; he just wanted to teach us the Hebrew alphabet, to lead us, as he kept saying, to a verse of the Bible.

So why was he afraid to fuss at us? It would have been better if he'd shouted. We weren't our parents—his "bosses," as he called them.

How horrid we were. We only pitied him when he was asleep.

I wanted to tell him that from now on I'd be a good pupil—I'd swear it—and not bring him so many glasses of tea. I was afraid I was whispering so loud I'd wake him up. I sat as quietly as I could.

"Oh," I thought, "suppose Abrashka comes out now and disturbs him! I do want him to get a bit of rest here. He probably stays up all night studying the Torah."

Suddenly the smell of chocolate wafted in through the open window. It was so strong I instinctively looked to see if it had wakened the old man.

The sweet fragrance hovered like a cloud around my head, filling my nostrils and making my mouth water. Intoxicating!

How annoying I wasn't out in the yard! I knew that in the baker's kitchen, underneath ours, they were making chocolate icing and piping it onto the cakes. If I'd been out there, the cooks would have called me and let me lick the big wooden spoon. The old baker, of whom I was so frightened when he

44

came out into the yard, was sweeter, in his warm kitchen, than the cakes he made so skillfully. His broad smile showed black teeth decayed by all the sugar he'd tasted; his white apron was daubed all colors of the rainbow with the icing he used to decorate the cakes.

I could see him now, putting his long horn to his mouth and blowing into it. Out came a thick, colored cream, and on the cake underneath appeared here a red flower and there a green leaf.

Then he picked up another horn and blew in it, and a little angel with wings emerged from the top of the cake. With a wooden spatula he made it stand up straight, and smoothed the cake all over, scattering crumbs of sweetness as he did so.

He knew I regarded him as a magician.

"Pretty, isn't it?" He smiled. "Would you like the left-overs?"

That was what I'd been waiting for. He held out handfuls of crumbs.

But when I opened my hand, it was empty. I looked about me: the teacher was still asleep.

Oh, when would he have rested enough? I was going to miss the leftovers! I'd be too late, the kitchen would be dark and shut. Should I sneak off? But what if the teacher woke up?

"ZZZZzzzz." Was that sudden sound the wind, or the rebbe whistling in his sleep?

I leaned out of the window, and almost fell through. A cloud of little white leaves was falling down from the flat where the photographer lived. Crumpled and bent, they fluttered like white doves over the yard and the steps.

I stretched out my hands, trying to catch one. I knew they were portraits that the photographer was throwing away. They were yellow, faded, spotty: a bit of an eye, a shriveled cheek— scarcely recognizable as parts of a human face.

Yet there had sat a girl with bulging eyes, her high collar choking her. And there had stood a soldier with a long mustache and a frightened expression, as if he'd just caught sight of a general coming to yell at him.

Oh, I'd caught one! I looked at it. What luck! A naked

infant lying on a white sheet. It was as plump as a little pig, but it would have broken its skull if it had fallen down to the ground.

"Play with me! Smile!" It did begin to smile.

Then I caught another picture, this time a whole family. How could the photographer throw them all away? A grandfather and grandmother; another grandmother; an uncle and aunt, father, mother, sons and daughters—the married and the single—some children. There weren't enough chairs for everyone, and those who had to stand behind looked cross. The children sat in front on the floor.

One day I'd gazed for a long time at a group like this, and felt I had to go and ask Mother why we couldn't have our photograph taken like that.

"The photographer lives in the same house as us," I said, "and we could see our picture in his showcase by the front door."

Mother gave me a look. "Are you crazy? What an idea! What, go and have our photograph taken like maids and their boyfriends in the army!"

Why was Mother so angry? Grandfather had his photograph taken once. True, it was done by a trick: while he stood unsuspecting behind the counter, they'd told him not to move—they had to measure the shop. So why shouldn't the photographer come and pretend to measure the shop, and take a photograph of us at the same time?

"Bashenka!"

Abrashka finally emerged from his hiding place.

"Has the rebbe gone?"

"Ssh!" I waved him back. "Quiet! He's asleep."

But Abrashka had woken him up. Fortunately, his sleep seemed to have refreshed him. He came to, saw us, and took hold of his book as if he'd been wide awake all the time.

"Now, children, where were we? Alef, bet . . ."

"Alef, bet, gimel, dalet," I chanted, glad that he wasn't cross with us.

"He, vav!" Abrashka broke in.

For the first time we repeated the alphabet from beginning to end. The teacher beamed with satisfaction.

"You're not too tired, little ones? You've been very good pupils today. Perhaps that's enough, eh?"

He put on his old overcoat and went quietly away.

The New Year

The Days of Awe came, and the whole house was astir. Every holy day brought its own atmosphere, and that of Rosh ha-Shanah was clear and pure, like the air after rain. Like a bright sunny day, the New Year followed the somber nights during which we prayed for forgiveness.

The Ten Penitential Days were full of agitation. Father got up in the middle of the night and woke my brothers. They dressed in silence and crept out of the house like thieves.

What were they looking for in the cold and in the dark streets? It was so warm in bed! And what if they never came back? How Mother and I would weep! I started to cry at the thought, and snuggled deeper into the blankets.

In the morning Father looked pale and tired as he drank his tea. But the turmoil before the high holy days drove away fatigue.

The shop was shut early. Everyone was going to the synagogue, and got ready as carefully as if they were going for the first time. Everybody wore something new: one had a new tie, another a new hat, another a whole new suit.

Mother put on a white silk blouse, and reborn, with a new soul, was eager to go to the synagogue.

One of my elder brothers leafed through the big prayer book and turned down the corners of the pages where she had to pray. Years ago each one had been marked with the word "Here" in my grandfather's writing.

Mother recognized the lines she'd wept over the year before. She trembled; tears came into her eyes. But she would go to the synagogue and weep again as if every word were new.

A whole pile of books was soon ready for her. She wrapped them in a large shawl and took them with her. After all, she had to pray for a good year for the whole family.

Father's prayer books and shawl had been collected and taken to the synagogue by the beadle earlier in the day.

I was left alone. The house was empty, and I felt empty too. The old year seemed to be lurking forlornly outside the window. The coming year would be bright and shining. I went to bed, to get the night over with as soon as possible.

The next morning I too went to the synagogue. I too was dressed in new clothes from head to foot. The sun shone. The air was clear and brisk. My new shoes clacked on the pavement. I went along as fast as I could. Perhaps the New Year had already arrived at the synagogue, perhaps the ram's horn—the shofar—was already being blown. My ears tingled. It was as if heaven itself bent down and hurried along with me to the synagogue. I made for the women's section. When I opened the door, a wave of oven-hot air surged up and took my breath away.

The synagogue was crowded, the tall desks covered with books. The old women sat all hunched up, so that the younger ones stood out high above their heads. The children crawled about among people's legs.

I wanted to go over to Mother, but she was a long way away, in the front, by the window overlooking the men's section. As I tried to make my way forward, a woman turned an angry red face toward me and hissed reproachfully, but with the aid of some unexpected shoves from behind I reached the

edge of the balcony safely. Mother gave me a look that meant she was glad I'd come, glad I was near her. But where was the shofar? Where was the New Year?

I looked around the men's section. The ark of the Torah was invisible, the curtain drawn. The two gold-embroidered lions watched over it, silently, peacefully. The men, though, were active, busy with something else. Had I come too soon? Or too late?

Suddenly a hand emerged from beneath a prayer shawl, holding a ram's horn. The shofar rose and hung poised for a moment. All eyes turned toward it. The voices fell silent. Everyone waited.

The shofar let out a smothered sound, as if short of breath.

The congregation stared. There it went again, even more hoarsely. A murmur ran through the synagogue.

"What's this? Call that blowing the shofar? Better get someone else."

Then, suddenly, as if the player had driven away the evil spirits blocking the horn, a clear full sound rang out. Its cry swept through every corner of the synagogue. The congregation let out its breath in relief: some sighed, some nodded their heads approvingly.

The sound swelled forth, reaching the walls, reaching me and the railing in front of me, rose up to the ceiling, clove the heavy air, and spread out to fill the whole room. It penetrated so deep into my ears and mouth it gave me a pain in my stomach. When would the sofar stop? What did the New Year require of us?

I went over all my sins. God knew what would become of me, I'd accumulated so many in the course of the year.

I could hardly wait for the afternoon, when I would go with Mother to the Tashlich ceremony to cast my sins in the river.

On the way we met other men and women, all going through the narrow street down to the riverbank. They were all dressed in black, as if they were going, God forbid, to a funeral. The air was cool; a crisp breeze was blowing from the public gardens on the steep riverbank. Red and yellow leaves fell from the trees, flitting like butterflies, twirling around us, then falling to the ground. Did our sins fly away from us in the same way?

The leaves rustled and stuck to our shoes. I tried to make them cling on, to make the Tashlich seem less frightening.

"What are you dawdling for? Let the leaves alone," said Mother, dragging me along.

Soon everyone came to a halt. The street seemed to break off. The deep, cold water lapped at our feet. Dark-clad groups of people were gathered on the bank. Bearded men leaned over the water as if they wanted to see right to the bottom.

Suddenly they turned out their pockets, and crumbs and bits of fluff fell out of the linings. They prayed aloud, casting their sins into the water at the same time as the crumbs.

But how was I going to cast away my sins? I had no crumbs in my pockets. I didn't even have any pockets.

I stood at Mother's side, shivering in the cold wind that blew up our skirts.

She whispered the ritual words to me, and my sins fell with the prayers out of my mouth into the water. It seemed to me the river swelled with our sins, that its waters suddenly turned black.

Home I went, purified. Mother sat down and began to read psalms. She wanted to make the most of the day, and make more requests of God.

The murmur of her voice filled the darkening room. A fine mist hung in the air, blurring her glasses. She wept, swaying her head from side to side. What was I to do?

It was as if the shades of our grandmothers and grandfathers rose out of the hollow chanting. They wavered, grew long and thin like threads. I was afraid to turn around. Perhaps someone was standing behind me waiting to grab me.

"Mother!" I couldn't help it, I had to pull her sleeve.

She looked up, blew her nose, stopped crying. She shut the prayer book and kissed it.

"Bashka," she said, "I'm going back to the synagogue. But we'll soon be home again, all of us. I'd like you to set the table."

"For the blessing of the first fruits?" I asked.

As soon as she'd gone I opened the cupboards, got out the big paper bags of fruit, and turned the contents out onto the table. They lay before me as in an orchard: great green melons; white and red grapes; juicy pears. Sweet apples had a golden sheen, as if already dipped in honey. Dark-red plums rolled here and there over the table.

What new fruits were we going to bless? We'd been eating fruit all year!

But suddenly I saw another bag, and out of it emerged something like a pinecone. A strange and unknown fruit—a pineapple.

"Sasha, do you know how pineapples grow?"

"How should I know?" She shrugged her shoulders. "I've got other things to think about."

No one knew where the pineapple came from. Its scaly skin

made it look like some curious fish. But its tail stuck up like an open fan. I touched its rounded belly and it toppled over. I hesitated to touch it again, it sat there so regally. I cleared a space for it in the middle of the table.

But Sasha ruthlessly started to cut it up, and under the knife it groaned like a live fish. The juice was white blood spurting out over my hand. I licked my fingers. They tasted sour and sweet at the same time. Was that how the New Year would taste?

"Dear God," I whispered, "think of us. Father and Mother have spent all day at the synagogue praying we may have a good year. Father thinks about You all the time, and so does Mother. She remembers Your name with every step she takes. You know how overworked and worried they are. Dear God, You can do anything. Please give them a good year."

I sprinkled the pineapple with plenty of sugar.

"Happy New Year! Happy New Year!" yelled my brothers, rushing in.

They were soon followed by Mother and Father, looking pale and weary.

"A good inscription in the Book of Life!"

My heart turned over. Was God speaking through their mouths?

The Day of Atonement

The eve of the Day of Atonement had quite a different atmosphere, heavy and oppressive.

All the shops had long been closed, their black shutters up as if forever. The sky was black too, as if, God forbid, it had been abandoned by the Almighty. People were afraid to go out in the street. Perhaps God would punish them and they would break a leg.

I started, hearing raucous laughter in the distance. The Gentiles weren't afraid. They laughed even on Yom Kippur.

The cries of Father's white sacrificial rooster still rang in my ears.

Late yesterday evening a thin, dark-clad slaughterer had slunk into our yard. A long knife glinted among the folds of his coat. He chased Father's rooster, which let out a shriek, setting off all the other fowls. Other cocks ran after the slaughterer with angry squawks.

The cook grabbed one cock by the leg, but it broke away. Feathers flew. The whole yard echoed with the poultry's warlike cries, like the sound of a thousand fire alarms.

But gradually their strength gave out and all was quiet again.

The two white hens destined for Mother and me had taken refuge in a hole, in which they could be heard clucking and whimpering softly.

The cook scooped them both up at once and laid them down in front of the slaughterer. Blood spattered all over the place. When I came out of my daze, all the cocks and hens were stretched out dead. Blood oozed from their scraggy necks, blood daubed their white feathers. They were left there to cool in the night air.

I couldn't forget how my little pullet had quivered as I followed the prayer in the book and swung the bird around my head by its legs. I trembled too. My fingers twitched when they felt its warm body. It clucked gently and fluttered above my head like a little white angel.

I looked up from my prayer book at the bird. It was clucking still, begging me for mercy. I no longer heard the prayers being whispered at me. I was afraid the bird in its fright might do something on my head.

Mother was calling me. I could see from a distance how her eyes shone, how her hands were moving gently as if to embrace someone. She asked me to hold the wicks for the big wax candles that would burn on the cantor's desk in the synagogue. She told hold of the first wick:

"For Shmuel Noah, my beloved husband. May he enjoy good health and live to be a hundred and twenty!"

She steeped the wick in blessings and tears, and pressed the wax around it as if to enclose it in gifts. "Hold the end tight, Bashenka," she said.

"For my dear son Isaac. May he be healthy and happy and live to be a hundred and twenty.

"For my eldest daughter, Chana . . ."

The names were called, the wicks were twisted, wetted with tears, and fixed in the wax. It was hard to hold all the ends and keep them from slipping out of my hand, but I clutched them as tightly as I could.

Mother prayed a long time for every child and every relation. I no longer knew what she was saying. At every name a tear fell like a pearl onto the wick and mixed with the wax. We soon had a big, thick candle. And still it went on.

"May we all live long! For my late father, Baruch Aaron Levant. May he rest forever in paradise! Father, intercede for us—for me and my husband and my children. Ask God for health and happiness for us all."

She was weeping so much she could scarcely see the wicks trembling in her hands.

"Long may we all live! . . . For my late mother, Aiga, may she pray for us. Mother, don't desert your only daughter, Alta."

She spoke to the wick. She'd have liked to linger as long as possible with her mother, and spread the wax slowly, slowly.

"May long years be granted to us! . . . For my little son Benjamin, who died." Her weeping broke out afresh.

At this point I couldn't help crying too, for the brother who died when he was a year old and whom I'd never seen.

Mother saw me through her tears, sighed deeply, wiped her eyes, and blew her nose.

More wicks, more wax. . . . The dead families of close and distant relations appeared before us, and Mother gave each a tear by way of greeting. I could no longer distinguish the names; I was in an unknown cemetery. All I could see was tombstones, threads of wick. I was frightened: so many dead relations were entwined in Mother's handiwork. Were we ourselves going to burn like the souls of the dead?

I was relieved when the beadle came to collect the candles and take them to the synagogue. I was exhausted and ready to go to bed.

Next morning we were routed out early. We were given a little snack to fortify us for the fast, and said another prayer. We did our best to perform good deeds. My brothers asked one another forgiveness for any offenses.

"Abrashka, you're not angry with me?" I hurried to my brother, remembering I hadn't always done as he wished.

Mother went down into the yard, to beg forgiveness of a neighbor with whom she'd quarreled.

The boys got ready to go to the synagogue, scarcely speaking, not playing at all, restrained by fear and awe.

They waited at a respectful distance for Mother to finish blessing the candles. Then they went up first to Father and then to Mother and wished them a happy New Year. My parents laid their hands on each one's bowed head and blessed him. It made even my grown-up brothers look like little children. I, the youngest, came last.

Father, eyes downcast, touched my head. I was choked with tears and scarcely heard his words of blessing. His voice sounded hoarse. I felt as if I were already beginning to burn in the big candle Mother had plaited. Purified, I left the magic circle of Father's white, warm hands, which shone like lights beyond the prayers, and took refuge beneath the trembling hands of my mother.

I felt better then. The sight of her familiar tears comforted me. I listened to her simple, heartfelt prayers and wanted never to leave the shelter of those hands. When her voice stopped murmuring her blessings, I felt cold.

Then we all set off for the synagogue.

"Happy New Year!" Father came over to Mother and held out his hand.

"Happy New Year," Mother answered, eyes downcast.

I stayed at home on my own. The candles burned, warm and holy. I went over to the wall to say the Prayer of Benedictions.

The words of Father's blessings were still in my ears. I beat my breast and acknowledged my sins, fearing I had more of them on my conscience than were listed in the book. The blood rushed to my head. The Hebrew characters expanded, getting wider and taller. Jerusalem appeared before me. I felt I wanted to support it with the big prayer book I clutched in both hands.

I called upon God, and didn't go away from the wall until I couldn't think of any more to ask of Him.

My brothers came back from the synagogue. The house was

dreary, the table empty. Only a white tablecloth gleamed wistfully under the half-burned candles, which had started to smoke. We didn't know what to do with ourselves. So we went quietly to bed.

When I awoke next morning, they'd all gone to the synagogue long ago, and I was alone again.

I remembered what I had to do, and washed only my fingertips and didn't clean my teeth. With a dry mouth I started praying again. Some gentile schoolmates came and wanted me to repeat my lessons with them, but I wouldn't stir from the wall until I'd finished my prayers.

Then I hurried around to my grandfather's. He was old and ill, and he too was alone in the house. The Rabbi of Borbruysk—Grandfather was one of his followers—had given him a dispensation from fasting. He was supposed to have a spoonful of milk every hour. I went to give it to him.

He was praying and didn't look at me, but broke into quiet weeping. The spoon shook in my hand, and I spilled some of the milk on my fingers. Grandfather's tears fell into the spoon and mixed with the rest. He hardly wetted his pale lips, and only wept the more. I went home very dejected.

"Bashutka, come and have something to eat." Sasha wanted me to come into the kitchen, where she had some cold chicken ready. "You must be starving."

I was angry at myself for not being allowed to fast all day. Every year I begged Mother to let me. Anyway, I couldn't eat after seeing Grandfather's tears, and then seeing Father come back from the synagogue, wan and exhausted, to rest for a while. With his pale lips, and flowing white robe and white socks, symbols of purity, he looked, God forbid, as if he were no longer one of the living. He seemed weightless, nothing but pure white spirit. With fresh fervor I started to pray again, longing to attain just a little of his ardent piety.

Mother stayed at the synagogue all day. Before the Afternoon Prayer I went to see how she was. The cantor was silent, the men's section half empty. Many had gone home to rest. A few sat on the benches, deep in their prayer books.

A few boys were playing in the yard outside. One was eating an apple, another a piece of Sabbath bread dipped in honey.

But the women's section was full of stifled weeping. Everywhere there was sighing and lamenting, and appeals to the King of the Universe.

Mother wept in silence, hardly able to see the words in her prayer book through her misted glasses.

I stood a little way off and waited. Mother lifted her head and looked at me as if to say she was all right, although she immediately began to weep again. I went closer. But what was I to do among all these weeping mothers? I looked down into the men's section.

The cantor's white robe and prayer shawl made me feel calmer. I looked for our own two among the rows of tall candles. They burned amid all the other tall flames on either side of the ark of the Torah.

Suddenly a whisper ran through the synagogue. It filled with people and warmth. The men pressed around the cantor and the heavy curtain was drawn aside. Silence fell; the air itself stood still. The only sound was the rustle of prayer shawls. The men approached the ark. The Scrolls of the Law were brought out of their cabinet like sleeping princesses suddenly awakened. Their white and deep-red velvet covers glittered with Stars of David embroidered in gold and silver. The silver handles were inlaid with mother-of-pearl and decorated with crowns and little bells.

The Torah was surrounded with light. Everyone gathered around, trying to get a glimpse of the holy scrolls or to blow them a kiss. And the scrolls themselves rose up above all the heads and all the outstretched arms as they were slowly borne around the synagogue.

I couldn't bear having to stay up on the balcony, in the women's section. I longed to jump down into the embrace of the Torah, to plunge into its light, be near it, touch it, kiss its rays.

But already the scrolls were being replaced in the ark. The candle flames flared up on either side, the velvet curtain was drawn. Everything went dark again.

The congregation started to pray loudly, as if to drive away the sadness.

I stayed by the window, fascinated by the men's section with its strong voices, its white prayer shawls rising and falling like wings, filling the synagogue and hiding all the dark places. Here and there an eye or nose could be seen. The black stripes of the prayer shawls moved in waves over their wearers' heads.

One of the shawls swelled out, then sank back again, stifling a sigh. The synagogue was getting dark, and I was growing scared. The shawls were bowing, rocking, turning in all directions. They sighed, implored, cried out. Suddenly my knees started to give way. The shawls fell to the floor like heavy sacks. A white sock showed here and there. Voices seemed to be coming from deep underground. The shawls pitched to and fro like a sinking ship amid tall waves.

I couldn't hear the cantor now; his voice was drowned by the hoarse cries of the congregation, enough to go through the roof. Arms were flung up. Lights flickered. At any moment the walls would open and the Prophet Elijah would fly through.

Men were weeping like children. I gave way, and wept and sobbed louder and louder, until at last I saw a living though tear-stained face under a lowered prayer shawl and heard voices murmuring.

"Happy New Year! Happy New Year!"

I hurried home. The others would soon be back, and I had to set the table.

"Sasha, quick! Bring the samovar!"

I got the big cake tin out of the cupboard and emptied it onto the table: cookies, tarts, honey cakes, gingerbread— everything you could think of. There was hardly room to put a glass of tea down.

Sasha lit the lamp and brought in the humming samovar. It too seemed glad to come to life again and be remembered.

Then I heard my brothers' voices. They rushed in one after the other like ravenous beasts.

Mother came in, weary and wan, and with a gentle smile wished everyone a happy New Year.

The cook came out of the kitchen, pale but affable, to do the same. We all waited for Father. As always, he was the last home from the synagogue.

Then we ate with a will. Many a glass of tea was filled and emptied.

We were saved. We weren't hungry anymore. God grant us a good year! His will be done!

Amen!

The Feast of Tabernacles

The morning after the Day of Atonement we waited for a messenger from God. Surely he was bound to come, after all our praying and weeping!

A cart loaded with pine branches drove into the yard. The carter tipped it up, and the prickly green branches fell out in a heap.

The yard became a forest, filled with the scent of pine and resin. The foliage was cool and fresh, as after rain. The branches lay there like big birds resting, giving off that strong aroma—or was it a song?

If you climbed on the mound of greenery, it creaked and groaned and gave way. And if you tried to swing on it, it collapsed.

"What do you think you're doing?" shouted my brothers. "It's not a haystack—it's to make the booth!"

They dragged the boughs from under my feet. It was hard to get them off the ground, and every needle quivered as they were moved.

I helped to carry them to the sukkah, or tabernacle. The

little booth was not yet finished. The planks of the walls were up and nailed together, but the roof was still open and the sky peered in. My brothers climbed up ladders and stood on chairs to pass the branches to one another, waving them about like the lulav, or palm branch, used in the holiday celebrations.

The branches were fanned out, and soon the booth would be wearing a sort of hat. It stood there in the middle of the yard, as inviting as a cottage in a wood.

The branches were piled so thick no star could shine through. A cool twilight reigned within. Only through the chinks in the walls could a few rays of light struggle in.

In the middle of the booth a long table was installed, with benches on either side. The floor was just bare earth, and the legs of the table and benches stuck in the damp ground, which clung to our shoes.

We stayed in the booth, pretending we were in the country. We lay on the benches, trying to catch the dancing beams of light, and gazing up at the roof as if it were the sky. We started if a drop of dew fell down on us. And to let everyone know that the booth was finished and the holiday about to begin, we sang a song.

Faces appeared in the windows around the yard.

"Look, the sukkah's ready!"

"The beadle's brought the lulav," someone called to us.

We rushed back into the house. It too had changed, and smelled of willow branches. The leaves were all over the floor and the scent all over the house. But where was the palm branch?

Ah, there it was, in the corner by the window, propped up solitary against the wall, its head bent as if looking through the pane to catch a glimpse of the sky of its native land. Its long narrow leaves were pressed together. I went over to it but was afraid to touch it. The tips were sharp as swords.

"Let me shake the lulav," I begged my brothers.

"What! Before Father?"

"I just want to see if it's alive."

The palm trembled in my hand, and I trembled with it. A

faint breeze seemed to sweep through it, and I felt as if I were standing on the soil of Israel under a rustling palm tree. How did the palm get here?

"What do you think, Abrashka?" I asked. "Did the palm come straight from Jerusalem? And what was it there—a tree, or only a branch broken off a tree? And who brought it here?"

"Anyone would think it was Passover, you ask so many questions."

Abrashka didn't know, and was trying to wriggle out of it.

"You know what?" he said. "I think the palm tore *itself* out of the ground. It wanted to see what goes on in the world, and so it ran away. And one night . . ."—Abrashka whispered, as if to scare himself—"one night it ended up on our windowsill."

I'd have liked to believe him, but I didn't want him always to be right.

"But they've just brought it from the synagogue," I said.

"Then what if I tell you it was packed in straw in a big wooden crate? I've seen stuff being sent like that at the railway station."

"No! Palm wouldn't travel with nonkosher goods. The rabbi would box your ears to hear you talking about the lulav like that. And look: It's all fresh and green. It would have been suffocated in a packing case."

I touched the palm branch again. Its narrow, smooth leaves vibrated like harp strings lightly brushed.

"Wait," I said, to comfort it. "Father will come soon. He'll pick you up and bless you, and then you won't feel so cold and strange here."

And where was the etrog, the citron?

It lay round and fat like a pharaoh on a soft couch in the empty sugar tin, giving off a delicate kingly scent. And where did the etrog come from?

Then Father came in, followed by my brothers.

"Come, children, and we'll bless the palm."

Father looked first at the palm, and then at the citron, then took the etrog from its bed and put it by the fan of palm leaves. They nestled against one another: they came from the same country.

Father, head bowed, recited the blessing aloud as if he were swearing an oath, lifting up the palm, then lowering it, holding it to his heart, then away from him to right and left. The palm straightened up, trembled, and shook its head, its narrow leaves reaching out imploring hands. As soon as Father stopped, they all closed up again.

"Here, would you like to bless the palm?" Father held it out to my oldest brother.

It went from hand to hand. All my six brothers seized it, shook it, struck out with it as if it were a sword, broke it. Then, exhausted, it was put back in the window.

The sukkah was ready, but had to wait a whole day for people to come and eat in it. Meanwhile it steeped in the smell of pine, and the walls and floor dried out.

Toward evening Father and my brothers put their coats on as if they were going out. But they were going to have supper in the booth.

Neither Mother nor I nor the cook was allowed to go in. We stood outside the entrance to hear Father bless the wine.

The food was handed in, one plate after the other, through a little hatch in the wall. My brothers could have thought it came straight from heaven.

Did they spare a thought for Mother and me, all alone in the house? It was cold and empty; as if there were no windows or doors. We sat at the table and ate without appetite.

"Mother, why do we have to stay alone with the maids, as if we were servants too? What sort of a feast is that? Why do they eat separately from us?"

"Ah, my dear, they're men," said Mother sadly, and ate a mouthful of cold meat.

Suddenly there was a commotion in the kitchen. Chaya and Sasha were running to and fro between the booth and the house.

"It's raining!"

"Bring out all the rest of the meal now so that they can say the final prayer!" called Mother frantically.

I was delighted it had rained in the middle of supper. The

Feast of Tabernacles was a very dreary one for Mother and me.

A peal of thunder! I looked out to see if the booth was still standing. The rain poured down. In a moment the whole place was drenched. Water trickled down the walls and over the table, and streamed from the branches. Chaya and Sasha ran out, covered the plates, and ran indoors with them, the rain beating down as if to pierce through the covers.

Through the downpour I could hear Father saying the blessing, and my brothers' shrill voices chiming in. Then they ran from the booth with their collars turned up, one after the other. We looked at one another as if after a long separation. They rushed into the house as though from another world.

Several days went by. The booth was dismantled, plank by plank, and the pine branches strewn on the ground. The yard was full of their needles. The tabernacle might never have been. The palm branch was taken out of the window.

"Look," laughed my brothers, "it's dry and withered like a toothless old man."

"Make it into something for me," I begged. "A toy, a basket, anything."

Aaron set to work. He had long, nimble fingers. He stripped the palm branch leaf by leaf, making them rustle and bend. His fingers flew, cutting narrow strips, weaving little plaits, and soon it was done. A little basket, a trough, a table and chair. All that was left of the tall palm branch was a bare yellow stalk.

As for the etrog, we'd forgotten all about it. The cook had thrown it into a pot and scalded it alive. The plump and lordly citron had been turned into a saucerful of sticky jam.

My heart was heavy. The holiday was over.

I couldn't wait for the Rejoicing of the Torah, when the whole town would come to see us.

The Rejoicing of the Torah

Once a year we children were allowed to run wild in the synagogue. By the evening we were worn out and breathless.

The synagogue was packed, and there were so many boys there was hardly room to keep out of their way. Even the little girls were allowed in the men's section for the "procession" of the Torah. Boys and girls together got under the older people's feet.

The lamps seemed to shine with a new light. The ark was open, and the Scrolls of the Law in their festive covers were brought out one by one. The synagogue became a holy temple, with the men dancing as they carried the scrolls around and the children dancing with them or keeping time with their feet.

We ran like wild animals around the pulpit, then up one side and down the other, clattering on the wooden steps. Pushing and shoving, we rushed around it as many times as we could, not stopping for breath or to stroke the carved railing.

We waved rattles and made a terrible noise. Our paper flags fluttered and tore in the wind.

The beadle huddled in a corner, afraid we were going to tear the place down.

"Stop it, children! That's enough!" he shouted. "You'll ruin the whole synagogue!"

But we couldn't stop, though our heads were spinning and we could hardly stand.

I tottered wearily home behind my brothers, still clutching my tattered flag.

Next morning early, all the house was in a bustle. We were expecting visitors. We hurried to the synagogue and got through the service as rapidly as possible. Before the prayers were over, the men started to gather in groups and whisper.

"Is it settled whose place we go to first for the kiddush?"

"Ssh! Ssh!"

"Reb Shmuel Noah has invited everybody," someone said.

"Oh, then we'll get plenty to drink! What do you say, Reb Hershel?" asked a thin man with a red nose.

"I agree. We'll go to Reb Shmuel Noah's first. He's a very good host."

The synagogue emptied as they all poured out into the street.

"What are you waiting for? Come on! We've got lots of stops in front of us."

"Today the Jews are going to get drunk!" said Christian passersby, laughing. Even the cathedral on the corner seemed to make way for the revelers.

The whole congregation arrived at our house. The room grew crowded and hot.

"A happy holiday to the lady of the house!"

The women moved to the side of the room. The guests gathered around the table, consulting each other about what to eat, rubbing their hands with glee, moving chairs aside, examining the food. The table was laid out as if for a wedding feast, and groaned under the weight. There were slices of cake, honey cakes, gingerbread, dishes of pickled herring, chopped liver, eggs cooked in goose fat, calves' foot jelly, and fried cow's udder. And standing among all these like soldiers on parade were lots of bottles of wine and spirits.

"Hey, stop pushing! Let someone else have a chance!"

"Why do you always have to be first? You're not being called up to read the Torah."

"It's the wine he's after—let him at it!" said some of the others, laughing.

"Hush, here's Reb Shmuel Noah. A toast to your very good health, Reb Shmuel Noah. To yours, gentlemen."

Father, as always, was the last one back from the synagogue. In his long holiday overcoat and tall hat, he looked taller and broader than usual.

"To your good health. A happy holiday."

His hat wobbled. He took it off. His head was still covered by his skullcap.

"Have you said the kiddush?" he asked.

"What about you, Reb Shmuel Noah?"

Several of them blessed the wine together.

"Blessed are You, O Lord our God, King of the Universe, Creator of the fruit of the vine . . ."

The guests went around sipping the wine, going on to the spirits, and tasting every dish.

"To the health of the mistress of the house. This is what I call herring!"

"And the calves' foot jelly is delicious!"

Mother beamed with pleasure.

Suddenly up jumped the beadle like the master of ceremonies at a wedding feast.

"Who wants to start blessing the offerings?"

A man with a long white beard stood up, cleared his throat, and stroked aside his beard and mustache as if they prevented him from opening his mouth.

"Blessed be He who . . ." he intoned, swaying from side to side.

"Did you hear how much he's giving? How much did he say?"

The beadle ran from one to another, announcing the names of the donors and the amounts they promised, as if informing a bride and bridegroom of their wedding presents.

"Why is he throwing cold water on everything? Where can we get something to drink? Hand over that bottle! What are you holding on to it for?"

Empty bottles rolled aside, new ones were opened, as if the party had only just begun. Goblets and tumblers were filled. Wine spilled on the tablecloth.

Suddenly the old man with the long white beard banged on the table.

"Silence!"

He closed his eyes and gave a deep sigh, as if to bring forth a piece of his heart. The sigh was echoed all around the table. And then, softly, he began to sing.

At first it was only a murmur, as if from far away. His head swayed, his brow wrinkled, his lips and mustache quivered. Gradually everyone came under his spell. Pale faces grew flushed, eyes half-closed, and one after another all joined in the singing, louder and louder.

The melody swelled and surged like a fire. The men were borne along by it, eyes shut, swaying to and fro, banging on the table as if to make it rise from the floor and join in.

One let out a cry of fear; others wept or prayed or lamented. The song filled with unshed tears. The singers snapped their fingers, flung out their arms; one clutched his beard to his breast as if to still his bursting heart.

Suddenly the lamenting ceased.

"My friends, there is a God in the world!" said the old man, looking upward as if the Almighty had appeared to him in person. "Why do you just sit there? Today is Simhat Torah, and the rabbi told us to dance and enjoy ourselves."

Arms and legs sprang into action. Chairs and table were pushed aside. The cloth was yanked askew; food and glasses fell to the floor. The very walls shook. The men stood and marked time with their feet, coattails flying, then danced around in a ring. Hunching their shoulders, they held hands tightly as if, left alone, each one might fall to pieces. No one looked at his neighbor; no one saw himself. Boots whirled through the air; feet no longer touched the ground.

Someone would straighten up and throw himself into the dance with renewed vigor, as into a fire. Everyone circled around; no one was left sitting at the table, which shook as if it

would like to join in the dance.

"Reb Shmuel Noah, what are you waiting for? Come on!"

And Father, my quiet peaceful Father, stood up and entered the whirling ring.

From where I sat, I tried to distinguish him from among the rest. There was his head, slightly bent to one side. His eyes were downcast; his beard floated in the wind. He twirled around rapt, as if in a dream.

Father, dancing!

I couldn't contain myself.

"Mother, may I?"

The women, in their corner, beamed with delight: their husbands were happy and carefree at least this once!

"Mother, do let me! I want to dance with Father!" I tugged at her sleeve.

"My dear child, you'd get trampled on. Look!"

A tall thin man rushed in, gave a yell, did a somersault, and landed upright again. He wriggled along the floor, cried, "Look out, here I come!" and with one bound landed in the kitchen.

"Oh!" screamed the cook in fright. "Mercy, Reb Laizer, what are you doing in here?"

Chaya had recognized him as one of our neighbors in the yard. But he, taking no notice of her, seized a long shovel, knelt down, and drew a big earthenware pot full of kulai out of the oven. The pot overturned, and the dark sticky mess spilled over the man's head. He ran back into the room black as a Negro, causing even more hilarity among the tipsy guests.

The latter, so dizzy they could hardly stand, slumped—half sitting, half lying—onto their chairs.

But after a moment: "Come, friends," someone cried, starting up again. "We've still got to go to Reb Mendel's."

Up they all sprang, as if someone were after them with a whip, and tumbled out into the street, Father among them.

When the first star came out, Father too appeared, slightly unsteady on his feet from so much wine. He was embarrassed, and fell into bed like a log.

We were embarrassed too.

The First Snow

After the Days of Awe there stretched out a line of ordinary days—silent, sunless, flat, and gray. The rain fell ceaselessly, as if it had forgotten how to stop. The windows seemed to be weeping. Inside the house it was dark even during the day, which ended almost as soon as it began.

Even the clock ticked faintly, dragging out the hours and striking hoarsely. I was depressed, didn't know what to do with myself, and thought I heard a stifled sobbing in the rain.

"Chaya," I said to the cook, "someone's knocking. Open the door."

"Do let me alone. How could there be anyone in this rain?"

"Can't you hear? Something splashing?"

"No wonder, it's been raining for days. And the wind!"

"But I can hear footsteps. Lots of people coming through the yard."

"Listen to her! What would you do with the child! Go and look then, silly—you'll soon see. . . . What was that?"

Her jaw dropped. Two eyes gleamed from the dark hallway,

like those of a wolf skulking behind a tree. Two beards streamed with water.

"Robbers!" I clutched Chaya's sleeve.

"Now what?" Chaya's fright had turned to anger.

"Cabbages, lady—nice fresh cabbages," the beards breathed at us.

Two peasants, drenched to the skin, lowered their heavy sacks. The water streamed off them; even their boots overflowed. They stood in the entry, scratching their heads and waiting uncertainly now that they felt dry ground underfoot.

"What are you standing there for, you fools? Can't you see the door?"

They nudged one another and stayed where they were.

One of them spat. The sacks looked as if they were filled with stones, and the men, panting from the weight, breathed out over the landing a little cloud of mist.

"Here! Careful! Tsk, tsk, the dirt, the mud," grumbled Chaya. "You turn the place into a pigsty. Stop, don't go any farther with those boots! Put the cabbages down here."

Chaya stood in the middle of the kitchen barring the way.

"Fancy coming in this weather. Couldn't you have come when it wasn't raining? You've brought all the muck in the village with you. And I just scrubbed the kitchen. . . . And what's this? This cabbage is all rotten!"

The heads of cabbage tumbled out of the sacks, white and round, clean and curly, as if wearing crisp lace shawls. How had they kept so clean in the muddy sacks? Out they rolled, one after the other, bouncing over one another, then nestling together cheek to cheek. Soon there was a big heap of them in the corner.

From it arose a strong, fresh smell, as if a whole field of cabbages had been planted in our kitchen. The kitchen was brought back to life, and we with it.

Chaya set to work at once, rolling up her sleeves and fetching pails and barrels.

"Don't climb on the cabbages, children," she said. "Sasha, bring the little table up from the cellar and scrub it."

A long, narrow table with a chopper in the middle was set

up near the heap of cabbages. I quailed. The executioner seemed to have been installed in our kitchen. A cabbage was thrown onto the table, fell under the knife's sharp tooth, and was sliced up in a trice. Then came the next cabbage. The chopper rose and fell, and bits of cabbage flew like feathers and fell into the waiting barrels.

The chopped cabbage was doused with water and sprinkled with peppercorns. The water gave out bubbles as the cabbage fell steadily in.

The barrels and pails were soon full, slices of carrot relieving the white of the cabbage. Lids, each weighed down with a big stone, made sure the contents couldn't escape.

I accompanied the barrels down to the gloomy cellar. There in the musty air the cabbages, now living and firm, would turn soft and sour.

We children threw ourselves on the tender hearts that were left, munching the pale little leaves.

On the day the cucumbers were laid down, we were on the alert again.

"Chaya, give us one and we'll help you clean them."

"Oh, you've smelled them, have you? I know your tricks!"

She wouldn't have the smallest mark left on any of the cucumbers, and so we used to polish them like shoes until they shone. I felt sorry for the polished vegetables in their gleaming green skins when they vanished one by one into a little vat, strewn with sprigs of fennel and other pungent herbs, to lie in a sort of wet grave.

We would all look for an especially shiny cucumber, pick it out of the vat, and crunch it up like a nut.

"Good-for-nothings!" yelled the cook. "What did I tell you? There won't be any left."

"Old witch!" we shouted back with our mouths full. "You'd like to make them all soft and sour in your brew, and then no one will remember what a real cucumber tastes like."

We ran out of the kitchen, a faint taste of vinegar still in our mouths. The rain was pouring down. We felt as if we were beginning to go moldy too.

82

Suddenly, one morning I woke up to find a dazzling light in my eyes. A miracle! It had stopped raining, the whole room was bright. The windowpanes were dry and gleaming. There was a white glow everywhere.

"Snow! It's been snowing!"

We couldn't tear ourselves away from the windows. The yard! It was no longer our old familiar yard. The day before it had been gloomy and dark; now it was all clad in white. The snow was falling over it like a shimmering veil; it must have been falling all night. There were thick eiderdowns of snow on the roofs and balconies, drifts of it by the doors, a heavy white carpet on the stairs.

And still the snow came down, the flakes glittering as if, in broad daylight, heaven were still scattering stars. The first snow! Looking at it, my eyes seemed bright and clear. Or had I been given two new ones, fresh and clean?

The little birds had flown away, but still seemed to sit looking down at us, frozen, from branches covered with tufts of snow.

"I wonder who'll be the first to walk on it?" said Abrashka, pressing his nose to the pane.

"Look, some snow has come in through the window!"

A long strip of cotton decorated with streaks of silver lay between the double windows, glistening like real snow. Out of it grew, timidly, a few little pink-and-red paper flowers, as if surprised at being there.

My brother breathed on the windowpane and with one finger drew a big head with tousled hair. We laughed so loud the paper flowers trembled. Abrashka, the rascal, was always glad if he could shock someone, even if it was only a paper flower.

"Come away from the window, you scamps! All we need, in this cold, is for you to break a pane."

They chased us away. Suddenly it felt as if the cold snow were falling on our backs.

The Hanukkah Lamp

"Children, where are you all? Mendel, Avremel, Bashenka, where are you hiding?" Mother was calling from the shop. "What have you been doing all day? Come along, Father's waiting with the Hanukkah lights!"

Where should we be? We were huddled around the stove keeping warm. The day was almost over. It was dark. We were waiting for the shop to close.

Mother hurried into the house and said apologetically, "I still have a lot to do in the shop, but this is a sort of holiday. I'd like to be with the children at least when the Hanukkah light is lit."

We all went into the study. Although it was a very large room, it had only one little window, and as Father was standing with his back to it, there was not much light. We waited in the dusk for the small flame to be kindled.

Father's head was bent over the Hannukkah lamp. His shadow fell and wandered on the wall, like another Father seeking something. When he moved his head aside, the somber silver of the Hanukkah lamp shone forth, a sleeping moon emerging from its hidden cave.

The lamp was small, hardly more than a toy, but what was not carved all over its silver surface!

In the middle were two lions with flowing manes and gaping jaws. In their upraised paws they held the Tablets of the Law. These were bare, without any writing on them. But they were radiant, as if steeped in the sanctity of the Law.

The lions were surrounded by a paradise of plants. There were flowers, little vines with grapes, all kinds of fruit. Two birds peered from the branches of a tree. There was even a big snake lurking nearby.

On either side, like sentries, stood two silver pitchers; these, though small also, were round and full-bellied, so that paradise should never lack for oil.

And so that the lions and birds might see plainly, there was a little bridge underneath with eight tiny cups waiting for a flame to flare up in them.

Father's white hands moved over the little cups. From one after the other, in order, he drew a small wick, then poured in a few drops of oil from one of the pitchers. The wick absorbed the oil and grew soft and white, almost like a candle.

Father recited a prayer and lit a wick. Just one. He didn't touch the other seven little cups. They stood there, apparently useless, empty and cold.

This wasn't a real festival, with just that one lonely little light! It was disturbing, as if the small flame—God forbid!— were a mourning candle.

The flame was so frail it could have been snuffed out with a breath. Its light didn't reach the murky floor or illuminate all the little paradise. Only one of the lions reflected back a touch of warmth; the other didn't know a light was burning near it.

My parents and brothers went away. I went nearer to the lamp. I wanted to straighten up the wick and make it burn brighter. But I couldn't get hold of it properly. I only burned my fingers.

The little flame flickered, sank, blinked, and wavered. It was

going out! No, it struggled and tried to flare up higher, just enough to lick a grape in the silver garden or warm the foot of one of the lions.

Suddenly thick drops of oil started to fall from the wick, choking the opening in the cup and stifling the little flame. The lamp began to smoke, and a dark stain spread on the woodwork behind it, overlapping the stain left by the Hanukkah lights of the year before. The stains shone almost as bright as the little flame itself.

Then the big ceiling light was lit, and its brightness killed the Hanukkah lamp, which gave a faint sigh and expired.

Why were Mother's Sabbath candles so tall and fat? And why did Father, who was so tall, bless such a tiny Hanukkah light?

The Fifth Light

One little light was lit after the other, and now all five of them burned together in the Hanukkah lamp. Each wick fanned its neighbor on either side, and five flames now warmed the silver paradise.

The children, large and small, were gathered around the dining table. The ceiling lights gave out a holiday glare. From the kitchen came promising smells, each more enticing than the last.

The pike was cooling in a little lake of thick gravy, together with slices of onion that looked as if they'd been trapped in the ice.

The grieben had gone hard and black, although they were still bathed in their own fat. A pan of fat simmered on the glowing stove. It was hot in the kitchen, and Chaya's face glowed too. She stood in front of the stove, holding an iron hook, shoving the pots and pans back and forth, heating up one, rubbing another with greased paper, now pouring a spoonful of batter into the bubbling fat, now lifting out a crisply cooked potato pancake. The chubby pancakes, dotted with beads of fat, jumped up and down over the fire like new babies being slapped into life.

We gazed at the cook as if she were a magician.

"Chaya, that big thick one's for me, isn't it?" Abrashka asked, his cheeks already bulging.

"You're going to have a stomach ache! How many latkes do you mean to put away? You don't give me a moment to breathe, you rascal!"

Chaya grumbled, but kept on cooking and piling up a huge plate of pancakes.

We roared with laughter and licked our fingers. The pancakes slithered about in the pan. We nibbled grieben. What could we do next?

Suddenly someone poured a heap of little round bits of wood like tiny barrels out on the table. A game of lotto!

We were each dealt a piece of cardboard marked out with rows of black figures all mixed up together, a two by a nine and a seven by a three. The game ended when all the numbers on one of our cards were covered with little wooden barrels. It was a game of chance, and whenever a number was called everyone trembled as if his fate depended on it.

"Eleven! Four! Seven!"

"Here! I've got four!"

"Who's got seven?"

No one could find it.

The little bit of wood twirled in my brother's fingers and rolled like a black devil over the table, under the lamp. The figures swam before my eyes and got mixed up with the pieces.

"Idiot! You've got the seven. Why didn't you say so? You have to have everything stuck right under your nose before you see it!"

Abrashka was looking over my shoulder.

"Have I won?"

"Silly! The game's not finished yet."

Everyone turned on me.

"Always dreaming! Look, she's asleep already."

"She's eaten too many latkes. You can see by her eyes."

"She doesn't know what a seven looks like."

"Of course, that must be it!"

That was too much.

"The teacher says I'm a much beter pupil than you!" I shouted. "And I can recognize a seven very well—it's a lucky number."

"But you nearly slept through your luck!"

"Look, she's trembling like a leaf!"

In my excitement I'd kept my eyes fixed on the little piece of wood, and now I suddenly jumped up, shouting, "I've won! I've won! You can say what you like! I've won! Look!"

They all turned toward me, and they and I together gazed at my card, marvelously covered with pieces.

"Fools are always lucky," said Abrashka.

They were all jealous. Even good-natured Mendel banged on his now useless card as if it were my knuckles.

"I only needed one more number to win. Just one," he moaned.

"Never mind, you'll win another time. It means a lot to her to win these few kopeks." Abrashka gave me a wry look.

My brothers had spoiled my pleasure. The money I'd won burned a hole in the palm of my hand.

"Come on now, watch my top!"

Abrashka spun his lead top onto the table. The tip hardly touched the smooth oilcloth, and the top began to whirl around frantically, hissing and humming like the wind.

All eyes were riveted on it. Where were its four sides? Where its four letters? The Hebrew letters gimel and nun appeared for a moment and then vanished.

But then the top seemed to flag, the whirlwind collapsed, and the little foot turned more and more slowly. The sides and their letters could be made out once more. All four characters—gimel, shin, he, and nun—twinkled at us as if they'd just returned from afar.

"I'll bet everyone the top stops at gimel," said Abrashka.

"It can't do anything else if you say so."

We all stared at the gimel, willing it to win. Soon it looked as though the top really was going to stop at gimel, which

meant "good," but at the last minute it wobbled, tripped up by the character shin which came after it. The gimel fell face downward, and shin, which meant "bad," lay uppermost in the middle of the table.

"Like to bet again?"

"What's the point? Listen, it's Hanukkah. We're allowed to play cards."

We threw ourselves on the cards with renewed energy, captivated from then on by the painted faces. The queen was the only card in the pack that was smooth-faced and slim. The king, on the other hand, filled the whole card, as if using his massive frame to show his dignity and importance. The jacks, who were younger, tried to distinguish themselves by their artfully curled mustaches. One card was divided between two jacks with their legs cut off. They looked as if they were jostling one another to get into the middle.

It was an art in itself to learn the value of all the cards.

"Shall we play twenty-one?"

My brothers grew excited. One of them shuffled the cards, shuffled them again, flicked the edges as if to air them, spat on his hand, and shuffled them a third time.

"Draw!"

A little heap of cards lay one on top of the other.

"Cut!"

"Stop giving orders. Anyway, they've been shuffled enough. What do you want to do, whisk them or something? They're not pancakes!"

"One, two . . . one for you. . . . One, two, three . . ."

The cards lay scattered as on a battlefield. We held our breath as we watched them flashing out from my brother's fingers. We sat like cats on hot bricks, afraid to see what cards we'd been dealt. "All the others will have got better ones," we all thought, concealing our hands so fiercely we bent the cards. It was as if the whole secret of winning lay in not letting anyone else see them.

The trick was to let the cards lie on the table, not looking at them but keeping them in your head. They lay in rows face downward, and everyone waited for a miracle. Perhaps he'd win! If any of us saw that our neighbor had a king, we felt a pang; now we *couldn't* win!

"Don't look so pleased with yourself. Sometimes a lower card is better than a king."

"How do you know I've got a king?"

"You may be dumb, but the cards aren't."

"Who needs kings? I've got a better card, better even than a queen."

"Show! Show!" Everyone fell on the boastful Abrashka.

"What a showoff! Don't believe him, he's cheating. What are you looking for under the chair? You made me drop one of my cards."

"*I* made you?" Abrashka mimicked him. "Don't talk non-sense. Your cards drop out of your hands from fright."

"Oaf! Give me my card back or I won't play any more."

"You don't say! Wait a minute." Abrashka rolled about on the floor, crowing with delight. He'd peeped at all our cards. "I've got you all! Here's the queen!"

"Give it back! It's mine! Cheating isn't allowed! That game doesn't count!"

"How do you know what's allowed and what isn't?"

"What a lout! He messes everything up."

Then the boys started to scuffle all around the table, sending cards and chairs flying. They pushed and slapped and cuffed each other, boxed one another's ears. From the racket you'd have thought a real war had broken out.

"It wasn't your queen anyway."

"Why not?" Abrashka wouldn't give in. "A queen's a queen, whether it's on the table or on the floor."

"Take that, you devil! This time you're not going to get away with it!"

"Quiet, children, quiet! How long are you going to keep up this noise? We can't get to sleep, and it's almost midnight."

My brothers all fell silent and looked at each other in confusion. Father's voice coming from the bedroom had the effect of a cold shower.

I gathered up the cards in silence. But they still whirled around in my head.

I couldn't sleep for thinking of the few kopeks I'd won. They lay under my pillow, but kept slipping out and whispering in my ear. I was afraid to touch them, as if they'd been stolen.

I could hardly wait till morning, to give them to the first beggar who knocked at the door.

Hanukkah Money

Mother had once told me I was born during Hanukkah, on the day of the fifth light.

But who knew it, in our house? None of my brothers cared in the least about when they'd been born.

"Right, you were born. So what? Do you want it to be a public event?" My brothers laughed at me. "What do you want? To be born again?"

And Father thundered, "What, another holiday all of a sudden? Only a silly little ignoramus could think of such a thing!"

So I made the most of Hanukkah, if only for the two ten-kopek pieces—the "Hanukkah money"—we got from Father and Grandfather.

We could use the money to hire a sleigh and go for a ride. A ride with a real horse—we were always ready for that. And so the two silver coins jingled in our ears like the little bells of the sleigh in which we remembered dashing through the town. The coin we got from Grandfather was particularly bright, as if he'd polished it for us on the eve of the holiday.

At Hanukkah, Abrashka and I used to hurry to our grandparents' house early in the morning. If Grandfather was still asleep, we woke him up. Perhaps he'd forgotten that the whole world was celebrating Hanukkah.

For some reason or other, Grandfather lived in a street entirely inhabited by Gentiles. It was called Offizierskaya, Officers' Street. He'd probably chosen it because it was near a big square surrounded by synagogues.

It was a street of little white houses. Everything about it was white, and it was the quietest street in the town. Not a single shop; no trade, no noise. Nothing to stop you from falling asleep. If anyone dared to laugh out in the road, old ladies in colored caps would emerge from behind the flowerpots in the windows, shake their heads, and call out, "Disgraceful! Stop it at once!"

As if there were a sick grandfather in bed in every house.

The houses were so low you probably had to lie down in them anyway. What happened if a tall man tried to stand up straight in them? He probably had to go about bent double. This explained why my grandmother and grandfather got smaller every year.

Some of the houses seemed to have collapsed, as if the old people who lived in them were slowly sinking into the earth. You couldn't tell whether the flowerpots were on the windowsills or the floor, and you could neither see nor hear what went on inside.

All the little houses were wrapped in a thick, warm coverlet of snow. The wind blew the snow against the windows and into all the chinks in the walls, but the old lace curtains betrayed no movement. The smoke from the chimneys wavered over the roofs like a drunken man, as if escaping from the overheated rooms to burst forth and expand in the open air. Under their mantle of snow the little houses seemed to give off a white mist of perspiration.

"Hey, dreamy! What are you staring at?" Abrashka laughed and pelted me with snowballs.

"Idiot! Be quiet. Everyone will come rushing out."

"In this cold? I bet they don't. Want to bet?"

Behind a fence stood a tree, probably an old one, covered

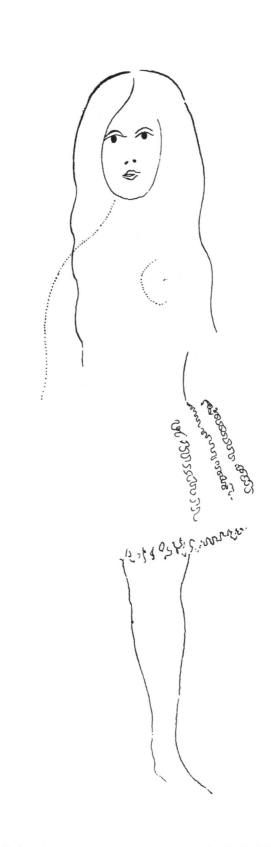

with snow as Grandmother's bed was covered with pillows. The branches could hardly bear the weight. Abrashka climbed onto the fence, then onto the tree, and shook the boughs. The whole tree shivered. Great lumps of snow fell like stones. A leafless branch cracked and broke.

"Monster! Isn't there enough snow for you in the street? What harm does it do you on the tree?"

"The tree's as much mine as yours. Or is it some relative of yours?"

I'd have liked to run into one of the little houses. Perhaps inside there was an old grandmother behind whose full skirts I could hide from Abrashka.

Grandfather's house was at the very end of the street. It was just like all the others: the same pots of flowers, the same shutters with barley-sugar rungs and snow in all the crevices, and the same streamers of smoke over the roof. But Grandfather's house seemed whiter and warmer than the rest.

As soon as he reached the door, Abrashka pulled the bell. It gave a hoarse cough and fell silent again.

"Is that you, children? I meant to go to the market first, and here you are already for your Hanukkah money!"

Frieda, Grandmother's old cook, stood in the doorway, a shawl over her shoulders.

"Brr, you've brought the cold with you. Come in quickly. Is it very bad out? Should I put another shawl on, Bashenka?"

She stamped her feet, and the freckles on her face wobbled up and down. In the winter they looked like little blobs of fat she'd forgotten to wash off. Frieda was always in a hurry, always busy and bustling. She said she was going to the market, but she'd certainly have the meal already in the oven. We could hear something frying in the kitchen.

"Frieda, can we have some fried potatoes?"

"How do you know I'm making any?"

"Frieda, is Grandfather still asleep?"

"Asleep? What do you mean? He never does anything but study the Torah. . . . Shoo!" She chased the cat out of the shopping basket. "That's a new trick!"

The cat, rudely awakened, glared at us out of bright slits of eyes. She saw the snow on our shoes, lifted her tail, twitched her whiskers, and prowled around us, licking the strange whiteness. The snow melted at the touch of her warm nose and made her sneeze.

"Silly puss," said Abrashka, getting hold of her by the tail. "Stop that, and go and tell Grandmother we're here."

"Don't bother her, she's lazy. *I* can run faster than she can."

There stood Grandmother. She'd come in so quietly it was as if her footsteps were muffled by the sweetness of her smile.

"Fancy coming in this cold, children. You must have something important to tell me!" she said, laughing. "Take off your shawl, Bashenka, and get warm by the stove. Be careful not to scorch yourself—I've just increased the draft."

Grandmother hovered around us, torn between helping us off with our outdoor clothes and getting us something to eat.

"Would you like a glass of hot milk? It's so early—what can I offer you?"

Her face and hair were white and shining. Little flowers bloomed on her cap as if it were summer. She was soft and plump and warm as the white-tiled stove.

You could scarcely move in her house. Every nook and cranny was crammed full, as if Grandmother, with her constant fear of catching cold, saw any empty space as a source of drafts.

"It's Hanukkah today, Grandma," Abrashka reminded her.

"You don't say! But gently—you don't have to knock your grandma over just because it's Hanukkah. My goodness, how you've grown lately."

She tottered a bit on her short legs, and Abrashka was afraid she might be angry. But she smiled.

"But I know you're a good boy, Avremel," she said. "It's kind of you to come and bring us the glad tidings so early. If it hadn't been for you, I wouldn't have known! Come, you little rascal—you can start by kissing the mezuzah, as I'm sure your teacher's told you."

"And me, Grandma? I want to kiss it too," I said.

"Out of the way, midget!" said Abrashka. "You're only a

girl." And he chased me away, along with the cat, which had got between my legs.

He was lucky. He was a boy and could throw his weight about. Perhaps it was better to be a cat than a girl who was short and always being made fun of.

"Stop teasing her."

Then Grandmother clutched her head, as if she'd forgotten something.

"You haven't caught cold, have you, Bashenka? Come along and let me give you something."

"Some raspberries, Grandma?" I ran after her, for I knew that whenever she talked about catching cold, she got a pot of raspberry preserves down out of the jam cupboard.

"Here, Bashenka, take that, and tell your mother to give you a glass of tea and some raspberry jam before you go to bed. Tell her it's good for everything, and the best remedy of all for colds."

"Where's Grandpa, though?"

"He's in there by the stove."

Through the half-open door we could see the big, white, shiny stove, and beside it, Grandfather swaying to and fro like a black shadow. And we'd thought he was still asleep! It was as if he'd been there like that, without going to bed, ever since we'd seen him last Sabbath. He wore the same coat of dark alpaca, long, black, and wrinkled as his brow. The same coat summer and winter. But of Grandfather's thin body, nothing was visible; he might have had no body. His face shone, his eyelids blinked reflectively, with one hand he smoothed a whisker in his beard, and with the other he seemed to be tying a sort of knot in the air, swaying back and forth as he did so. Perhaps he was pondering a passage in the book that lay before him on the table, and turning its meaning over and over in his head.

He did not see us two children. His eyeglasses had climbed up his forehead, and his bushy eyebrows hid his eyes. His beard lay on his chest like a snowdrift, and the cheeks emerging from his sidelocks were also snowy white. Through the delicate skin glowed a few little red veins, warmed by the heat of the stove.

We were afraid to approach. The shadow moving back and forth in front of the white stove seemed far away, as if it already had one foot in another world.

"Look, Bashenka," my brother whispered, clutching my sleeve. "The ten kopeks are on the table."

Dear Grandfather! He'd remembered! And I'd imagined he thought only of holy things.

But he didn't turn his eyes away from the window. They reflected the sun as if trying to drink in all the light of heaven. In the window stood the Hanukkah lamp of dark old silver, its little cups still empty, waiting for the lights. But Grandfather's eyes lit up like a match, so that to me it was as if all eight candles suddenly burst into flame.

"Grandpa!"

We couldn't contain ourselves, but then at once fell silent, startled by the sound of our own voices.

"Eh? What's that?" Grandfather seemed to wake out of a deep sleep. "Aiga, I think there's someone here. Would you go and see?"

"But it's Alta's children—Avremel and little Bashenka!" cried Grandmother.

Grandfather turned his white head toward us, saw us, and smiled. He was transformed. All the pensive wrinkles were smoothed away like wax.

"And I was thinking," said Grandfather, letting his glasses slip down onto his nose and looking through them at my brother, "I was thinking that, God willing, Avremel would be bar mitzvah next year, and had forgotten all about Hanukkah money!" He pinched Abrashka's cheek affectionately.

"Come here and let me test you a bit. How far have you got in the Five Books? You've been studying with the rebbe for a long while now."

The ten-kopek piece glittered on the table, taunting. The silver coin lay within arm's reach. Abrashka could almost touch it, stroke it. He was dying to know what was stamped on the other side. The usual eagle, or something else?

Grandfather's voice was buzzing in his ears, but Abrashka's hand twitched. He wanted to roll the coin just once over the table. But the oilcloth was slippery, the money might roll off like a wheel. It might fall on the floor, and you'd have to look for it down all the cracks.

Abrashka's eyes bulged at this possibility, and he thought to himself: "I must get hold of the ten kopeks fast, before Grandpa asks me about all the things I did know once but have forgotten again."

And what should he do if Grandfather suddenly took it into his head to get the Five Books of Moses down out of the bookcase? Then Abrashka would have to recite just as he did for his teacher. The whole day could go by like that, and then where would he find a coachman or a horse? Why should they wait for him? All the other boys had piled into their warm sleighs and set off long ago. And he . . . Abrashka felt a pang. He would fall asleep beside his grandfather in front of the stove. The old man's face was as red and shiny as the wood burning in the stove. He felt sorry for him. Grandfather's hands trembled, his eyes glittered like two ten-kopek pieces.

"Ten kopeks!" thought Abrashka. With the other ten from Father, he'd have enough to ride right through the town. What driver would refuse? He'd only have to flash a coin at Ivan and his eyes would pop out. He'd get excited, the old peasant, and claim that no one had a horse and sleigh to equal his. They'd been left to him by a landowner!

"There's a fine black fur rug in my sleigh," Ivan said. "It doesn't matter if it looks like an old dead goat—that fur has warmed the children of the gentry!"

And his horse! Ivan whistled to express his enthusiasm. If you only knew how to tickle him, he'd fly like an arrow! And it wasn't just any old horse: the landowner's wife had always used it whenever she went for a drive.

"And what about my bells? They sound like all the church bells ringing at once. Get in the sleigh and let the horse show his paces!"

Ivan's rough voice boomed in Abrashka's ears. He could restrain himself no longer. He stretched out his hand and grabbed the money.

"Hey, hey, not so fast! There's plenty of time. Why are you

in such a hurry? You'd do better to hurry up and learn your bar mitzvah speech."

Abrashka looked up. Who was talking to him like that? Not Ivan! It was Grandfather's thin hand that was laid on his anxious fingers.

"Baruch," said Grandmother, "give them their ten kopeks. It will bring the children a taste of happiness. You can see they're bursting with excitement. The boy can't stand still, and the girl doesn't know what to do with herself!"

I held my breath. And then, swift as the wind, we rushed out of Grandfather's overheated little house. Abrashka clutched the ten-kopek coin in his hand.

He ran through the streets as if the snow burned his feet, whirling his hands around and around to make the coins jingle inside his gloves, asking himself: "Will there be a horse and sleigh left?"

I stopped for a moment. One of my galoshes was loose.

"That's what you get for taking a girl with you!" cried Abrashka, instead of helping me. "Stop dawdling! First Grandpa, and now you and your galoshes. All the sleighs will have been taken."

"It's not my fault my galoshes work loose. They're new." Then, to be unpleasant: "Grandpa must be angry that you wouldn't read for him."

"That's right, keep on at me! You'd do better to help me choose the driver. Who shall we go with, Ivan or bowlegged Berel? Berel limps."

"But you can't see it. He just sits there. And his horse's legs are straight enough."

"Who knows? Perhaps the horse limps too. Berel's a rogue!"

"Avremel! Miss!" The coachmen had seen us. They knew us; they were always there at the corner. From cold or boredom, they blew into their hands and flapped their arms.

"Got your Hanukkah money? How much? Show it to me. Right, get in. Jump in, miss."

The drivers jostled one another for our business. One, who

was obviously freezing and who was older than the rest, breathed out a dense vapor as if to warm himself, and when he spoke his little beard went up and down like a small ax chopping off every word.

"Come with me! Don't bother with him—you can see his horse is as decrepit as he is!"

"What! My horse could swallow ten like your nag! The angel of death take you!"

The drivers went on cursing and insulting one another.

"Come, young sir, they're all trying to cheat you. But you always go with me. Just see how warm you'll be under the nice fur rug, miss."

Ivan rushed out from behind the other sleighs and slid to a halt in front of us. He looked like an overstuffed sack, but with a supple bow he whisked back the motheaten sheepskin as if we were his old employers, the landowners. And before we knew where we were, we were sitting in his sleigh.

"Ugh!" The other drivers spat. "What can you do with him!"

Ivan cracked his whip just once, and the horse quivered and lifted its tail up like a cat that's had a pail of water thrown over it.

"Gee up, you lazy old nag!" cried Ivan, bouncing off his seat in his eagerness. The bells jingled, and kept on jingling.

"Hup, hup!" shouted Ivan.

The whip whistled through the air, marking the little horse's cold rump like a red-hot iron. The horse twisted and turned to escape; its own tail whipped it more than Ivan's thong. Its gaunt hindquarters rubbed against the shafts as if trying to scrape the skin from the bones.

We lurched about behind. At one moment the sleigh sank in a snowdrift, at another it tossed us up in the air. Scarcely able to catch our breath, we rushed along as if we had wings.

"Come on, you plague—hup, hup!" Ivan was yelling himself hoarse.

He whistled, clicked his tongue, bobbed up and down. A mountain of snow fell off his back and onto us. A cloud of snow rushed past and after us.

Snow spurted from the horse's muzzle and hung from its

eyelashes. Snow sprayed from its head and back. It breathed white steam and drunkenly tossed its mane. The bells jingled.

We swam along in its wake. On either side the town flew by, one street fading into another. The snow enclosed us as if someone was emptying a sack of flour. Where were we?

In a flash we'd flown through the park. A moment ago we could see its tall trees on the hill; now it had vanished like a snowflake in the air. And where was the cathedral? Who could have moved it? Its white walls, detached from the earth, hovered in a whirl of snow. Its gold cross flashed forth for a moment and vanished into the sky.

My cheeks were burning. I stretched out my hands to catch some houses, some streets. But everything fled—windows, shops, shop signs—carried away by the wind, swallowed up by the sky. We were far away from the town now. We seemed to fly through the air. I couldn't see anything. The snow clung to my eyelids and pricked my forehead. My head was frozen, my hair stiff with snow. You could have cut it with a knife. My neck was clammy—the snow had gotten down my collar.

The fur rug was drenched long ago and made me colder instead of warmer. I tried to stamp my feet, but they were like blocks of wood and I couldn't lift them. I shook Abrashka. What was the matter with him?

The wind blew so loudly I couldn't hear him. A minute before, he'd been neighing like the horse. Why wasn't there a cloud of steam coming from his mouth anymore? My face started to burn. Were we going to be frozen to death? Mother! Where was Mother! Had she disappeared into the sky too? She'd scold us. Where did we think we were off to? The ends of the earth?

"Whoa!" The sleigh stopped with a jolt. We nearly fell out.

"And where are the ten kopeks?" Ivan's gruff voice woke us out of our dream. He stuck his mitten, like a great bear's paw, in front of our noses. With one pale finger he extracted the ten kopeks from Abrashka's glove, stuck his whip in his belt, spat first into one hand and then into the other, and tossed the coin back and forth as if to weigh it. Then he bit it, smiled, and said: "Real silver, hard as iron!"

"Ivan, where are we?" I cried.

"Back home, little miss, back home!"

I looked around. It was true. Behind me, as always, stood the cathedral. Its walls and roof and cross had all come down from the sky again. And the sky itself was wrapped in darkness; all the clouds were gone. Just one small star twinkled on high.

The trees had all grown again on the hill in the park. The houses, shops, and windows were all back in their places.

We slithered out of the sleigh.

Where had we been?

Ivan had brought us back to our own wide street.

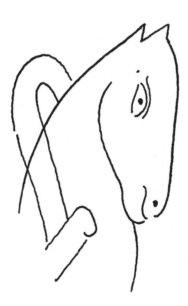

The Shop

A completely different world opened before me when I pushed ajar the heavy door separating the house from the shop.

The door was studded with big iron nails and had no handle; instead, a large key was always in the lock. The back of the shop was dark, and at first I groped my way blindly along the walls. Rough brown paper rustled underfoot.

Clocks still in their wrappings lay on the floor waiting to be hung on the wall. They lay silent, not ticking, as if buried alive. But the gloomy air was thick with noises from the shop.

A hum of voices beat like waves against the wooden wall and then ebbed again. I stood behind the tall partition and tried to make out who was speaking. When I heard my mother's voice, I was pleased.

But wait! Did her voice sound calm and peaceful, or—God forbid!—angry? On that depended whether I went in or not. But those high notes were encouraging. I drew aside the curtain over the last door dividing me from the shop.

At once I was dizzy with the clamor of glass and mirrors.

The ticking of all the clocks danced around in my head. Silver and gold, blinding as flames, were reflected in the mirrors and flashed from the glass showcases. Two large gaslights hanging from the ceiling breathed audibly, sighing over their woes. The fine mantles over the flames only just held back the sparks.

Two high walls were covered with glass cases, so close-fitting they seemed to have grown into the ceiling. The panels slid open and shut without a sound. Through the glass you could see quite clearly—almost touch—all the things on display: cups, glasses, sugar bowls, dishes, little woven baskets, milk jugs, water jugs, boxes to hold the ritual etrogs, fruit dishes. Everything glittered and shone as if newly polished. Whenever I moved, everything seemed to follow me as if in a mirror. The light of the gas lamps and the sheen of the silver crossed like swords: now the first would absorb the second, now the second would shine forth brighter than before.

On the opposite wall there was another showcase, with articles not of silver but of pewter, shining with a quieter and more modest luster.

In the middle of the shop, three smaller walls seemed to grow up out of the floor; they were long counters with drawers, dividing the room into separate parts. They were fitted with glass tops, beneath which lay objects of pure gold, sparking like magical arks of the Torah. Stones of every color set in golden rings, earrings, brooches, bracelets—all flamed like matches just struck.

With all this glitter and light, you scarcely noticed that the floor was dark. Even in front of the counters, where the customers stood, silverware shone through the glass and was mirrored in their well-polished boots.

The third wall was dark even in the daytime. It was covered with big clocks and looked like a forest of somber trees. All the clocks were different. Some had big wooden cases and thick chains bearing heavy brass weights. Others were slimmer and more elegant, with lighter chains and smaller weights. But under the belly of each hung a daggerlike pendulum, swinging ceaselessly, restlessly back and forth.

Hidden away among the larger clocks were some small or even tiny ones. You could see only their white dials, their round moon faces. They had no wooden bellies, and their thin chain legs hung out in the open for everyone to see. The whole wall of clocks sighed and groaned. From every case came a stifled cry, as if every minute, on that dark wall, someone were being slain.

Suddenly I started. One of the big clocks had woken up and was moaning like an old man getting out of bed. The sound was so heartrending I looked around hastily to see if it hadn't fallen to pieces. But heavily it struck the hour, and my heart thudded with it. I was glad when the minute hand moved away from the other: I had time to get my breath back before the old fellow started to groan again.

Another clock sounded as though it were blowing its nose or laughing hoarsely. The small clocks had high, thin voices: children waking up frightened in the dark. All the clocks groaned and sighed and swung their pendulums day and night without cease. When did they ever rest?

Suddenly several struck at once. Were they doing it purposely, so that I couldn't make out which was which? I looked from one to the other, bewildered, and heard some voices that seemed to come from the earth. It was a few little alarm clocks lying in cardboard boxes on the floor. Noisy brats, keeping the old folks awake!

I hurried over to twist their little heads and make them be quiet. But halfway there I stopped, rapt. A faint song tinkled through the air: a music box. I opened the lid, and the sound flew out like a bird from its nest. The box was crammed with wires and springs and wheels. Like waves they climbed on tiny cylinders, then rolled off the other side and swam along in the current of the melody. Each spring and each little wheel swam in one note, and kept it up till it was out of breath.

I went up close to the music box to let it know that I was listening and that it should go on playing. But all of a sudden, silence. I didn't close the lid. I waited. Perhaps it would decide to sing again.

Such a warm world had risen up out of the darkness and

spread all through the shop. Even the old clocks on the wall were holding their breath.

Every night before we went to bed, one of my brothers did the rounds of the shop. My parents sent him to see that—God forbid!—no thief had broken in. I wanted to have a look at the shop in the dark too, to see what all the gold and silver things were like when they were asleep.

But as soon as the big key creaked in the heavy iron door I quaked, even with my brother there beside me. What if the angel of death and all the spirits of evil were hidden there?

But it wasn't quite dark in the shop. A little light was kept burning on a table all night. The wick was twisted, and the sooty flame made our shadows long and flickering. The wall with the silverware was veiled in smoke: only here and there a sleepy eye opened—an engraved flower sparkled or an ornament shone. Then suddenly there was a blaze of silver, like the moon breaking from the clouds.

I was afraid to go near the wall with the clocks. They hung on their black nails as though eternally crucified. I seemed to hear sighs coming from open graves. The clocks scarcely moved: their pendulums limped, and the white dials with their little black marks winked with spectral eyes.

From a distance I listened to them all, and sighed when they did. I felt they were calling me, touching me on the shoulder. With a heavy heart I forsook them.

There was a wall clock in our dining room too. But it was shut up in a tall carved case: you couldn't hear its heart beat, you couldn't see its legs. And when it struck the hour, it sounded dull and indifferent.

A Wedding

The house was always dreary toward evening. Everyone stayed late in the shop; they'd all been in and drunk their tea long ago. The samovar was cold and stood there like a dead soul. The chandelier hummed and cast long shadows over the table. All day the dining room had been full of activity; now it was a dark abyss, and I was afraid of falling into it.

It seemed to me that if I stayed where I was, the light would get angry and grab me up to the ceiling. And who would hear me if I shouted? Even the glasses left lying on the table wouldn't stir to help me. I was frightened of the chandelier and of the cold samovar, and dared not look in its brass belly and see my pale face reflected there.

If only someone would come!

Where were my brothers? Where did they go every evening? Out in the street it was windy and cold, yet they came home cheerful and loaded down with new stories.

"Where have you been, Abraska?" I'd ask.

"Nowhere."

"What have you been doing?"

"Nothing." And he'd smile.

I'd sit at the table, my head propped in my hands, and hang on my brothers' lips.

They would all laugh. Then one would interrupt the other: "What's that you're trying to tell me, sheep's head?"

"I saw it with my own eyes!"

"Idiot! Does that mean it was true? I know the fellow better than you do. I . . ."

Yes, when my brothers were around it was amusing and I was never afraid. I envied them. They could go wherever they liked and Mother would never scold them.

But I? Where could I go? Into the kitchen? I was tired of the kitchen—all day long it was full of the smell of food, and now, with only the one little light, it would be gloomy. No, not the kitchen.

What about the shop? It was certainly light and cheerful there. But as soon as I put my head around the curtain everyone yelled, "What do you want? Go home! We have enough to do here without you."

I was always in the way. Don't touch this! Don't stick your nose in there! So I let the curtain fall and went away.

In the half-light of the hall I could see my coat hanging on the wall, with my white hood sticking out of one sleeve.

What about going out?

With my outdoor clothes half on and half off, I went down the short flight of steps that led to the ground floor. Behind me the steep, dark stairway wound upward like a snake.

I opened the big front door. A snowy white path lay enticingly before me. The cold made my nose tingle. Light flurries of snow scattered little beads of ice. I drank in the fresh air like water. The street was quiet, as if the snow had buried all the voices.

Frozen flames burned in the white, snow-covered street-lamps. The coachmen stood at the corner of the street, mounds of snow. Under their wet sacking their horses seemed to have stopped breathing and to be standing there lifeless.

There were only a few people about. The snow creaked as they walked along. I decided to follow them, and went along the broad street. In the distance I could see a big courtyard all lit up, and in it a two-story building behind whose windows lay suites of large rooms. Reception rooms.

Every night a wedding was held there. Even from outside, the place looked festive. Two big sconces flanked the entrance like rampant lions.

There must be a wedding that evening. Whose?

The snow began to fall more thickly. A lump of it fell off one of the sconces and dropped at my feet.

I could hear footsteps. Who was it? I looked and saw people coming through a gate. Two men were carrying a big copper container on their shoulders like some great dead animal. They came nearer. A thin jet of soda water squirted into my face. I was startled and didn't know whether to laugh or cry. What had they got against me? I hadn't done anything to them. I sneezed right in their faces.

They guffawed. "What a funny girl! Can't keep away from weddings, and washes in soda water!"

Waiters came and went. They were all carrying something. One had a cake still warm from the oven, another a jar of pickles you could hear slopping about. Others followed with trays of pastries.

Wide planks and trestles were brought in, swung through the air, and then fixed together as tables.

"What's that you're carrying?" I wanted to see everything.

"Oh, all sorts of things—fancy rolls, stuffed fish, everything your heart can desire." The waiters smacked their chapped lips merrily.

I moved aside to let them pass. The doors opened wide before them. The tables were shoved through, letting in a draft. I could see chairs placed along the walls. One corner was made into a little garden with palms and other potted plants. Under their leaves' green shade stood a chair like a throne with a red rug in front of it. The chair was waiting. For what bride?

It looked like an old man with sunken cheeks. A thin fringe hung from the thin upholstery.

How many brides had sat there? Each had left there her own fear and trembling.

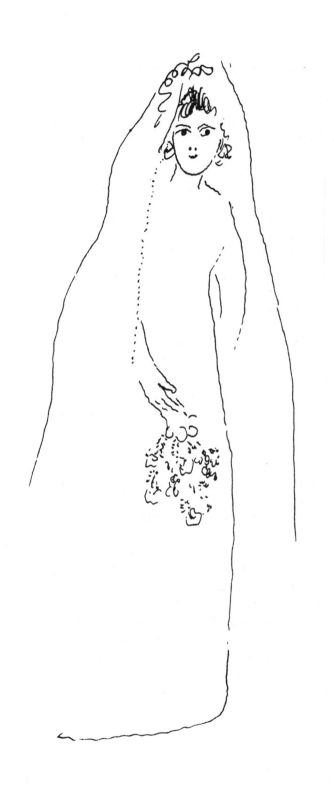

All the other seats could be moved about, but the throne with its flattened cushion stayed where it was and waited. For what? For the white bride, for the light in the darkness.

But when the bride came it would revive, breathe a sigh of relief, fill with air and whiteness. The carved heads on its back would bend toward her, and when she sighed the chair would moan too. If she wept, its arms would embrace her. And whether she was pretty or plain, in this embrace she would certainly burst into tears and pour out her heart.

The chair was ready. As soon as the bride raised her handkerchief to her eyes, it would absorb the warm tears and store them in the old wood. But they would occupy only a tiny space. The bride who sat there tomorrow would know nothing of the tears of the bride of today. For she would see nothing; she would walk blindly with downcast eyes up to the chair, and, as soon as she sat down, her white veil would be spread over it. As if poised on wings for flight into another world, she would be unaware of the sobs of her sister of yesterday. She would weep for herself, and leave behind on the old chair a part of her own weeping heart.

But where was she? The chair still stood empty, slightly embarrassed. Everyone was a little afraid of it and gave it a wide berth.

Women jostled each other and roamed about aimlessly. It was time for the ceremony. Why was it taking so long today? They whispered to each other, breathing audibly in their stiffly ironed dresses.

"She's very pretty, isn't she, the bride?"

"Yes, God bless her."

"Amen to that!"

But why didn't she come?

She was probably still at home, still being dressed in white. Her black hair had already been brushed, braided, and arranged in a coronet. But young smooth hands and old veined ones were still fussing over it.

"Pass me a hairpin," said one.

"Here, Manishka, you know how things should be done—you fix her veil."

What did she look like?

A bride was first and foremost a long white dress that trailed along the ground like something living, the whole covered by an airy veil. Through it, as through glass, the bride herself seemed far, far away.

Perhaps now she was riding through the dark streets, her veil overflowing the narrow sleigh and mingling with the blue-tinged snow. Her old mother was with her, holding her tight, unwilling to part with her. Hadn't she herself been a bride once, white and young?

The sleigh drove on.

"Are you sure you're not cold, child? Take care not to catch cold."

I was beginning to feel cold too. Something flashed by the windows; and had I heard the sound of a silk dress going past? Could I possibly have missed the bride?

Then I saw that the waiters were spreading big white cloths over the tables. They rustled as they fell in folds at the corners and hid the dark floor. The waiters laughed as they bustled back and forth, and you could hear the clatter of china and cutlery.

"Make way for the stuffed fish!" called one thin fellow, wriggling like a live fish himself.

"And for the chopped liver!" yelled another.

"And here comes the calves' foot jelly! Stand back!" cried a third.

Guests were arriving. The stairs groaned under their feet. The women filled the air with their puffing and blowing. I pushed my way through them and onto the porch. That was the best place to wait for the bride, to see her descend out of the air and set foot on earth again.

I hid in a corner. People shook the snow off their furs onto me. White beards turned black. Wigs emerged from wet shawls. The women they belonged to were adorned with flowers and pearls. Single snowflakes glistened in their hair, snow melted off their feet.

I felt wet and cold. A sleigh drew up right in front of me. Could this be the bride?

A couple of fat sacks rolled out: two little girls with little red faces.

"Whew!" They blew into their gloves. Unwound from their shawls, they revealed naked arms and shoulders and shiny pink and blue dresses. They must be the bride's sisters.

"Rosa, look how pretty it is! And the lights! I can hardly see, they're so dazzling."

"Quick, Rivka, let's go and find out what's going on upstairs."

"That's right, children, go in before you catch cold." And the older women hustled them on in.

These ladies really did need as much space as they could get. Their fox capes fell from their shoulders like gates flung wide; the little warm tails waved about and tickled me.

No one took any notice of me. I knew why: wrapped up in my hood, I looked just like a stranger standing and watching. I felt embarrassed when I looked down at my weekday dress. What a pity I hadn't changed! I looked up the stairs and saw the long white stockings peeping out under the girls' skirts. They were going to enjoy themselves, and dance about merrily on their short white legs!

I couldn't hold back my tears. I was angry that I wasn't one of the guests. I could have worn my pink silk dress. Sasha could have brushed my long hair and plaited it with flowered ribbons. My dress would have billowed out when I stood on the tips of my black patent-leather shoes. As soon as the music began, I would have gone into the middle of the room and kicked up my heels like a little goat.

Sometimes, when I was with my brother Abrashka, people would ask us to dance. "Move back, please," they'd say, "and let the children dance. It's a real pleasure to watch them."

Then they'd sit in a circle, making a ring with their outspread skirts.

I would bend one knee and bow my shoulders as if about to fall down. Then I'd glance at Abrashka, rise up on tiptoe, and look away. Abrashka would hold me tightly, and then we'd keep on dipping and rising. The fiddle played, and suddenly you heard the beat of the drum. The lights burned brighter. I couldn't see any faces, only the bodies of the women swaying in time to the music. They smiled, trying to lend us their energy. We seemed to be swept up into the air. I tossed my disheveled hair back like a shadow.

Then the music went wild and started to play a mazurka. Our feet carried us away. Abrashka stamped his feet and twirled me around. It was as if we'd left the room far behind us and were dancing somewhere else. Then the mazurka stopped as suddenly as it had begun, and we were left standing.

Hands stretched out and drew us toward them.

"How old are you, little girl? Oh, it's Alta's youngest!"

They patted us on the shoulder.

"Such nice children. May they be safe from the evil eye. And imagine a boy dancing so well."

They pinched our cheeks. . . .

But now the music had stopped, seemingly forever. I was still standing outside the reception rooms. The air was growing colder. An icy wind blew in my face. I was still by the open door, and through it there now came a mountain of snow. Once inside, the snow melted and was scattered like rain, as out of the mountain came a tall man.

"Hello, Bashenka, what are you doing here? . . . Hasn't the bride come yet? Come along, let's go upstairs. Why are you standing here in the cold?"

He blew into his frozen hands.

"Hey, Bashenka, don't you recognize me? Just wait—I'll soon be leading you under the bridal canopy too!" And he burst out laughing.

He was shaking all over. I watched his Adam's apple bobbing up and down. Of course I knew him. He was the master of ceremonies. I'd been just standing and waiting for the bride, but he'd been specially summoned. As he took me along with him, he sniffed the nuptial air with his long nose. His ears waggled, he shook his head, his neck was strained like the strings of a fiddle. So why did everyone start to weep when he, who was so merry, called out, "Bless the bride!"?

He had a voice that went right into your heart. He knew every family: each aunt and cousin, whether the bride had a father and mother, what everyone did for a living, whether they were happy or not.

He could draw everyone into the middle of the room, manipulating them as if they were on strings. Then he called out the names of those who were to bless the bride. The name would echo around as the aunt it had summoned lumbered forward, tottering a little, brimful of benedictions.

When the master of ceremonies gave his voice free rein, everyone grew tense. When it vibrated even louder, they were frightened. It was as if the aunt were approaching a corpse.

The lighted candles held around the bride would tremble in the people's hands, and in their midst the bride would sit like a scared white bird. The aunt approached and lifted her arms as if she were blessing the Sabbath candles. The bride hung her head even lower and groped blindly for her handkerchief, knowing she was near to tears. The aunt pitied her. She didn't touch her, but blessed her from a distance, like a star. The master of ceremonies looked around and called out other names. Everyone breathed again. You could hear people blowing their noses.

Everyone tried to cheer the bride up, fanning her, straightening the veil that had slipped and gotten rumpled, blowing at the strands of hair clinging damply to her forehead.

The master of ceremonies was clutching my hand and dragging me up the stairs.

"What are you doing? What's going on?" he demanded as soon as he reached the door.

The groups of women dispersed. I skulked along by the wall. But what was that? I hurried to the landing. A white cloud was floating up the stairs. A light breeze began to blow. The sound of a violin cleft the air and turned into a tune. The drum and the cymbals joined in.

Here she was at last—the white bride, light as air. With every step her heart beat faster. The music played all around her, decking her path with kisses. On the top stair she stopped. Should she go on?

Everyone had drawn back against the wall. She could have found her way to the throne blindfolded. She just looked down at her white slippers gliding like little boats across the floor.

I stood there, pressing behind the others. We all pushed forward, as through trying to guide her safely to shore.

A little way off stood a row of men dressed in black. They were led by a young man who walked with hesitant steps and whose tall hat trembled with him. He drew near the whiteness of the bride. He seemed as scared of her as she of him.

The rest of us held colored confetti; the master of ceremonies sang. The bridegroom and his men came nearer and nearer, and the red carpet was covered with black shoes.

The bride drew herself up and waited. We backed her up.

With a slight movement of his hands, the bridegroom lifted up the veil and threw it over her. It was as if both he and his bride were suspended in midair.

We showered them with confetti like stars. Some of the colored dots fell on us.

A little red sky had been unfurled in the middle of the room, held up with long poles. The bride stood like a bright cloud in the middle of the dark floor. We hurried over and supported her from all sides. Almost fainting, she was led under the bridal canopy.

Purim Gifts

White snow, pale sun. Purim had announced itself with the dawn: the frost had painted heroic knights on white horses on the windowpanes. A light wind blew. Today was Purim, the feast of Queen Esther.

Abrashka and I ran to meet it. We had our Purim money—we could hear it clinking in our hands—and couldn't wait to get to the market.

Already it was as busy as a fair. The rickety old tables were spread, as if for a wedding, with snowy white cloths with holes in them. Women and children crowded around like men in the synagogue about the Torah.

The tables shone enticingly, spread with a whole world of little figures made of icing. Tiny horses and sheep and birds, dolls in cradles—they all winked at us out of little red dots of eyes to show they were alive despite the cold. Little golden fiddles lay there as if lulled asleep by their last tune. Mordecai and Ahasuerus sat proudly in their saddles.

Now and then a pale sunbeam fell on all the fabulous Purim gifts, too feeble to warm them. Abrashka and I pressed up close against the tables, as if to rescue the frozen toys by thawing them with our breath. We'd have liked to take them all away with us; here they would surely freeze to death.

"Make up your minds, children. Choose your presents and go home!"

The shivering vendor broke into our dreams.

As if it were so easy to choose! We looked at the Purim toys with beating hearts: perhaps they'd tell us which of them wanted to come and which to stay.

How could one bear to part with them? And what should one take, a big horse or a small one? My friend Zlatka might think I was showing off if I gave her a big one, but she might like it better than the other. I fingered the little horse.

"Bashka, what are you doing? It's dangerous to touch," my brother teased me. I let go of the horse before it could bite me.

My teeth were chattering, either from cold or at the wicked thought that all these little horses and fiddles were the sweetest of sweets, and I'd like to pop them straight in my mouth and eat them alive.

"I'll deliver your Purim presents if you like," said a tall, thin boy, coming up to us.

"All right, come along."

I was drawn by his sad round eyes, like those of a beaten dog.

"What's your name?" I asked.

"Pinya," he said.

"Pinya?" That was a funny name. Like the name of a bird. I asked him if he could whistle.

At home we spread our Purim gifts out on two plates, one for Abrashka and one for me. The small sugar figures seemed to come to life again in the warmth. Their little cheeks began to shine. I blew on them, afraid they might melt. A fine thing if the Purim gifts dissolved into little bits! More than once we exchanged plates and rearranged the presents. Above all I felt I couldn't part with the little violin. It clung to my finger as to a bow, wanting to play a tune.

124

If I sent it to my friend, I'd never see it again. My heart sank.

But Pinya, waiting to deliver our Purim gifts, was shuffling his feet impatiently. Trembling, we looked one last time at our plates, then wrapped each one up in a handkerchief and tied the ends together.

"Here are the Purim gifts, Pinya. Don't run with them, will you? And be careful not to slip on the snow. And look where you're going—someone might bump into you. Come on, wake up!" And we clapped him on the shoulder.

Pinya leaped up and started to run. The plates tilted in his hands.

"Gently, Pinya, there's plenty of time. No need to rush. Hold on tight to the knots," we called after him.

That boy will cause trouble, I thought. Those long legs! He'd drop our presents, for sure. And suppose one of the horse's ears broke off, or a bit of the violin? What would our friends think? That we sent them presents in pieces?

"Where are you, Pinya?" I said aloud.

But he was gone.

Now, I thought, he's turning into the lane where Zlatka lives. Now the black latch is being lifted and Zlatka appears in the doorway, as if she'd been waiting.

"Are they both for me?" she'd ask, stretching out her hands.

"No, this one's yours."

He'd probably mixed them up.

Zlatka snatched the plate and ran with it to her bedroom, leaving Pinya standing there.

Zlatka's mother was busy in the kitchen. With a long iron hook she lifted a big black pot off the stove and put it into the oven. Pinya's mouth watered. How delicious the roasted meat and potatoes smelled!

"What's taking you so long, Zlatka? The things children get excited about! Skipping about like goats over nothing."

Then she turned to the boy. "What are you standing there for, silly? You can sit down for the same money."

Zlatka was a sturdy little girl with short legs and a long pigtail. She walked so slowly I couldn't bear to watch her.

Even her great big eyes scarcely moved and looked as though they were frozen. The Messiah could come before she finished with the Purim gifts! She was probably looking at my plate from every angle, and holding the horse and the little gold lamb to her nose and ears. Her long pigtail would be waggling to and fro, as if trying to help her think. But she wouldn't be able to make up her mind.

Suppose she wanted to keep the whole plateful?

But what was I thinking of? I was ashamed of my suspicions. She was probably only going to the drawer where she'd put her own Purim gifts, spreading out her own little horses and lambs and comparing them with mine.

"Will she take the dear precious violin?" I wondered, quaking. And what would she put in its place? Oh, why didn't Pinya come back? Had he vanished forever?

"What do you think?" I asked Abrashka. "Do you think Pinya's got to your friend by now?"

But he laughed. Being older than I was and a boy as well, he thought he was entitled to make fun of me.

Let him laugh, then! I knew he was waiting for Pinya too, and dying to know what would be brought back on his plate and what gifts would be added to it. Whom was he trying to impress? I could see he kept looking out of the window.

"You know, Bashka," he said, "Pinya probably won't be back for an hour or so. My friend Motka lives on the other side of the river, and by the time that dreamy Pinya has crossed the bridge we'll be fast asleep ourselves. He's bound to stop and see what's happening. Perhaps the ice is breaking!"

What if Abrashka was right? I was nearly bursting with rage.

"Yes, with Pinya anything can happen," I agreed. "He'll dawdle by the river and not even be back before supper."

"Silly ass! You believe everything you're told. I just made it all up!" And he rolled about laughing.

Then suddenly he shoved me out of the way and in one catlike bound was down the steps leading to the kitchen. Pinya was knocking at the door.

"Why do you brats have to make all this noise?" yelled fat

Chaya. "You hang around all day doing nothing, and then come and get in the way. Out of my kitchen!"

We hauled Pinya inside, examining first him and then the plates. He was bound to have seen the presents sent in exchange for ours.

Well, I knew my violin was gone—I could see it in Pinya's sad eyes. I undid the handkerchief. Yes, she'd taken the pretty little fiddle, and I hadn't received another. What good was the doll she'd sent? I had two of those already—Abrashka had given me his. And this was what she'd been messing about over for a whole hour! I bit my lip with vexation.

And there was Abrashka laughing again, and that stupid Pinya too. I couldn't bear to look at them.

Abrashka could afford to be cheerful. Motka had put a large horse on his plate, and he was whinnying with glee. I burst into tears and ran to the kitchen.

"Why have you got such a long face?" asked Chaya, chopping onions. "Don't you like your Purim presents?" She jabbered away as if she were chopping with her tongue, and bits of moist onion spattered my face.

"How terrible! Let's hope you don't have any worse troubles before you're a hundred and twenty. Silly girl, you'll have forgotten all about it long before you're married."

Whether it was what she said or the onions, I began to shed real tears.

"Here's a little hamantash for you," she said, pressing into my hands a triangular pastry full of poppyseeds and heat. My fingers felt damp and warm, as if they'd been kissed.

"You see, Bashutka, no need to cry." Sasha smiled consolingly. "Do you know what? When I've finished my work, I'll pop out and change your doll for a little violin."

My darling Sasha! I hid myself in the folds of her skirt which from underneath looked like an overfull wardrobe, and wiped away my tears on her sleeve.

"Now, now, Bashutka, that's enough. I have to get on with my work. It'll soon be suppertime, and I can't do with you under my feet."

And she pushed me gently away.

In the dark of the room at the back of the shop, I bumped into something hard. It was a wicker basket. It must be Mother's Purim gifts for our aunts and uncles. It was crammed with delicious things. How could Mother send them away so heedlessly? There'd be red and white wine, little flasks of sweet liqueurs, big pears, wooden boxes of cigars, tins of sprats and sardines, and a new red tablecloth with colored flowers.

Mother was busy in the shop as usual, and had probably forgotten all about her Purim presents. Was it possible that she didn't even give them a thought? When the basket would be taken away at any moment! Wasn't she anxious at all about the presents she was going to get herself?

I pictured how pleased my good Aunt Rachel would be with my mother's gifts.

"God Almighty! So many beautiful things, and all for me! Oh, Alta, you do spoil me."

Aunt Rachel's frail heart beat with joy. She sniffed at the basket and closed her eyes, drunk with all the wonderful smells.

But what was this? As if awakened from a dream, she felt the tablecloth, lifted it up, and stroked it. Then, as if in benediction: "A thousand thanks, Altinka. May God in heaven grant you many happy and healthy years. How did you guess? A new tablecloth was just what I wanted for all my Passover guests."

Suddenly she thought she saw a speck of dust on the new cloth. She blew it away, and, lest the cloth get spoiled before Passover, carefully folded it up again.

How many baskets of Purim gifts had been sent through the streets from one house to another! And all the things they were full of! The gaunt old woman who delivered them could scarcely carry them.

"Is Isaac at home?"

I suddenly heard an unfamiliar voice in the kitchen. A little old woman wrapped in a large shawl stood in the doorway.

She was holding a yellow sugar horse as carefully as if it were a new baby.

"Happy holiday, Bashenka." She smiled at me with her thin lips. "Is Isaac in? Here's a Purim present for him."

She held it up to show me how large and beautiful her gift was. And indeed the horse seemed bigger and fatter than she was.

A strange woman, like someone out of the madhouse. Had she really once been my brother Isaac's nurse? He was so big and tall—how could this little woman ever have been his nurse?

He'd been living abroad for three years studying medicine, but every Purim the old woman came to bring him a present. And each time the dried-up old nurse said she wanted to see her baby.

Mother pressed a silver coin into her hand and said softly, afraid of frightening her, that Isaac wasn't at home. She should take the little horse away again and, God willing, it might come in useful next year, when Isaac might be here.

And every year the little horse grew yellower.

One day Isaac was there when the old woman came. But when she reached the door and caught sight of the grown-up young man, she was so frightened she ran away as if someone were chasing her, and forgot to give him the little horse. No one stopped her, and after that she never came again.

Mother gave Purim gifts to the servants and the people who worked in the shop. Something glittered in her hand—a pair of gold earrings and a ring showing through the tissue paper. Presents for the maids. Every holiday they were given something made of gold, which they happily hoarded away, although they never got married.

I looked at our bookkeeper. He was usually quiet and reserved, but now he'd become quite talkative. His mustache quivered as he stroked a new silver watch.

Huneh the clerk quietly folded a white silk scarf Mother had given him for his young wife.

But Rosa the salesgirl deafened the whole place with her rapture. She turned this way and that in front of the mirror, and boasted to everyone about the beautiful pendant she'd been given as a Purim gift.

The cashier had been given some money. Although she worked on a full till every day, she herself was hard up.

The clockmaker had a couple of bottles of wine—he had plenty of watches in his drawer already.

All of them beamed as if a wedding party were being held in the shop. Father's voice rang through the hubbub:

"Shut up the shop! Nearly suppertime!"

The Book of Esther

After the deep frosts the winter suddenly withdrew. The snow began to dwindle, the ice lost its luster. Blustering winds brought new scents and drove away the cold.

And with the wind came Purim knocking at the door.

One evening a gaunt old man appeared at our kitchen door like a weary messenger after a long journey. His hair almost hid his face, and his black beard was a thicket through which no wind could blow. His sidelocks hung down like two small braids from under his cap and lost themselves in his beard. Bushy eyebrows jutted out like a gable over little, deepset eyes.

He stood breathing heavily in the doorway, his beard panting with him. His large nose, curved like a shofar, blew into his mustache and whiskers as if to try to air them

"Well, if it isn't Reb Leib," cried the cook. "Oi, and me with my hamantashen still in the oven!"

She hastily wiped her hands, took off her greasy apron, and put on her holiday face.

The man at the door was not a beggar come for alms but Reb

Leib the Megillah reader. Every Purim he came to our house to read the Book of Esther. To read it, that is, to Mother and me and the cook. For the shop stayed open, and Mother didn't have time to go and hear it read in the synagogue.

"Why are you standing there in the doorway?" asked Chaya. She was glad of the chance to talk to a man of piety and show him she was pious too.

"Come in. The mistress is waiting for you. Thank God we've lived to see Purim come around again! May the Almighty perform a miracle every year and save us from all suffering!" And she suddenly gave a sob.

The man blinked uncomfortably. Perhaps he was late?

Chaya grew more and more expansive. For a moment it seemed to her that Reb Leib had come just for her, to tell her a beautiful long story.

"Sit down, Reb Leib," she said. "You're on your feet all day. We're only human."

She pushed up a chair. Her legs were always swollen, and all she thought about was sitting down. Whenever anyone came, the first thing she did was offer him a chair.

But the man stood there as if she weren't talking to him, and didn't even look at her. Eyes downcast, he stood chewing his beard, propping himself up on his long, knock-kneed shanks.

No one set eyes on him the whole year, but on the eve of every Purim he looked so tired you thought he must have wandered all over the world since the last time. Did he tell everyone about the miracle of Queen Esther, or was he searching for other wonders to tell us about?

He took a pinch of snuff, coughed, sneezed, and took out a big red handkerchief and wiped his mouth.

"May you be safe from the evil eye, Bashenka," he said, casting a brief glance at me. "How you've grown since last year! Have you got your rattle? You're so big and clever now, you'll be able to shout Haman down all on your own, won't you?"

At every word his mustache jumped up and down, and his big yellow teeth stuck out like the keys of an old piano.

I ran to fetch Mother from the shop.

"Hurry, Mother, the man's come to read the Megillah!"

"What, already? Is it as late as that?" She dropped every-thing and shouted some instructions to the staff. "Keep an eye on the stuff lying about, all of you. I won't be long. Anna, don't let any customers go before I come back, will you?" And she hurried out.

I rushed after her.

"Mother, do you know where the rattle is? Reb Leib was asking for it. He wants me to drown Haman!"

"You and your questions! Don't bother me. If you can't find the rattle, you can always stamp your feet."

When the man saw Mother he stepped forward and bowed his head. "Good evening, Alta."

"Good evening, good evening, come in, Reb Leib. It must be late. I suppose they've already finished reading in the synagogue?"

Instead of answering, he smiled shyly into his beard and sidled by so as not to touch us, God forbid. But as soon as he was past us, he strode through the house as though he were out in the street.

"Here's your rattle, Bashenka," whispered Chaya, pushing a wooden noisemaker into my hand.

"But it's last year's! It doesn't work anymore."

"May all my enemies be struck as hard as you'll strike Ha-man with it! Reb Leib will tell you the same."

The reader was standing in front of the bookcase. He opened both doors wide and reached in with a hand as wide as a spade. Without looking, he drew the scroll out from the corner where he'd left it a year ago. The quiet bookcase trem-bled, and a few books fell on their sides, sending up an angry little cloud of dust.

Reb Leib picked up the scroll and bore it in front of him like a treasure. The silky white cover with its embroidered gold letters and crowns cast a bright ray of light on his dark face. Even his beard shone.

Cheerful, revived, he went over to the table. He didn't look at us. He took off his cap, and his black velvet skullcap lent him new luster. His short prayer shawl lay on his shoulders like a pair of white wings.

"Quiet!" He banged on the table with his hand, probably imagining himself at the lectern of a crowded synagogue.

"Quiet!" He banged again, though we were all three standing there in expectant silence.

He gathered himself together, bowed to the scroll, kissed it, and removed the cover. And like Samson casting down the pillars of the Temple, he took hold of the rollers of the Megillah and unfurled it to right and left. The yellow parchment gave off a musty odor.

A heap of black letters arranged in rows like stairs lay on the table. Reb Leib lifted his head and stretched out his goose-like neck.

"Ahem! Aha!" He lengthily cleared his throat.

The lamp hanging from the ceiling shone on his face. He looked into the light, and his face lit up as if it had absorbed its warmth. He swayed back and forth, and then in a high, chanting voice began to read out the first verses. And all three of us repeated them after him.

Once started, the reader didn't stop. Riveted to the table, propped on the handles of the scroll, he swung back and forth as if propelled. The stiff parchment rustled in his hands; he was enveloped in sound.

It was as if the whole mountain of black lines had been set in motion and was spinning around like a wheel.

Then King Ahasuerus came down from his palace with an army of warriors. They seemed to ride over the lines, the horses' hooves trampling on the letters as upon cobblestones.

The reader read faster and faster. With every breath he drew in a whole lot of letters, as if Ahasuerus and his army were after him and each word was a step gained.

He crumpled the pages, snatched out the lines, and tossed them into the air on his trembling voice, each following like clockwork the prescribed tune. Now it soared slowly up and was stretched out, now it sank back again. Next Reb Leib would swallow a few lines, then the melody would rise and fall again. He veiled the whole story in a kind of wavering cloud.

Now and then he would force a note, as if to give Ahasuerus himself a shove.

We listened with bated breath. I tried to catch the moment when the king rode by and when Mordecai appeared on his white horse.

Mother held her Yiddish text and nodded her head in approval. Chaya, crammed in the doorway, sighed and snapped her fingers. You could just hear her voice: "It's true—all he says is true."

I stared into the reader's mouth, but couldn't keep up with his tongue tapping against his teeth like a little hammer, or make out where he had got to in the text. Hardly had he reached a passage than he'd rolled it up and his eyes had sprung to the next.

I was on tenterhooks for the name of Haman to come. I mustn't miss it, God forbid! It was up to me to shout him down all on my own.

The rattle was clammy in my hand. I only hoped it was going to work.

I went nearer to the scroll and touched the silver handles flanking the yellow parchment like two great columns. There must be pillars like this, I thought, at the entrance to the king's palace, to light Esther on her way. Soon she would appear with her long robe and golden hair. The lines were already farther apart, leaving a bright empty space. I could see Esther's radiant face. . . .

Suddenly Reb Leib gave me a push, probably to shove me out of the queen's way. I glared at him angrily. But his neck was stretching up toward the ceiling, and his voice thundered out:

"Haman, Haman, son of Hammedatha!"

Mother and Chaya stamped their feet.

Of course, I *would* choose now to be dreaming about Esther! There was scarcely time to wield my rattle. I banged it crossly on the table.

Reb Leib took a breath and plunged into the Megillah again. I didn't take my eyes off him now.

"Haman, Haman!"

He nodded to me as if to say that Haman had escaped from the book and I was to strike him down on the spot.

I banged the rattle on the table, stamped my feet, and yelled with all my might. If Haman escaped me, Mother and Chaya must catch him.

"Haman, Haman!"

Now he was shouting it over and over again, as if not one but a thousand Hamans had emerged from the scroll.

We were making a fearful noise. The reader added to it, undoing the scroll: every page let out a sigh.

Would we really be able to kill Haman? Or would he run us through with his sword?

Esther, Esther, where are you? Come and perform your miracle!

Then Reb Leib actually stopped shouting and swaying, as if Esther had risen up to shine upon him from the page he'd just unrolled. He lowered his voice, decorated the melody, and bowed as if to kiss the hem of her robe.

"Esther's come, thank God!" I whispered to Mother.

We were all relieved. Mother sighed; Chaya raised her eyes to heaven, praising God, perhaps, for having shown His mercy in time.

Esther, rising out of the chanting, went down the steps of the lines on the page. Her long train swept behind her over the empty spaces, leaving pale folds in place of black letters, as if, in honor of the holiday, white candles had been lit upon the scroll.

"Amen, amen!" we all chimed in and ended with the reader.

The melody had run its course, and Reb Leib fell silent. His hands still rested on the scroll. I stood and waited. Perhaps some word would issue from his closed lips, from the beard now suddenly black again.

But no—all was still, as though something had died.

The reader kissed the scroll quietly on both sides, as if on

both cheeks, and rolled it up tight. It became old and arid again. He took it back to the bookcase. We followed it with our eyes. We wouldn't see it again for a whole year.

When he returned from the bookcase, Reb Leib suddenly stood still and stared at us. Had he been reading just for us three? It seemed to him the whole world had heard him.

The Purim Players

The house was in a bustle the whole day of Purim. Until suppertime, presents were being wrapped up and taken away. Here someone was filling a basket with good things. There someone else was unpacking gifts sent by relatives.

The old messenger woman was exhausted. "Phew, I can hardly stand," she sighed, setting her basket down on the table and sinking onto the chair.

"Dvosha, you can rest for a whole year," said the cook. "There's another basket still to be delivered. But hurry, it'll soon be time for supper." She didn't give the old woman time to catch her breath.

In the dining room the lamp was lit and the samovar brought in, hissing and shining as never before. The shop was shut too, and Mother hurried in.

"Where's Dvosha?" she asked. "Dvosha, have you taken all the presents? What about Aunt Zipa? And my elder sister-in-law? Do you remember the trouble we had over her last year? Think, Dvosha—are you sure you haven't forgotten anyone?"

The old woman—the same one every year—knew all Mother's relations by heart.

"With God's help, Alta," she said, "I've taken care of them all. They were all very pleased with their Purim gifts, and wished you even more good things than they'd put in their baskets!"

"Good. So here's your Purim gift, Dvosha. Have a good holiday." And Mother pressed some coins into her hand.

"Thank you, Altinka. A happy holiday to everyone. With God's help, may we all live in health and happiness till next Purim!"

Father sat at the table in his long silk coat. His beard had been combed so that every hair was in place. His face shone in the light of the chandelier, which scattered little circles of brightness here and there over the tablecloth as the lamp stirred. At the other end of the table, Mother's tall candles burned. The festive board was ready.

The beadle from the synagogue came in, followed by the director and a neighbor who lived on our courtyard. They came to wish Father a happy holiday, and he asked them to stay to supper.

"Sit down, Reb Ephraim. Sit down, Reb David. We'll have a glass of tea while we're waiting for supper."

They sat there and drank their tea as if it were wine. With every glass they grew more lively, melting with warmth and well-being.

A little heap of silver and copper coins lay on the table near Father's hand. He pushed forward a pile of small change for every beggar who came in.

"Happy holiday, Reb Shmuel Noah. Happy holiday, ma'am," they all said, bowing.

All the town and its beggars passed through the house. The door was never shut. We might have been sitting in the street with all the people going by.

A tall man with a black beard came and stood before Father. I thought it was King Ahasuerus in person: everyone would get up, even Father, and give him the place of honor. But the man went away, not at all like a king but with bowed head.

The little hill of coins grew smaller. Who was still to come? Whom was Father waiting for?

Suddenly the glasses on the table shook. There was a noise as if people were fighting in the kitchen, with plates and cutlery falling on the floor. There was stamping and whistling and laughing. Father and the visitors exchanged glances.

"It must be the Purim players," whispered the beadle.

The door flew open and a rowdy company burst in. Tall, short, fat, thin. They seemed to come not only through the door but also out of the walls, out of every nook and cranny. The doors and windows rattled.

Strange heads popped up everywhere. One was like a blue sugarloaf, another had an enormous nose, another swollen cheeks. But there were no feet to be seen.

Where were their feet? They never kept still for a moment. One climbed onto another, dug him in the ribs, tripped him over, then fell down himself, dragging the other with him, and both turned somersaults. We were bent double with laughter.

"Attention!" One man emerged from the rough and tumble holding a false red nose to his face. His real nose was probably even uglier, or why would he be trying to hide it?

"Happy holiday, gentlemen! Here's the merry Purim, and I'm Red Nose." And he whistled through his ample nostrils.

Father and the guests nodded their heads.

"Happy holiday," all the Purim players chanted together.

Red Nose whipped up the enthusiasm. "Come on, friends! Why have you stopped? Let's dance and make merry." And he started them off by singing and stamping and clapping his hands. His boots thumped the floor like hammers.

They all whirled around the room, reeling as if they were drunk, falling down, turning somersaults. One voice rose above the rest:

"Hey, Mendel the Drum, where are you?"

A fat round drum came forth, followed by feet that seemed not to belong to it. From one side a long hand stretched out and banged it on the belly; from behind, two cymbals came and boxed it on the ears.

A trumpet blared, a horn blew, and high above the others sounded a flute.

They seemed to circle around over my head, and I didn't know which to concentrate on. It was as if they were all protesting at Red Nose, who pushed them around and wouldn't let any of them show off his tricks.

"Quiet!" he roared. "Here comes King Ahasuerus!"

And he stepped forward, took off his red nose, and put a golden crown on his head. It always had to be him!

"Him and his big boots! Perhaps he's going to play Esther too," whispered the others.

Then someone sprang past him, riding a white stick and crying, "I'm Mordecai!"

Another, wearing a pointed tin hat with bells on, shook his head and made them tinkle. It was as if his whole body were covered with bells.

This was too much for Father, who laughed so heartily that he had to wipe his eyes.

The fat director rocked back and forth, his belly shaking with laughter. "Mordecai's a bit early—he's shouted down the king instead of Haman!"

"That'll be enough!" Father brought them all to a halt. "You've still got to go around the rest of the town." And he stretched his hand out over the table.

Red Nose—King Ahasuerus—leaped nimbly forward and grabbed the whole heap of money. The troop of players were furious, and began to fight in earnest.

Father's voice brought the row to an end.

"Alta," he called, "let them have something to drink."

A glass of brandy was poured out for each of them. They gulped it down as if they were going to swallow the glass as well, and at once they were all on fire again. They leaped and danced. Eyes sparkled, the drum rolled, the cymbals clashed, the flutes trilled, the bells tinkled. They called us, pulled us, took hold of us all. My head was swimming. I started toward them. . . . But what had happened?

The bells sounded fainter and fainter, smaller and smaller,

far away. I looked around. The Purim players were gone, all somersaulted away. The noise died away too.

Where were the players now? Vanished, as if they'd never been. The house was silent, more silent than before. Only the light shed its brightness, trying to keep up the holiday spirit.

Drinks were served. The table was laid. More guests arrived. I looked at the door, wondering whether the Purim players might come back.

"Father," I asked, "where are the Purim players now? Are they dancing somewhere else, or are they just going quietly through the streets like other people?"

Father smiled around at the guests.

"Let's sit down to supper, shall we?"

They all moved toward the table. I followed, but in my ears the bells were tinkling still.

Dinner

"Sasha! Chaya! Have you gone to sleep, or what?" my brother Israel called out from the dining room to the kitchen. "Didn't you hear me come in?"

He was always grumbling, my brother Israel. He was irritable, and exploded if he thought he was being neglected or that someone else got a better helping than he did. He sat at the table picking at the food with his fork, then pushed his plate away.

"Look at the bit of meat you've given me. Nothing but bones."

A growl started to gather in the kitchen, then approached with Chaya's heavy footsteps. She poured down a hail of reproaches on Israel. "What have you all got against me? Do you want to worry me to death? Leeches!"

She was shaking all over; her face was as red as a beetroot. She wasn't afraid of us children.

"You're not an only son, you know," she bawled. "Putting on airs like that! Is it my fault if you come in after everyone else? Chaya here, Chaya there! Chaya, I want a veal cutlet.

Chaya, I want a sweet-and-sour puff. And I want some potatoes with prunes. One wants an omelette, another wants meat, and another wants something made with milk." She imitated each one.

"And if you won't give them what they want, they snatch it out of your hands! It's all I can do to save something for the master and mistress."

She clutched at her heart. Her chest heaved. Suddenly she stopped, biting her thick lips.

"Perhaps you think I've eaten all the meat. As God is my witness!" She clutched her stomach now. "As if I could eat anything with my bad stomach." She squeezed out a tear. "A whole family breathing down my neck. I work like a horse. And no one ever feels sorry for me."

"All right, all right, that'll do." Israel was unmoved by her tears. "The best thing for you to do is to go back to the kitchen and get me a better piece of meat. And don't forget," he called after her, "bring me some warm vegetables—the others have gotten cold."

On weekdays we all ate separately. You felt at a loss, sitting alone at the table. My brothers might have nothing to do all day long, but they all wanted to show the maids that they were the boss, that they were as busy as Father and Mother and had no time to wait to be served.

Mother really didn't have time to eat. She was in the shop from first thing in the morning, and stayed there until Father and all the staff came back from dinner and business got a bit quieter. Then she'd snatch a moment and hurry in for a quick bite.

Only on the occasional happy day free from trouble did she allow herself a meal at the proper time. Usually she came in late, harassed and tired. Then it was better to steer clear of her.

She would hurry through the back of the shop where the bookkeeper sat. She didn't look at him. It was as if she were ashamed to be going to sit down and eat in broad daylight.

"Sasha, is there anything to eat?" she called. "Hurry up and put it on the table. Quick, I haven't much time!"

The maid hastily cleared a corner of the table and set out bread and salt, spoon and fork. Mother went on scolding the maid as she washed and dried her hands.

"My God, Sasha, why do you take such a long time? Where are you? Have all the children had their dinner?" Then, suddenly remembering me: "Has Bashka had anything?"

She knew the boys wouldn't have let themselves go short, but I was a pale little thing and the youngest, and she thought I ought to be fed by force.

Everything was now on the table. Sasha gave Mother a plate of soup.

"But," she said wistfully, "the meat will be cold by the time you've finished your soup."

Mother sat on the edge of her chair, listening to the sound of voices from the shop.

"Hush," she said, "my head's bad enough without you. I think I heard someone just come into the shop."

About to fly off again, she hastily swallowed the last mouthful.

Then the shop boy panted in. "The master's asking for you, ma'am."

Mother jumped up at once.

"Shall I bring the rest of your dinner into the shop?" asked Sasha sadly.

I was left alone at the table. There was no one there to tell Mother I wasn't eating anything. Sasha kept putting things on the table.

"I don't want any more," I told her.

"Bashutka, God preserve you, what are you saying? It's so nice. Smell! Just taste and see how it melts in your mouth. Hey, Bashenka, you're not ill, are you? Wait a minute, I'll fetch Chaya."

She knew I was more frightened of Chaya than I was of her. In came the cook, smelling of onions as usual. She fell on me at once.

"What's this? Why don't you want anything? Now, no nonsense, please! When are you going to learn to eat like everybody else? No wonder you're so pale. And your mother will say I don't give you enough to eat."

"All right, all right," I said. "I'll have something, but leave me alone."

I ate a bit of meat just to make her go away. I couldn't bear her smell of onions and dirty crockery.

"God Almighty, even the child is against me." Chaya drooped, wiped her bleary eyes with her greasy apron, and went back to the kitchen.

I was alone again. I swallowed a mouthful and looked at the door. If only someone would come. . . . I counted the days until next Sabbath, when all those empty chairs would be around the table again, and Mother and Father and my brothers sitting on them.

Suddenly the door opened and Abrashka flew in like a whirlwind.

"What are you sitting around for, you daydreamer? Look, there's the ice-cream man!" He pulled me over to the window.

We looked out at a man who was going around the courtyard like a wandering iceberg. He wore a loose white smock and balanced a tall tub on his head. The tub was swathed in white cloths, which hid his face, and looked as if it were his real head, wrapped in a towel because it hurt him.

He strode through the snow on his long, strong legs. The tub moved in time with his shiny black boots. Then he stopped in front of our window. Probably he'd seen us. He craned his neck like a cock before rain and crowed:

"I-i-ice cream! Sweet i-i-ice cream!"

The very windows shook. Abrashka leaped to the door and then back again.

"What are you standing there for?" he yelled at me. "Go and ask Mother for five kopeks—he won't give me any more credit."

"I think she's busy."

"Well, silly, at least go and get some glasses."

He flew into the kitchen, where he seized the cook from behind and hustled her over to the window.

"Chaya," he said, shaking her, "you must give us five kopeks. There's the ice-cream man!"

"God Almighty, is the boy crazy? You'll get five kopeks, I

don't think! You've only just been eating meat for your dinner!"

"That? I've forgotten it long ago."

"Oh, yes, poor little orphans! I starve you, don't I? Why, you've just guzzled down three cutlets, and you have the nerve—"

"Oh, cut it out! You'll keep it up all night, and the man will have gone."

"Yes, and a nice one he is, your ice-cream man, coming here and leading Jewish children astray. You're lucky your teacher isn't here—he'd give you what for, and all your nasty ice cream would melt—"

"I-i-ice cream! Sweet ice cream!" sang the man in the yard. Abrashka racked his brains to find a way of getting around Chaya.

"His ices aren't made with milk, you know." Then he tried to wheedle her. "I'll knead the dough for you, Chaya, without being asked, and I'll fetch the pickles and the sauerkraut from the cellar."

"Thanks for nothing. And what's the use of sticking to me like a leech? Where am I suppose to get the money?"

He could hear her weakening.

"What, do you mean to say you haven't got five kopeks' change from the marketing? Why should you be so stingy with Mother's money?"

"Oh, so your mother's money doesn't matter? We're supposed to throw it away, are we? And how am I to square my accounts tonight, may I ask?"

"I-i-ice cream! Sweet i-i-ice cream!" The voice of the ice-cream man wafted in through the kitchen window.

Chaya was beset on all sides.

"Ai, what would you do with the brat? He wears you down. Here, you rascal!"

She rummaged among her skirts and brought out her purse.

"Eat the nasty stuff, then! Ignore the dietary laws!"

Hunting the Hametz

The eve of Passover was approaching. The whole house was in an uproar. Even the air throbbed.

"Have you scrubbed here? What about the corner? Make sure you dust the shelves properly. And here are the Passover towels."

Chaya tormented everyone within range.

"As for you, Sasha," she told the little gentile maid, "to the devil with you and your leavened bread! Take it to the cellar and eat it with Ivan."

She collected all the dishes that had had yeast in them and stowed them away in a dark cupboard. They were things she used all year round, but now she couldn't bear the sight of them and almost kicked them out of the way. Suddenly she stopped in horror: she'd caught sight of a smudge of flour in the black tin she used for baking cakes and biscuits.

"If your father were here, he'd burn even that!" And she put it in the cupboard, out of sight. She scratched her hands trying to get shreds of radish out of the scraper.

"This cursed leaven, there's no getting rid of it. Children, didn't your teacher tell you to turn out your pockets? So what are you waiting for? Your father will soon be here to burn the hametz."

She turned out our pockets herself.

"Hey, careful, you'll tear the pocket right out!" It was no easy matter to empty our pockets. All year we filled them with anything we found indoors or out. So the boys watched to see whose would have the most crumbs.

"Quick, here's Father!"

And our pockets were hastily turned the right way in again.

Father had come to burn the hametz, and Chaya relaxed. Father's face was grave, as though something had been lost and he had to find it. His black hat overshadowed his face, but someone handed him a candle and the little flame lit up his pale features.

"Have you got a feather duster?" he asked softly. All the children followed him in silence; we could hear ourselves breathing.

Father, with the candle and the duster in one hand, and a wooden spoon in the other, inspected every ledge and corner, though they'd all just been scrubbed. He even rummaged through the bookcase and looked under the Talmud, as if someone were trying to hide something from him. Suddenly he spotted a few crumbs that had been overlooked in all the washing and wiping. Or perhaps Chaya had left it there on purpose, so that Father wouldn't have to search too long!

His eyes flashed, and so did the candle, as if he'd found a treasure.

He put all the crumbs he'd collected in a piece of paper and bore it like an offering to the stove. The flames devoured the little parcel—and the hametz—and were reflected in his eyes.

"Thank God," sighed Chaya. "We'll have a kosher Passover!"

Preparations for Passover

The first person to be caught up in Passover fever was Chaya, our fat cook.

Ever since Purim she'd been going around in circles. Ordinary weekdays meant nothing anymore. Her only thought was of a kosher Passover.

Early in the morning she'd come rushing into the dining room. "Come on, children, you've been dawdling around long enough. Finish up your breakfast and get out of here—the painters have come."

The boys started to grumble. "What, already? Do you know when Passover is? There's time for the Messiah to come before then!"

"Yes," Chaya snapped back at them, "and the place has to be painted for him! So instead of chattering, help me move the wardrobes away from the walls."

"Is that all? Just a little thing like that? What will she think of next? They weigh a ton."

We all heaved together against the wardrobe. It just moved. Inside were Father's black suits, together with his pelisse and

Mother's fox cape. The long hairs of the fur tickled the other clothes. We kept pushing, and the wardrobe creaked and groaned with every shove. The legs scratched the floor, leaving white streaks.

"Hey, stop!" cried one of the boys. "See what you've done, Chaya? One of the legs has come loose. How are we going to get it back again?"

"So what do you want me to do? The wall's got to be papered."

"Perhaps you ought to go to the rabbi and ask him if you

should move the walls instead," they jeered.

"Very clever! But I've been cleverer since before you were heard of. I've got more brains in my little toe than you have in all your heads put together. What I should really ask the rabbi is how such heathen come to live in a good Jewish family!"

"There, she's angry! Let's go and watch them make the matzahs."

Then Chaya turned toward the open door and called, "Reb Yidl, Reb Nahman, you can come in now. You'd better begin with the little room next to the dining room."

Two white shadows emerged as if from a mist. Apparently they'd been waiting for her to call them. They were white from head to toe: shoes, hair, cheeks, and eyebrows—all were spattered as if with flakes of snow. One had a ladder over his shoulder and a bucket of paint in one hand. The other needed both hands to struggle with numerous rolls of wallpaper, like holy scrolls.

As soon as they crossed the threshold the painters took possession of the room. We cleared tables and chairs out of the line of march. They were soon in complete control. One climbed up the ladder and scraped at the cornices; the other got on the table and scrubbed at the ceiling with a big brush, bringing down bits of plaster.

"Want to taste the whitewash, miss?"

The younger of the two painters smiled down at me from the ladder. His little beard was covered in whitewash and seemed glued to his white lips.

It was so cheerful with the painters there! First one and then the other would burst out laughing. They sang and whistled and stirred the paint and dipped their brushes in. Paint was spattered around.

Suddenly one of them began to paint the ceiling, back and forth. The other followed, and both dabbed with their brushes like birds pecking with their beaks.

Then it was the turn of the walls. It was as if the painters wanted to tear them down. The old wallpaper rustled to the floor, bringing with it lumps of crumbling plaster. The walls were left bare and rough and ugly. Everywhere underfoot

157

there was paint and torn wallpaper, its flowers damp and bedraggled. But the painters skipped over all that, and cut up new lengths of wallpaper with new little flowers and pasted them on the walls.

The paper cockled up and wouldn't stick. So the painters dampened it with a wet cloth and it spread smoothly from top to bottom.

The little room, freshly painted and papered, shone as if to welcome a bridal couple. But it wasn't kosher enough yet for Chaya. She draped the walls with white sheets like prayer shawls. She even spread one on the floor. It seemed to me the place was fit to hold the ark of the Covenant.

The first thing to be brought in was baskets of unleavened bread—two tall, wide baskets swathed in linen napkins. It looked as if each matzah was wrapped in a sheet. Chaya ran ahead to show the way.

"Careful, mind the steps. Put the baskets down gently so that the matzahs don't get broken, God forbid!"

She ran around the baskets, touching them, almost whispering a blessing. With the matzah a bit of Passover had already entered the house.

A third man with a fine long beard brought a small basket of special matzah for Father. He held the basket in both arms, as if he were carrying the Torah.

He didn't say a word, but looked around, saw a hook in the ceiling, and hung the basket on it. Now no breath with a hint of leaven in it could touch the special bread. The basket was so shrouded in white that the wicker was invisible.

From then on no one was allowed into the little room. Only Chaya in her felt slippers could linger there. She became its mistress, and all the family submitted without a word.

When Chaya went through the house in a white apron with a white kerchief on her head, we all knew where she was going: to the little study. Her face was tense, as if she were on some world-shaking errand.

We would sneak after her, but she locked herself in. The latch clicked in our faces. We sat down on the step outside and listened to the pounding of the wooden pestle.

"Chaya," we begged through the keyhole, "let us in. We'll help you pound the matzah."

The pestle banged away as if it were clouting us on the head.

"Chaya, our hands are clean! We swear! We've just washed them."

Perhaps she couldn't hear. The pestle was louder now. So we rattled the latch at every stroke.

"Chaya, just let us help for a minute."

Suddenly the door flew open and we leaped back, almost falling down the steps. On the threshold, like a thundercloud, glowered the cook. She was unrecognizable, as white with flour as if she'd just emerged from a mill.

"Why do you keep pestering me? Leave me alone, can't you? Do you want to spoil even my Passover?" As she panted, she breathed flour too. "What, let you in to pound matzah with unclean hands? I should say not! Can't you wait? Clear out!" Another blast of meal. "And don't you dare go near the baskets!"

Having vented her wrath, she went back inside. The latch banged to. Again we gathered around the door and put our ears to the keyhole. Now we could hear a sound like running water bearing sand along with it.

"Chaya, please, let us sift just a little bit of matzah flour. Please!"

She stuck her red face around the door and burst angrily out of the little room.

"Will you stop it? Leave this door alone!" she yelled.

A big sieve full of still unpounded matzah was clutched against her stomach so that the fine meal sifting through it seemed to be coming out of Chaya herself.

One of the boys tipped the sieve upside down.

"You wretch!" bawled Chaya. "May your hands shrivel up!"

She started to strike out at him, then remembered she had a Passover sieve in her hand.

"God Almighty! Haven't I got enough to do already? Why must you keep on pestering?"

"We only want to help!"

"Never mind what you want! And how come you're suddenly so thoughtful? Well, we'll see who gets his own way! If any of you tries to get in here, I'll . . ."

What a woman. When she got worked up it was best not to cross her. She'd box your ears as soon as look at you—and tell the rebbe. She knew he and my parents would side with her: Passover had to be kosher.

So we let her alone.

She calmed down then and trudged back to the kitchen, leaving white footprints like the tracks of an animal in the snow.

Soon we heard her returning. She was carrying a barrel of beets on her back, and slopping the red juice onto the floor.

She was so tired; her feet were swollen. How could we help her? She thought we were unclean, and she wouldn't let us touch anything.

"Hey, Chaya—what if we lapped up some of the juice? It'd make the barrel lighter!"

We pranced after her.

She shook her head. Her face turned from red to black. Her eyes were like sacks of damp ash—one squeeze and they'd overflow with tears.

"Oh, my feet! They're killing me!" she groaned.

Then, before she reached the little room, she dropped the barrel.

Chaya stood there in a daze, signing to us not to come closer.

My brothers tried to shove one another forward.

"Go on—you say we're sorry."

"No, you—you'll do it better."

Chaya wrung her hands.

"Keep away! Your hands! They're probably covered in hametz!"

"How could they be? It's ages since we had anything to eat."

And the barrel was picked up.

Chaya gulped back her tears. She'd have willed us to be kosher if she could.

"My God, these kids! All they think about is food!"

The little room filled up with dainties. We were fascinated.

Why should Chaya be the only one to taste the goodies? But she watched us like a cat, afraid to leave the little room unguarded. Perhaps she even slept there at night!

If we started whispering together, she'd loom up and want to know what we were up to.

"Nothing. Just standing."

"Why here? You must be going somewhere!"

"Now where could we be going?"

Then she'd go off, grumbling, to see that all was well with the little room. Every day something new was brought in: sugar, salt, nuts, prunes, almonds. There were sacks of things in every corner. Chaya seemed to delight in hoarding them just to tantalize us.

What a funny woman. On the first day of Passover she'd stuff us to the gills, but now she made us suffer tortures.

Every day it was the same.

Abrashka would hang around the door, then run and report.

"Bashka—I think they've brought the raisins today."

"No—I can smell prunes."

Then Chaya would catch us and ask what we were sniffing around for.

"Can't a person even sniff?"

"Go and poke your noses somewhere else! If you keep hanging around here I won't need to do any baking—there won't be anything left to cook."

Then she began to scour the pots and pans. One copper vessel after another would vanish from the kitchen. All the year round they stood on the upper shelves like generals on parade, darting fiery glances down below. By Passover they had grown dull, and Chaya lifted them down by their blackened handles and took them away to be cleaned. Even the old Sabbath jug and the samovar that hadn't had a drop of water in it for years were made as kosher as the samovar that boiled and bubbled every day. They might just have a speck of hametz in them!

The purified vessels looked as if they had a new skin inside them. Chaya took them to the little room and wrapped each one up separately in a white cloth. All those shrouds seemed to waft a sense of anguish through the house.

"Bashka, you're a big girl now. Here's the key—go and look through the glass cupboard. I think a few wineglasses got broken last year," said Mother.

Chaya too wanted errands done outside her own preserve, the little room.

There was a special Passover cupboard built into the wall of the dining room, but it was always locked, so that you forgot it was a cupboard. I opened the doors. There was a smell of old, imprisoned things. But now the captive glasses, plates, and goblets woke up.

What was missing? A wineglass? A cup?

I climbed onto a stool so that I could peer over all three shelves. I counted the glasses. Would there be enough to go around? I worked it out, imagining us all already sitting around the table.

The whole cupboard glittered with glass and china, plain or decked with gold. One shelf was full of wine glasses, thick, thin, tall, short. They dazzled me and reflected one another like mirrors.

On one side stood red and blue Bohemian goblets, deep in thought, in a world of their own. They still gave off the scent of last year's wine.

Taller by a head than all the rest stood the cup of the Prophet Elijah. I touched it gingerly. Every year I trembled in case it broke from all the wine poured into it. Even empty it sparkled with red lights like drops of wine.

I fancied I was sitting in a tree, with strange red and blue birds singing and pecking at the branches. The big decanters added to the glow. Their thick glass could turn even plain water red as blood. What would it be like when all the decanters and glasses were on the table, full of wine? The white cloth would catch fire!

My smarting eyes turned to the next shelf. Here stood a big soup tureen, painted with red flowers and too heavy to lift. Now I understood why Chaya's arms ached when she carried it in, full of soup and dumplings, and set it in front of Mother. Next to the tureen were piles of plates—a whole shopful! I picked out some small ones, for I was in charge of the refreshments and it was my job to set them out. I had to calculate which plates to use for candied fruit and which for cakes and almonds. Every plate had an apple or a pear painted in the middle. They fascinated me, smelled like real fruit, and upset my calculations.

Suddenly I noticed a milk jug with a broken handle standing to one side as if it were ashamed. I looked around and saw there wasn't another. But if I went into the shop and told Mother we needed a new milk jug, she'd be angry.

"Why do you come bothering me about a milk jug? We slave away in here to earn a few pennies, and back home everything gets stolen or smashed to pieces!"

Better not tell her.

Where could I get another blue jug to match the blue sugar bowl?

I felt lost in the china shop.

All the glass seemed to tinkle, I was reflected in every mirror. One showed only half my face; in another I had a long nose, in another a flat one. The owner of the shop, a tall stout man, walked around with me, his black coat obliterating his wares. He moved around lightly, surveying all, every so often flicking a glass with his finger. Was it to make sure all his goods were as they should be, or to show them off to me?

The glass he'd tapped gave off a little cry that ran through the whole shop and made all the rest vibrate. But as soon as he took his finger away, the sound died out in some corner, and all was silent but for our own footsteps.

I forgot what I'd come for. Oh, yes, Chaya had asked me to get her something for the kitchen.

"Look," whispered the shopkeeper. "Those liqueur glasses! Just in! Aren't they pretty?"

He said it quite casually but my eyes opened wide. The little glasses beckoned like exquisite flowers. They were so fragile a puff of wind could have blown them off the shelf. You longed to hold them against your cheek or touch them to your lips.

I could just hear Chaya.

"What do we want with more liqueur glasses? There isn't even anywhere to put them. But of course you've forgotten to bring me just a couple of ordinary plates!"

I could see her holding one of my purchases up to the light.

"Just look! It'll melt in the dishwater. And how many glasses like this have come to pieces in my hands when I'm drying them?"

But they were so pretty! I hadn't the heart to leave them in the shop.

Let everyone be angry with me! There were plenty of other unnecessary things in our house!

The Seder

From early in the morning I'd been studying the ma-nishta-nah: as the youngest child, I had to ask Father the Four Questions.

"Every year you make the same mistakes," grumbled one of my brothers. He didn't like having to hear me rehearse.

"Why are they the same questions every year?" I asked.

My head swarmed with not four but forty questions I'd have liked to put to Father. But what was the use of asking him anything? All year I was scolded for asking questions.

But now Father wasn't there, so I *could* ask.

"Father, why do you suddenly become king for the Seder? And how is it that when the two days of Seder are over, you aren't king anymore and our kingdom is gone? Why doesn't the Prophet Elijah sit beside you during the Seder? He could be a king too—his cup is the largest and most beautiful. Father, why does his cup stand in the middle of the table untouched? Why doesn't he eat with us, and why don't we open the door and call him until after the meal? Father, why does he promise us 'Next year in Jerusalem' every year? Every year the same promise, while he hides in the darkness. Why? Why?"

"Why do you always get stuck at the same place, dopey?" my brother complained. "Here's what you've got to say. Repeat it after me."

Once more I said the Four Questions from beginning to end.

The house was in turmoil, and I walked about in it as carefully as if I were balancing a pitcher full of questions on my head, whispering them to myself for fear they might spill out of my memory.

The day went by. Smells of Passover foods wafted in and out. Chaya flew like the wind from kitchen to dining room and back again, occasionally standing still and counting on her fingers.

"The chopped nuts and apples . . ." and she crooked one finger. "The stuffed chicken necks . . ." She crooked another. "The hardboiled eggs . . . And what else? . . . But where's Sasha? Whenever you want her, she's nowhere to be found. Seder or no Seder, it's all one to her. Bashenka, go and see if she's still with Ivan in the cellar having supper . . ."

And Chaya spat, as if it made her quite ill to think of their ungodly food.

I hurried off. The cellar was unrecognizable. Its black walls shone. Sasha had scoured it so thoroughly it seemed large and spacious. It was clean as a new pin, and no longer smelled of kerosene, moldy sauerkraut, and pickles. The barrels were hidden behind piles of firewood. In the middle of the floor a kind of dining room had been arranged for Passover week.

There, sitting on a large log, Sasha presided like the lady of the house, and beside her on another log was Ivan the porter. Above their heads, jutting out a short distance from the wall, hung a little tin lamp. The wall was damp, but the glass chimney was so bright the tiny flame inside burned bright and cheerful. It blew to one side and flickered over Sasha's dress, trailing on the earthen floor.

The table was groaning with food. Sasha was stuffing herself till her cheeks bulged, and laughing. Black-bearded Ivan looked like a bear in his sheepskin coat, and kept wiping his damp mustache.

"Like a bit of leavened bread, Bashutka?" he guffawed.

I turned my back on him.

"Sasha," I said, "Chaya wants you. Everyone's here. The Seder will soon begin."

I tugged at her sleeve. I didn't want to leave her alone in the cellar with Ivan when he was drunk.

She gathered up her skirts over her arm, laughed once more at Ivan, and hurried out with me.

"Are they really all there, Bashutka? Quick, then!" The stairs shook under her feet.

Up in the dining room a holiday atmosphere reigned. The table stretched the length of the room, a white Seder cloth reflecting the glow of the red wineglasses. Candlesticks shone, bearing tall white candles not yet lit. Even the ceiling reflected the brightly polished chains of the chandelier.

Heaps of matzahs were covered with napkins that looked like little prayer shawls. The plump white cushions on the chairs seemed embarrassed to contemplate the flat unleavened bread. The Haggadahs—the books containing the story of the exodus from Egypt—were resplendent with the golden letters on their bindings.

Mother came in first, wearing her holiday clothes. Her face shone. With her hair piled up, she looked taller. Her dress was long and full, trimmed with lace, buttons, and ribbons. It trailed on the ground and filled the air with its rustling. She went over to the candles and lit them, circling them with her hands as if blessing the whole table.

The air grew warm and clear, as if not only Mother's seven candles but hundreds of others had been lit. Just as they'd been caressed by Mother's warm hands, so they in turn seemed to fondle the cold sheen of the tablecloth.

Other candles had been lit at our neighbors' in the courtyard. All the beams crossed, splashing the darkness with gold. They were reflected in the windows, danced over the table, over the cloth's embroidered flowers, the waiting bottles of wine, the red glasses.

One little flame after another licked at the white table. But the table was not quite ready. It was still being set. No one thought to wonder whether it could bear all the weight.

"Chaya, have you shelled the eggs? Where's the salt water?"

Mother bustled around the table, trying to take everything in and see that nothing was missing.

"Fetch another cushion—there's a guest I'd forgotten. Put a clean cover on!"

More white cushions were set out. The chairs looked pregnant.

"Who's coming, Mother? How many will there be of us?"

"Oh," said Mother, "why count? Especially on a holiday. . . . Ssh, they're back from the synagogue."

An unfamiliar voice was heard, and in came one of the guests.

"A good holiday!" he said.

"A good holiday! How are you?"

"Are these your boys? Are they all bar mitzvah?" And he gave them all a friendly pinch on the cheek.

This first arrival was a distant relation of my father's, a peddler in the neighboring villages. He knew that for us a relative was sacred, so he'd invited himself to our Seder and was making himself at home. He walked around humming a tune, blew his nose loudly, lectured people, and offered advice. He was the first to welcome each new guest with open arms.

Soon there was a noisy crowd, all waiting for Father and passing the time with stories and jokes.

"What are you studying, Bashenka? Are you good at Russian?" someone asked me.

"What sort of marks do you get?" A brother and sister who'd come from some distance away joined us.

I looked at them as if they were strangers too. I didn't see them all year. My brother was studying abroad, and my sister lived in another town. This year she'd brought her two little boys with her. They climbed onto everyone's knees—long legs particularly appealed to them—and pestered to be bounced up and down.

Everyone was cheerful. Only one bachelor had a sad, wistful

look. He watched the children playing, and remembered he too had once had a father and mother, and a home. He withdrew into a corner, like a little boy.

"A good holiday!"

Three young soldiers, all spick and span for Passover, came in and stood in a row. They'd been lured in by the noise.

"Quick, here's Father!"

The noise stopped dead.

I hardly recognized him at first. It was a new Father. In the doorway stood a king, dressed in white from head to foot. He was lost in his loose white silk cloak. The material shimmered and fell in ample folds, held in by a wide belt. The sleeves hung down like wings, long and full, covering his hands and fingers. A white silk skullcap shone on his white hair. All in white he looked taller, stouter. His face beamed. He seemed to give forth a white radiance. If he as much as moved his arms, he'd take off like a bird. I looked into his face. Yes, he was king for today!

"A good holiday," said Father.

"A good holiday," we all answered.

The Seder began.

Father sat by himself at the head of the table. Leaning against his two big cushions, he really was like a king on a throne. Everyone jostled to the table after him, pushing the chairs this way and that, crowding around. Some perched on their fat cushions as though suspended in midair.

Father was the first to pick up his napkin from his plateful of Seder fare and give it a searching look. Mother's eyes followed his gaze. Could anything have been forgotten?

From under the special matzah, like moss from an ancient roof, emerged sprigs of bitter herbs, a little mound of horseradish, a stuffed chicken neck, and a hardboiled egg.

The other plates were then uncovered and found to be laden like Father's.

"Arka, can I have some of your bitter herbs?" Abrashka called to his eldest brother across the table.

"Glutton! You only think of one thing, holiday or no holiday!"

"What about you, barking like a dog! I only asked for some herbs."

"You'd stuff yourself with anything. I know you!"

"Quiet!" said Father. "What's all this noise? Fill the glasses and pass them around to our guests."

Bottles passed from hand to hand, were snatched from one to another, spilled onto the tablecloth.

"Mm, delicious!" Someone had found time to taste it. "May my luck be as good!"

"Don't forget the Prophet Elijah."

But Father shook his head. And Mother said, "Use this bottle—it's better."

A bottle was tilted forward, and the tall red cup of the Prophet Elijah, a moment ago standing still and pensive, was filled to the brim.

The wine began to fizz, and my head to spin with the smell that arose from the glasses. Suddenly, from the pages of the Book of Exodus, over which all heads were bent, a breeze seemed to waft up, bearing the first prayers.

I was crammed into my usual place between my parents. It was more of a squash than usual because of Father's cushions. They seemed to be giving off heat. I was stifling. My head was heavy with wine. The cushions invited me to rest on their soft down. But I knew that soon, after the first prayers, Father would bend toward me as if it were he asking me the Four Questions, and not I him.

Already he was making signs.

"Well?"

Silence. Everyone was looking at me. I hid my face in the scriptures. Everything was upside down, inside my head and out. I ran my finger along the lines, trying to make the letters stop dancing about and stand up straight. I gulped, then was startled by the sound of my own voice.

"Why is this night different from all other nights? . . ."

Father prompted me softly. I thought I could hear smothered laughter from the other end of the table. I got more confused than ever. I crept miserably from line to line, but the questions came out all muddled. And I'd learned them so well, and had so many others to ask!

As soon as I'd brought out the last word there was a cry of relief, and everyone plunged into his own Haggadah. The whole long table took off smoothly, each chanting to himself, trying to catch up or overtake all the rest.

The voices echoed back from the windows, climbed the walls, and woke up the portrait of old Rabbi Shneerson, which had hung there for years. The rabbi looked down out of his green eyes and listened to every voice as though he were testing us. On the other wall, the aged Rabbi Mendele couldn't go on hanging quietly either. With his white cloak and long white beard, he seemed to step thoughtfully down from his frame as if summoned to the reading. The bare walls listened, the ceiling bent down to hear the Haggadah and carry each word back up to heaven.

The words poured out, page after page, like sand in the wilderness. I was tired just from looking at everyone. Where had we got to in the text?

My brothers raced along like a team of horses. Suddenly came a phrase that was not in Hebrew.

"Silly fool, you skipped a couple of pages!" It was Mendel scolding Abrashka.

But whom was he trying to cheat? And what was the hurry? Heaps of lines and letters piled up and ran up and down stairs. I got lost in my Haggadah. I touched its yellowed pages. Here was a wine stain; underneath it a crumb of last year's matzah. Suddenly I came on an illustration: a Passover table surrounded by sorrowful faces.

I felt a pang. There they were, our honored grandfathers and grandmothers. How tired and withered they looked. I stroked them, and turned over page after page looking for them. The piece of matzah on the Haggadah was like the sands of Egypt under my feet.

"We were slaves . . . " I murmured.

The pages started to sigh, and the desert wind sighed in my

ears. The pale shapes in the illustration drew so near me I could feel their breath. As soon as I touched them with a word, they poured out their hearts and told me all their woes: how they'd wandered in exile through the desert, halted, gone on again, for days, nights, years, without water, without food.

Their sufferings rent my heart. I could hear them panting along step by step, backs bowed.

My own shoulders drooped, as if I were dragging myself through deep sand. My mouth was dry. I could hardly speak. The words sealed my lips like lumps of clay. I whispered, bent over the Haggadah, trying to enter into it, to set out with them on their long journey, to say a word to them, to help them carry something.

Suddenly a thought struck me. They probably had children with them. How they must have howled!

How far had the others got in the reading? It seemed to me they were all quite carried away. I'd never catch up with them.

Where had Father got to? The best thing would be to listen to him. His voice was calm. Every word rang out like one step after another. He walked an even road. I'd like to walk with him. Fortunately he paused for breath.

"Now the plagues." He signed for a bowl into which to pour the ten symbolic drops of wine.

"Water . . . blood . . ."

His voice rang out like a bell. Each plague was drowned in a slow drop of wine and pushed aside, as if he'd like to drive every trouble as far away as possible. He poured out his whole glassful.

Mother then took the bowl and slowly poured one plague after the other into it. She was afraid of naming them too loudly, and anxious too not to spill wine on the tablecloth.

Everyone grasped his glass as if ready to do battle, took the bowl, and poured in the wine as if spitting in the face of the enemy. They all aimed their curses at the middle of the bowl. At last it came to me. By then so many plagues were swarming in it, the wine had grown quite thick.

"Blood . . . frogs . . . insects . . . disease . . . Take that, and that, and that!"

It was as if I were throwing stones. I poured out all the wine in my glass—I couldn't hold it back. The earthenware bowl changed into the head of the wicked Pharoah. I'd have liked to pour out all the plagues on him at once, to dash my glass to pieces against him and soak him in the red wine as if it were blood.

"Locusts . . . darkness . . . And take that for my grandfathers and grandmothers you persecuted. . . . The slaying of the first-born . . . And take that for the murdered infants! . . ."

I was terrified myself by the curses and the red stains on the tablecloth. I poured out the rest of my wine as fast as I could.

The Prophet Elijah

Exhausted with eating, exhausted with reading the Hagga- dah, we chewed our bits of matzah. Soon Father would hide a piece of matzah—the afikoman—for us children to "steal."

Only Father behaved like a king. Reclining on his cushions, he chewed his matzah peacefully, eyes closed, as if he were thinking, "Where will the Lord lead us now?"

Suddenly he opened his eyes and looked at Mother. She pushed back her chair, opened her Haggadah, took a half- burned candle from the candlestick, and turned to me.

"Come along, Bashenka. And bring your Haggadah."

I sprang to my feet like a spark flying upward. My heart contracted with both fear and exultation, because I—and I alone—was going with Mother to meet the Prophet Elijah and let him in.

Each holding an open Haggadah, and with Mother holding the candle too, we went quietly out of the dining room, leav- ing the men sitting around the table. None of them moved, but they all watched us, following us with their eyes, dispatch- ing their messengers with their blessing.

We hurried through the dusky parlor. We mustn't be late! Suppose Elijah were to come to our house and find the door shut! We went so fast the candle's little flame was swallowed up in its own wax and scarcely lit our way. Tears dripped from the candle as if it too were afraid of the dark. When we reached the hall my heart beat faster. It tried to leap out of my body and up to the sky, but fell back in terror to the murky floor.

"Careful! Here, hold the candle," said Mother, opening the door to the street. The black night rushed in like the wind, blowing into our faces and up our skirts, almost putting the candle out and making us stagger back.

"Now the Prophet Elijah's nearly here," I thought. "He'll arrive at any moment. It's the wings of his chariot that are beating the air as his fiery steeds speed through the clouds."

I was afraid to look out of the door in case anything was lurking there. Shadows stirred at our feet. I could see only a patch of sky, gleaming like black velvet. The whole street was black. In the black sky a little star splashed about like a fish in water, scattering light. Suddenly it looked in at the door and stopped right over our heads.

Mother's eyes were cast down and she saw nothing. Suppose the little star flew in through the door, and the Prophet Elijah—or even the Messiah himself—leaped past us in one bound?

I trembled, and strained my ears. Everything was still. Silence hung from the sky and over the street and houses. No footstep was to be heard. The streetlamps burned with a meager flame.

Through the windows of the house opposite came the gleam of another candle. Was there a door open now in every house? Did a mother stand at every threshold with a little girl holding a candle in her hand?

Suddenly there was a noise behind us. Chairs were being pushed back. It sounded as though the table had fallen to pieces. It was the men, who'd heard us open the door, and stood up and started reading the Haggadah loud enough to awaken the night itself.

Marc Chagall

As we stood there submerged by their voices, I huddled close to Mother. I'd have liked to cling to her skirts, so that if the darkness seized us I'd at least be with her.

The light of the little white candle wavered to and fro. I shielded it from the wind with my hand. God forbid we should be left in the dark, right by the gaping black hole of the doorway.

Mother recited to herself from the Haggadah, as if she thought the silent night would listen more kindly to unspoken prayers. Her lips scarcely moved. Her face was drawn; her eyeglasses were slipping down her nose. The candle was going out. We seemed to be standing there forgotten.

I put my head under the Haggadah, under Mother's hands, so that her heartfelt blessing might fall on me and I wouldn't be afraid any more.

"Have mercy, Prophet Elijah," I prayed. "Come down quickly. It's cold and dark. Come to our house. Everyone's waiting for you. And you'll be warmer too. Can't you hear Father praying? He never raises his voice ordinarily, yet today he's praying so loudly. Come on, Prophet Elijah! Please!"

A gleam of light shot through the doorway, cleaving the darkness. I wanted to look up and see what Mother was doing, what was going on in the sky. But my eyes were full of darkness and I couldn't open them. I felt they couldn't bear the blinding light.

"Next year in Jerusalem!" A final shout went up from the dining room.

Then the chairs were drawn up to the table again and there was silence.

"Mother," I asked, "has the Prophet Elijah already gone in?"

"Next year in Jerusalem!" she said to the open door in answer.

I looked out into the street. The wind had dropped. The sky was full of stars large and small, come from the ends of the earth and hanging like lighted candles with their heads down. Their beams intertwined, and they swayed together in the vault of the sky like a bridal canopy. Soon the white moon would come and shine among them, a bride in all her glory.

Mother closed her Haggadah and made a gesture of stroking the air, as if to bring something down from heaven. Perhaps she didn't want to leave the open door. One more caress, like a kiss, and she shut it.

We went silently back, the cool night air following us and reaching for our shoulders with invisible hands.

Back in the dining room it was light and warm. They were all sitting with lowered eyes, intoning the Haggadah. No one even glanced at us. Mother sat down without a word. The vibrating air swallowed me up, drew me back into the yellowed pages of the Haggadah.

I looked around.

Had the Prophet Elijah really come?

The excitement in my heart flickered out.

The Afikoman

"Sasha," called Mother. "Take this cup of wine to Ivan."

"*Spasibo*—thank you!" came Ivan's hoarse voice in the distance. He was the porter, and supposed to protect us from thieves and robbers.

"Will he drink it all up, plagues and all?" I wondered fearfully.

"Fill the glasses," Father ordered.

We started reading the Haggadah again. A voice rose, then faded away as if it had fallen down a well. One guest mumbled into his beard; others gabbled as fast as they could. They were probably hungry.

Father was the first to rise from his seat. He went to wash his hands. The children rushed to the washstand and struggled for the jug and the wet towel. Then they rushed back to the table and snatched at the pieces of matzah Father threw for them. Each hard bit of bread skidded over the table until someone caught it and held it tight.

"Here, Bashenka, you like horseradish, don't you?"

Father gave me a second helping, which I spread between

two bits of matzah and ate like a kind of bitter sweet. Egg yolks crumbled under Mother's fork and turned the salted water yellow. Everyone wrinkled up his nose as he sipped a spoonful of the mixture.

Meanwhile I'd forgotten to watch where Father was hiding the afikoman. His cushion was stuffed as full as a round belly. How could I find it in all that?

The fish was being served. Mother reached out over the table, and all the plates were held up toward her. Then came the kneydlakh, the matzah balls that slid down smoothly with the golden soup.

"Who's got a dumpling he doesn't want?" the children asked one another.

"Hurry up and finish eating," said Father, "or else it'll be too late for the afikoman."

He'd stopped eating already. We sat looking at him, tired and full and longing to go to bed. He shifted about in his chair, turning the cushions over and looking for the afikoman.

"Oh, you little wretches, you did manage to steal it!"

And he smiled.

I sat there baffled. I hadn't seen where he'd hidden the afikoman, nor who'd stolen it. I looked angrily at each of my brothers in turn.

"I got it!" cried Abrashka, holding the afikoman up in triumph.

"Right," said Father. "What do you want for it?"

"Oh, I'm not giving it back except in exchange for . . . for . . ."

He tried to think up something enormous.

I stared at him, almost glad I hadn't managed to steal the afikoman. I'd only have asked for some trifle in exchange. During all the rest of the year, no one would have dared to ask for anything. And now Abrashka—what nerve! But Father, like a real king, wouldn't dream of haggling.

"All right. You're no fool. Have your own way. But now hurry up and give me back the afikoman. It's getting late."

Tisha be-Av

I'd spent almost all the summer in the country. There were swarms of buzzing flies. The sun shone in bright round patches through the branches. You couldn't catch those little moons—they slipped through your fingers, slid from under your feet before you could tread on them. I forgot the city, and seemed to turn into a plant or a blade of glass.

I went barefoot and began to smell of earth and rain. I lingered along the hedges like a red berry. Blue flowers like tiny hats winked at me between the ears of corn.

I went into the woods and clambered over the tangled roots of felled trees. I looked for blueberries and collected them in a little basket. When I glanced down at my bare legs, they seemed longer and stronger. I drank my fill of sun and air. I didn't notice how the days and nights were going by; nor how the sun was drawing away somewhere, ever farther and deeper; nor how, each dusk, it cast a longer shadow.

"Bashenka, come home. Tomorrow's Tisha be-Av." This was Mother's message from the city.

I was glad. I'd been away from home a long time.

"Oh, how you've grown!" Sasha would exclaim. Mother would conceal her joy and hardly look at me, so as not to tempt the evil eye.

So I came home full of happiness.

Then stopped in the doorway.

Had someone died? Why was everyone weeping? Why had Mother told me to come home? I'd fallen out of a bright sky into a dark pit.

I stood and looked at Mother, who sat with bowed head at the table, reading a lamentation. She wept in silence, without looking up. The long white cloth stretched out over the table like a shroud. The burned-down candles smoldered in the candlesticks. A few sacred books were lying about. Father stood not far off. His white socks caught my eye. My heart ached.

Dear God, why was everything so gray and dark? Outside it was still summer, the sun was shining. Among the Gentiles, children and grownups were laughing, running about. But here . . .

Father and Mother sat on low stools as if on stones, weeping and lamenting. They themselves seemed turned to stone, and their tears streamed as though to wear it away. The floor was covered with dust and ashes.

What sins had my parents committed that they must pray to God like this? What misfortunes were they lamenting?

"We have lost our holy Temple," my brother Mendel told me sadly. "It was burned down. The land is laid waste. It's Tisha Be-Av."

Sadness crept over me. The little red and blue flowers still blossomed in my mind's eye, but at a blow my warm summer had been swept away.

Abrashka came running in and tugged at my sleeve.

"What are you standing here for?" he asked. "Come out in the yard and we'll throw burrs at each other."

I didn't care what I did. I let myself be dragged outside. Abrashka had a whole heap of burrs ready. If they all hit me, they'd tear me to bits. I held my hands over my eyes while Abrashka fired the burrs at me like cannonballs. They got into my hair and stuck to my clothes. I could scarcely move.

"That's enough Abrashka. Now it's my turn."

Almost in tears, I snatched up a handful of burrs.

"Take that! And that!"

I tore the burrs off my clothes and shied them at Abrashka; I didn't stop to see what he was doing. Abrashka was calmly picking them all up and sticking them on himself like buttons. He planted one on his cap. His whole chest was covered with them.

From the open window came stifled sobs.

"How doth the city sit solitary! . . . Shall joy never return to us?"

FIRST ENCOUNTER

The First Meeting

This is for you, my beloved.

"Thea, are you there?"
I knocked at my schoolmate's window.
"It's me—Bella."
The summer was nearly over. I was just back from abroad.
Every summer Mother went to Marienbad and took me with
her. I'd also been to Berlin and Vienna. I had so much to tell
Thea I couldn't wait.

I knocked again. Why didn't she open the door? And after
I'd hurried so! I'd run straight through the streets and over the
bridge without stopping.

Thea lived on the other side of the river, not far from the
railway station, in a quiet street lined on one side with low
stone houses. The windows gave directly onto the street.

Was that why they were always shut? The heavy curtains
muffled the noise from outside; the light too. The parlor was
always cool and dark. You couldn't hear the wheels of the
droshkies driving to the station, or the clopping of the
horses' hooves. Half of the street was paved with wood and
half with stones. How often had I felt a sharp point sticking

through my shoe as I skipped from one cobblestone to the next.

I peered in at Thea's window. It was like looking at yourself in a mirror. The panes shone hot in the sun. Between folds of heavy curtains, starched white lace billowed gently to and fro. On one panel was embroidered the figure of a king on a throne; on the other, a beautiful young queen wearing a crown. This was the first time I'd noticed them. You couldn't see them from inside because of all the flowerpots.

The windowsills were covered with flowers and plants. Others stood on the floor and in every possible nook and cranny. They grew on tables and stools, they hung from shelves. There were tubs of palms, some with foliage soaring upward, some with leaves outspread. There were even tin cans with bunches of leaves in them, and perhaps a few little flowers. Every day the plants grew denser and the light more dim. As if that weren't enough, Thea's mother never came home from the market without another bunch of flowers. If she couldn't find a vase, she stuck them in a bottle.

From the outside, their house looked like all the others. Yet there was a difference. Was it because of all the greenery inside the windows, or because of the music that could be heard through them even though they were shut? The strains greeted you as soon as you turned off the main street into their little alley. The neighboring houses stood silent to listen to the sonatas of Mozart and Beethoven. Passersby would stop for a moment by the windows, drink in the music, and go on their way refreshed.

All the way there, I'd been looking forward to hearing those sounds. In the parlor stood a big broad piano with a grid of tinkling wires beneath its gleaming black lid. Sometimes you could also hear a violin. When no one was playing it, it lay quietly on the piano, the bow waiting nearby like an outstretched arm.

There was no piano or violin in our house. At dusk, if I felt sad, I'd hurry over to Thea's. Her house was always full of people, fun, and laughter. I dreamed of living in a house like that.

Thea's mother was at home all day. She would bustle from one room to another. Now she'd run into the kitchen and bake a cake and some rolls. Then some visitors would arrive. She had a word for everyone. She used to talk to us children as if we were her own friends, and give us a taste of whatever she was cooking.

"Belloshka, have a blini. Don't worry, it won't do you any harm. What a pretty dress! Is it new? How's your mother, Manishka? Sonishka, you're late. Is it true your sister's getting married?"

And so Thea's mother flitted among us, smiling and encouraging.

Thea had had the same friends for years, so her mother knew us all, and all our families and relations. But no one could tell how old *she* was, that slight little figure, sprightly and cheerful as a bird. From her thin lips—always moist, like Thea's—poured forth a flood of words. Her nose was curved and sharp like a beak, and her dark eyes shone like drops of water.

Thea's brothers—there were three of them—were always cheerful and joking. They all played the piano or the violin, and would perform either together or alone. Friends would join in, singing, whistling, or turning the pages of the score. We often acted plays and charades. For costumes we'd ransack drawers and wardrobes, and Thea's mother would bring out her old dresses that had gone out of fashion. Sometimes we just pulled the flowered quilts off the beds. Nothing was forbidden. For me, a white sheet around my head was enough. I always had to be the bride or the innocent maiden; I don't know why. Perhaps it was because I had long hair and big eyes.

As soon as I entered their house, I felt different. The air was full of sounds. The front room was full of birds. They were everywhere, like the pots of flowers—in whole families or in pairs, in cages hanging on the walls or standing on tables. In the middle, a green parrot swung on a perch suspended from the ceiling, clambering about and showing off. All the birds cheeped and twittered and cooed, and as soon as you opened the front door they all swooped down on you, making so much noise you couldn't hear your friends bidding you welcome.

From the parlor came the sound of music, from the courtyard the din of Marquis barking. The barking grew louder and nearer, for Thea's big dog had to inspect every visitor. He knew us all quite well, but he still had to get under our feet and sniff us over.

Would Marquis know me now? I hadn't seen him all summer. And what about the birds? I gave them a whistle. I was longing to see them hopping up and down, pecking with their beaks to say hello.

But why didn't someone open the door? People going by began to stare. What was I doing, standing there all that time on the pavement like a fool? And yet I wasn't really in a hurry. Even standing out on the doorstep, I felt as if I were already inside.

There must be somebody at home. Thea's father was a healer, and so good at it that everyone treated him like a trained physician. No Jew who was ill thought he could get better unless he called in Dr. Brachmann. He always found the right remedy: first a careful prescription, then an apt saying that he seemed to whisk out of his pocket before he left. And the patient's family, reassured, would slip him half a ruble.

The peasants too liked to consult Thea's father. Some came in from quite remote villages, especially on market days. When they had to visit the town to sell a pig or a calf, they'd bring a sick child along too. Mother and child would both be wrapped tight in the same shawl, and often both looked ill. Sometimes it was an old man who was ailing, and who'd sit on the bench in the waiting room, staring guiltily at the floor. He might seem to be dozing, then suddenly start awake and spit contemptuously, as if at himself.

The people from the country all came at the same time and squeezed onto the benches in the front room. They'd rather have squatted on the floor; chairs were for the rich. But they sat and looked at the birds. They reminded them of their own villages and gardens.

The things Thea saw! Open, festering wounds; pale old eyes swimming in tears. She opened the door to the peasants, and went around the waiting room laughing and trying to cheer them up: it would soon be their turn.

But they knew that there were other patients waiting in the parlor, townspeople that her father would see first.

"Father will be free in a minute," said Thea.

"Yes, miss."

Relieved, they would stand up and thrust a little basket into her hands.

"Give this to your mother, miss. New-laid eggs, straight from the hen." They were paying in advance: perhaps they'd be remembered and let in sooner.

In the evening, when the last patient had gone, Dr. Brachmann went out on his rounds. The coachman harnessed the horses, and the doctor drove all over the town. Between professional visits, he'd drop in on a friend who had nothing whatever the matter with him. Why not? Everyone knew Dr. Brachmann liked a game of cards and a glass of brandy. He must have been a gay young man in his time, as you could see from his red nose and the pouches under his eyes. Those eyes still twinkled through his glasses, and his gruff voice often broke into roars of laughter.

As I stood there at the door, Dr. Brachmann was no doubt out on his rounds, and Mrs. Brachmann and Thea must be relaxing after letting patients in and out all day. Why hadn't they heard me knocking? I didn't want to ring. I never did that, in case Mrs. Brachmann thought I was a patient and, instead of answering the door, just called out, "The doctor's not at home. Come back in the morning."

But what was going on? I could hear a dog barking. Marquis at least must have heard me. He might be old, but he was still a dog. But if Marquis was at home, Thea must be there too. She never went out without him.

Didn't she sense that I was there, then? Perhaps she didn't think about me anymore; she hadn't seen me all summer. But I'd thought about her the whole time I was away. I'd missed her in all those big cities. I'd only seen Mother's friends, grownups who hadn't brought their own children with them. I wanted to tell Thea how dreary it was, dragging around those great foreign boulevards all on one's own. The houses were so tall you had to stretch your eyes to take them all in. Most of all, I'd been impressed by the flowers growing right in the streets. Whole squares carpeted with flowers, and the horses and carriages going around them, and the air full of different scents. And no one dreaming of touching.

Thea would have loved that. She adored flowers, and always had one stuck in her hair or her dress.

And if she'd seen the horses, the carriages! They were so tall, getting into them was like climbing a mountain. Our local coachman couldn't have managed them; they seemed to speed along by themselves.

As soon as I stopped to looked at the pedestrians, too, they were gone. All I could remember afterward was a coat or the feathers on a hat. Instead of a face, all I could conjure up was shiny shoes—black, brown, and red—all hurrying along the sidewalk.

If only Thea had been with me the day the man's boater blew off! One moment he was there beside me, and the next it was as if the earth had opened and swallowed him up. I looked all over the place for him. But no one else had even noticed.

And I wanted to tell Thea how I used to stand for hours looking in the shopwindows. Often they were larger than the shop behind them.

"Mother, Mother, come and look! All those things—we can get all our presents here." I dragged her over. "Look, a tree made of handkerchiefs! And there—a bride, right in the window!"

Mother was impatient. "It's ridiculous—who needs all those things? Let's go home, Basha dear. I expect you've forgotten the name of our hotel. But do you remember the name of the street?"

In one shop I saw a big Tyrolean cape with a green hat and feather to match. I wanted one.

"Why do you suddenly want to dress up in a cape?" Mother wanted to know.

Yet now here I was, wearing it. Would Thea like it? The green feather was perched on my head like a bird. You could see at a glance it came from abroad. Just try to find a feather like that in Vitebsk! I was sure everyone was looking at my hat.

"Welcome back," they'd said the day before. "Did you have a good time? What a lovely hat! May you wear it in good health! What beautiful things you can get abroad!"

If I'd stopped to speak to everyone, I'd never have got to Thea's today. But she didn't seem in any hurry to see me. I was getting tired of waiting.

But was that something moving inside the window? Yes, it was Thea! She ran through the parlor, disappeared, then came back and went over to the piano. Was she going to play? She lifted the shiny lid and gazed at the keys. She looked very thoughtful. Had something happened? Who could tell? Thea sometimes invented dramas for herself. She got bored when things were too quiet and peaceful.

She was standing with her back to the window and didn't see me. What was the matter? I couldn't stand it any longer and called out.

"Thea!"

She started as if it had been a clap of thunder. Why was she so on edge? Didn't she recognize my voice? Was she expecting someone else? She ran over and opened the window.

"Oh, it's you, Bella. How long have you been there? You frightened me."

"What's wrong with you, silly? Hurry up and let me in."

"What a pretty cape. Where did you get it?"

"Do you really like it?"

We kissed each other. She seemed to keep her arms around me longer than usual. She looked on the brink of tears.

"Theanka, darling!" I hugged her tighter. She was trembling, as if she had some great secret and was afraid of giving it away.

Wasn't she pleased to see me? Usually, when we met, she couldn't take her eyes off me. But today there was something different, something I didn't know about. That was probably why she'd taken so long to let me in. I waited for her to tell me what it was.

But after a while it was I who began.

"Thea, do you know what? . . ."

I told her one story after another, but she wasn't paying attention. My words floated past her across the dining room. She didn't sit down; she kept moving about. I was hurt. Wasn't she interested in my adventures? Usually she was all ears, but today she let me go on talking and never said a word.

I went on, but her silence alarmed me. The plants in the window were merging into the shadows. It was almost dark. My words weren't reaching Thea; they were hanging somewhere in midair, like the lamp over our heads. I suddenly had the feeling that we were not alone.

I was uneasy. The plants on the windowsills and the flowers on the little tables had stretched up and drunk in the dark air. I could hear them breathing. And another sound, like a bird stirring in its sleep. I looked around.

A ray of light fell from a chink in the door, piercing the dusk like a flash of lighting. I pricked up my ears. Had someone come in?

Another shadow seemed to have fallen over Thea. If only she would say something. Why didn't she speak? Usually she was very talkative, but today she was biting the words back. Her mouth must be dry. Her lips were usually moist, but now she kept licking them. I stole a glance at her.

She seemed to have filled out during the summer. She hadn't been all that feminine before, with her broad shoulders and her high forehead, her hair brushed straight back and hanging down behind in a childish pigtail. Her drab-colored dress was too small now. Her legs had grown longer—and she'd already been self-conscious about the size of her feet. She could race any boy, and sometimes even keep pace with her dog. Her hands were bigger than mine too. They were always moist, and she tended to keep them in her pockets. When she shook hands with me, she crushed my fingers. She was always cheerful, especially in company. She held people spellbound with her singing, and was so witty and vivacious they doubled up with laughter. So she was very popular.

She liked being with boys, and would kiss them, quite unabashed, right on the lips. She liked fighting them too.

With girls, though, she was gentle, and might spend hours gazing at a long neck or a pair of beautiful hands. Generally lively and serene, she was liable to become suddenly depressed, wrapped in a black shawl of gloom and singing sad songs in her husky voice.

There was nothing Thea couldn't do. She could play the piano; she could play cards. She spoke German, and would often recite by heart poems that had only just been published. She even wrote herself. Her letters, which always covered the whole of the paper, always included some of her recent poems. When she read them aloud, her voice was tense. And when she fell into one of her fits of melancholy, people regarded her with awe.

Was that the explanation now? But why was she so distant with me? We'd been friends since we were small. Every year at school we'd graduated together from one class to the next. Although we were so different in other ways—with different eyes and hands and feet—we'd had the same sorrows and the same joys. So why was she avoiding me now? She must be hiding something.

I tried to make her laugh.

"I wish you'd been there, Thea. I nearly split at my sides . . ."

But instead of going along with my story, she just said, "Really?" gave a wan smile, and turned, embarrassed, toward her father's office.

Who was in there? What was she listening for? Her father was out on his rounds in the town.

A shadow darkened the chink in the doorway. My laughter froze on my lips. Who was it? What was Thea hiding from me?

The door opened wider, without a sound. I felt hot with apprehension. I dared not move, dared not look around. I felt as if something were scorching me. Light spread over the walls, and against them appeared the face of a boy, as white as the walls.

Where had he come from? I'd never seen him before. He was not like my brothers' friends, or like anyone else I knew. He stood as if afraid to hold himself upright. Had he only just woken up? He lifted one hand and forgot to lower it again. It just hung there in midair.

What did it mean? Was he trying to say hello to me, or about to box my ears? Was it I who'd awakened him? Why was he sleeping here anyway, and in almost broad daylight? His hair was tousled. It grew in little curls all over his head, clustering over his brow and hanging down over his eyes.

When you did catch a glimpse of his eyes, they were as blue as if they'd fallen straight out of the sky. They were strange eyes, not like other people's—long, almond-shaped. They were wide apart, and each seemed to sail along by itself, like a little boat. I'd never seen such eyes before. Or perhaps I had, in pictures of animals in books. His wide mouth was open, with the corners stretching up almost to his ears.

I couldn't tell whether he was going to talk to me or bite me with those sharp white teeth. Then he coiled himself up, an animal about to spring. It was as if, in preparation for stretching out his arms and legs, he only bent them all the more. And all this time he was laughing. Was he still laughing in his sleep? Or was he laughing at me?

I was always sure everyone was laughing at me. And this boy was obviously delighted to meet a girl who was afraid of him. How could Thea play such a trick on me? Why hadn't she told me right away that there was a visitor?

I was angry. When I thought of the stupid things I'd been saying! He'd heard them all, and now he was laughing in my face.

Now I knew why Thea hadn't said anything, and had let me do all the talking. She was embarrassed because he was there. Or was she embarrassed because of me? Who was he?

I didn't know what to do with myself. I stood rooted to the spot. I'd have liked to run away from my altered friend and her odd visitor. He was still laughing at me with that mouthful of teeth, as if he'd like to grind me to pieces. What was he thinking? He seemed to be pondering something. His brow

furrowed, as if to make a path for his crowding thoughts. He came closer. I looked at the floor. No one said anything. We could hear one another's heartbeats.

I couldn't stand it any longer.

"Thea, I must go home!" I could scarcely move my parched lips. My head was burning, and my whole body felt as if I were being scourged.

Then the boy said, "Why? What's the hurry? You have such a lovely voice. I heard you laughing."

He was speaking! And to me! *He* wasn't overawed by the silence. But his words were killing me.

I didn't understand. He didn't even know me. What did he want? What was that he'd said about my voice?

I looked at Thea.

"This is the artist," she said, coming to life at last. "I told you about him."

I blushed to the roots of my hair, as if I'd been caught stealing. Thea was speaking hastily, defensively. A flood of syllables poured over me.

"Oh? Really?"

I didn't know what to say. Her words trapped me like a spider's web, winding around my arms and neck and skin as if to throttle me. I grabbed my hat and cape, and ran out of the room, out of the house, out into the street.

"Phew!" I felt cooler out in the breeze. My head was back on my shoulders. My feet were no longer like lead, and ran along of their own accord. But the boy's face ran along beside me like a shadow, blowing on my cheeks and whistling in my ears. If I chased it away, it came back from another direction.

There were several artists in our small circle. But none of them had a face like that. Victor, for example, was quite different: he had a strikingly good-looking, rather girlish face. But it was like bitter chocolate, and like his own painting: slightly repellent.

I'd always imagined that an artist must reach out and move people with his heart, since it was with his heart that he painted. But the painters I knew couldn't even create a ripple in the air. I didn't think I was mistaken. They painted their own portraits often enough. Each of them was in love with himself, and stood in front of a mirror saying, "Just look at me!"

But the artist whose image was pursuing me now was like a shooting star. You couldn't catch him. He burned with a fire that was hot and cold at the same time; then disappeared into a cloud, and yet lingered on in my eye.

And his name! I envied it. It rang like a peal of bells.

I thought of him as big and strong, yet as if he had no legs— as if it were his springy hair that bore him along.

No, that wasn't right. He wouldn't let himself be carried away so easily. He was odd somehow, as if his limbs were put together by chance. He might seem shy. But the way he laughed!

I was usually uncomfortable with boys. When they looked at me, I wished the earth would open and swallow me up. But this one seemed to revolve around himself. His teeth bit me only from afar. But how sharp they were.

I longed to get home. I hadn't finished the book I was reading. On every page I'd meet people who were familiar and yet distant. Their voices and footsteps vanished between the lines. But the voice of the boy I'd just met kept ringing in my ears.

What was the situation between him and Thea? Had they known each other long? I brooded, got all mixed up, felt like the ice in springtime melting in the first ray of sun.

Now I remembered. Thea had told me not long ago that Victor had introduced her to one of his friends. Was this he? I thought she'd said he was poor, so poor he didn't have a place to work in peace. When he wanted to paint, he had to climb on the stove in the kitchen. His family were afraid he'd spill paint over everything, and the only place he didn't disturb anyone was up there, with the kegs and the hens clucking all around. And when he finished a picture and brought it down off the stove, his sisters would grab it and put it someplace where it wouldn't mark the newly scrubbed floor.

Thea must have been to his home. Why hadn't she ever taken me with her? I'd have liked to see the house where he lived and the stove he painted on.

Thea was certainly good at keeping secrets. She'd only mentioned him once. What else did she know about him? I wanted to know it too. Probably they met quite often. They seemed to be quite good friends.

Oh, what an idiot I was! Why hadn't I thought of it before? There I'd sat jabbering, and all the time I was in their way! And yet I'd noticed how ill at ease she was; I ought to have understood and left them alone. Now it was too late. Perhaps Thea was angry with me.

And he? Well, he'd put in an appearance, laughed, and then goodbye!

But whose fault was it? How was I to know there was somebody else waiting to see her? She was so odd. Was I her friend or not? She could have told me the truth, and that would have been the end of it. But no. And what did it matter if a boy had a bit of a rest in her father's office? He probably didn't get enough sleep at home. If he had to work on the stove, he couldn't have had a room of his own.

In the office there was a long couch covered with black oilcloth like wet mud. During the day the patients lay down on it, but in the evening it wasn't used. The boy must have stretched out on it and just dropped off.

Now I understood. No doubt, when he fell asleep, Thea was scared and went back into the parlor, where I'd seen her through the window. That was understandable. Someone came to see you and suddenly dozed off, and heaven knew when he'd wake up again. Your mother might come in at any moment, and what would she say? You never knew where you were with a fellow like that.

When I thought about him, his face floated up before me, a face that kept changing as if he had several of them, one after the other. Now it would be bright, with sparkling eyes and teeth flashing out between his lips like a row of lights. The next moment a dark shutter would come down over it, the light would vanish, and I could see nothing.

Then I thought: but wasn't he like an animal? He sprang on you and his glance shattered you. His spring was as lithe as a cat's. Could it be that he was cruel?

But why did I keep thinking about him? I wasn't going to see him again. He wasn't the first boy I'd met at Thea's. And all of them had taken one look, and then goodbye!

It was funny, though: those two didn't really suit each other. They might want to be together, but they pulled in different directions. I wondered if he was very young. Why couldn't I tell? I remembered what Thea had said to me about his home and his work. I'd thought then he must have a hump, crouching all day like that on top of the stove. And she'd said his painting was to be taken seriously. So he couldn't be all that young.

Thea had been very enthusiastic about him, and kept on saying she had to help him. That was Thea all over. She wanted to help all the painters we knew.

"It's our duty to help them," she said to me once. "You can't imagine how difficult it is for them to work. Their families are all against them. They can't afford models—they cost too much. But we could help. They have to study the nude. We could pose for them."

She brought this out with a rush. I was flabbergasted. What would she think of next!

But now I saw it all. She didn't need me anymore. What was the good of a friend who took fright at a mere word?

I hurried homeward, trying to hide my face so that no one could guess what I'd been thinking.

Why did I have to go to Thea's that evening? I could have gone tomorrow morning when the boy wouldn't have been there. In the mornings Thea's father was there seeing his patients, so the boy couldn't have been lying on the couch. Anyway, he had to paint during the day.

Oh, well, there was no use going on about it. Here was the bridge, thank goodness. I was halfway home. Now I could stop for a moment.

The river, amply filling its bed from bank to bank, gave off a refreshing breeze which cooled my fevered head. The sky and the clouds seemed to have lost their balance and fallen in while looking at their reflections in the water. There was a little boat in the distance. Was it floating on the river or in the sky? I'd have liked to lie down on the cool waves too, and catch a piece of reflected cloud in my hands.

I leaned over the parapet.

Was that a shadow slipping over the elaborate balustrade? Had the clouds, trying to climb back out of the water into the sky, been halted by that barrier?

But I could feel something rubbing against my legs. It was Marquis, Thea's dog, licking my ankles with his warm tongue. I turned around and almost let out a scream.

There stood Thea and the boy. Where had they sprung from? Had they followed me here, watching me all the way, looking at my back and reading my heart?

They must know what I'd been thinking. That was why there was a smile lurking about the boy's lips. But I felt more like crying. Why were they dogging me like this? I'd hardly had time to get my breath back, and here they were again. His teeth shone as if he hadn't closed his lips since he first saw me. Was his mouth too small to hold his teeth? Did he laugh all the time? Or only when he was looking at me? Thea was smiling too. I was fed up. Let them laugh, then, if they thought it was so funny!

Of course they were playing tricks on me again. Couldn't Thea find some other stupid girl to make a fool of? And she was always telling me I was her best friend!

What did they want? I'd left them alone together in the house. I had the right to stand here on the bridge as long as I liked.

They hadn't even seen me to the door. That had hurt me. I couldn't raise my eyes and look the boy in the face. His eyes were now gray-green like the water beneath us. I didn't know whether I was swimming in them or in the river.

Thea and he stood one on either side of me, hemming me in. I couldn't move; I felt trapped. Then suddenly Thea's shoulders seemed to droop as if she felt sad, and her moist lips curved in a faint smile. I felt sorry for her. I wanted to put my arms around her.

The boy's voice leaped between us. "Let's all go for a walk."

How strange! Whatever he said surprised me. His words seemed to come from another world.

"Quick, look over there! That little cloud. First it's pearly gray . . . then dark gray, like steel. Look how it twists and turns."

He twisted and turned too, as if he were trying to catch it. I turned as well. A voice that was new was coming from him as if from a deep well. We both looked up at the cloud. It was rising, swelling up like a cushion, coming nearer and nearer. The wind was blowing straight into our faces, trying to push us away. Thea's dark dress had gone pale. A little while ago she'd been cheerful and lively, her face rosy and gay. Why was she suddenly so sad? Was she afraid of the cloud? Didn't she like me anymore? What had I done?

It wasn't I who'd made the cloud go dark. It wasn't I who'd made the boy come here. Who'd asked them to follow me? Was it his idea?

The things I thought of! It was quite simple. They'd been playing, having a race, and they'd just accidentally caught up with me.

Thea seemed to be finding it hard to breathe. There was a red spark wavering in her eyes. What's the matter, Theanka? I love you so much. And more than that—I can't bear you to be sad. I'd give anything to make you as cheerful as you were before. But what *can* I give? Have I taken something away from you? You know I always tell you everything. I can't bear it when you won't speak to me.

The pale moon rose in a corner of the sky, like a lighthouse lantern the keeper had forgotten to turn off in the morning.

I summoned up my strength and managed to blurt out, "I must go. Mother will be waiting for me."

"We'll come with you." The boy turned toward me as if my voice had woken him up.

"No, no, I must run. It's late. Mother's waiting. . . ." I couldn't think of anything else to say.

I fled without even saying good night. All I cared about was that they shouldn't try to stop me. Let them think what they liked. Perhaps Thea would laugh again and feel better.

I strained my ears. No doubt they had burst out laughing. Were they still on the bridge? Had they turned back? Had Thea taken him home with her?

I must run home and bury myself in my books. Forget everything. Forget what? That boys laughed at me behind my back?

Voices called out at me. "Where are you running to, miss? Don't worry, we won't bite you!"

Why did they have to tease me? They didn't know how much it upset me. I was tongue-tied with embarrassment and bathed in sweat.

Like a thirsty traveler coming to a stream, I sank into my window seat and hid myself beneath my books as under a blanket.

A breeze blew in through the window, coming from the street and the river. I felt as if I were still on the bridge. My hands were holding not the book but the cold parapet. My head was spinning. I wasn't sitting in the window, I was floating back up to the cloud. His cloud.

I fell into a long sleep. I began to live a new life.

A Glass of Seltzer

"Will you come out for a walk?" I asked my brother.

"Are you crazy? Who goes out after supper on Friday evening?"

"Why not? Come on, let's go and have a glass of seltzer." I knew Mendel's weaknesses.

Budrevich's bar near the station stayed open late, even on Friday. We walked along, up through some streets, horizontally through others; the little hills were like flights of steps. It was a cool night. Everything slept. Houses and shops were sunk in darkness. The street lights were out. Here and there a little flame flickered behind its smoky glass, casting more shadow than light.

We came to the wooden bridge, its planks gleaming in the darkness. I opened my eyes wide and took a deep breath. Above, the sky was full of stars. Below stretched the river, its waters apparently still. Water, sky—all was at rest. The weary moon had crept behind the clouds, to rest for the night on their downy feathers.

Only the stars were awake. They'd gathered from all over

the sky to frolic like children let out to play. They turned somersaults, danced, teased one another with their rays. If they'd dared, they'd have dropped out of the sky and jumped right down to earth. As it was, as soon as anyone stopped on the bridge, they pounced and flashed all around him, and he went on his way among their sparkling reflections.

We walked across the bridge slowly, afraid to move our heads lest we bump into the stars above, setting our feet down carefully so as not to tread on the little circles of light below. The stars went with us all the way. But as soon as we stepped off the bridge, they left us. Perhaps they were afraid of getting lost in the narrow streets, among the dark rooftops. They scampered back up into the sky over the bridge.

But as soon as we were off the bridge we ourselves plunged into the darkness. The street was swallowed up, the shops shut, their signs invisible. But I knew that here was a draper's, there a bookstore, and over there a photographer's shop with its display of portraits. How often I'd stopped to look at them, the chubby babies and the dressed-up ladies with their eternal fixed smiles. But now I could see no one: only empty space and a glint of gold frame.

Behind the draper's closed shutters, the models slept in the same finery as they wore during the day. In the bookstore you could buy stationery too. I'd often been in for pens and pencils and exercise books.

My eyes hurt from staring at nothing. But as we got near the railway station, long shafts of light fell at our feet. They came from the seltzer bar, attracting people like flies. And then we saw the shop itself, all lit up, and open. People were crowding in and out. A hive of activity. And practically in the middle of the night.

The seltzer fizzed in the glasses, all set out as if at a wedding. Around the walls big copper siphons, set slantwise in buckets of ice, seemed to be trying to melt it with their rounded bellies. They sweated great beads of moisture in the attempt.

Whenever anyone pressed the handle of a siphon, it gave a loud sneeze, and the seltzer spurted out like a fountain, whistling into the glass. Bubbles foamed up and exploded, tickling your nose and throat.

My brother wept tears of delight. He gulped his drink down in long swigs, puffing out his cheeks so that it looked as if it would all come shooting out of his mouth again.

It was too salty for me. I'd like it better with some syrup in it.

"Which will you have, red or yellow?" asked the barman.

"Which is sweeter?"

"How should I know? Taste both and find out!"

From the ceiling two big glass containers were suspended like sausages, one full of yellow liquid and the other full of red. In a moment my drink turned pink, and I too was filled with a delicious warm glow.

As we were leaving, feeling slightly tipsy, someone called out to us. "It's you! What are you doing out so late?"

I stood there as if someone had hit me on the head. I'd heard that voice before.

A ray of light fell on a thin, pale face, a pair of long eyes, and a mouth that was open over sharp white teeth. A body emerged from the dark.

It was he! My new acquaintance. Where had he sprung from? His voice sounded like that of a newly awakened bird. I glanced at my brother. He didn't know the young man. His eyes were nearly popping out of his head.

"What *is* this?" he demanded.

There was a drop of seltzer on his cheek, like a tear. My heart sank. What would he think? A boy coming up to me like this and talking to me as if he'd known me all his life. And where? On the other side of the town, in the middle of the night!

God, what was going to happen next? I was sure this wasn't going to be the end of it. The boy stood there quite calmly, as if he had a perfect right to dispose of me. And I stood there too, riveted to his side.

Had I been expecting him? Had I gone out to look for him? My teeth chattered. He was driving me crazy. There I was, always sitting quietly at home on the window seat with my

books, not wanting to meet anyone, not even scrapping with my brothers. Just as if I lived behind a curtain. And along comes this boy with his challenging manners and blows my serenity away like a whirlwind. What a night! If only morning would come!

My brother knew all my friends. They'd been the same for years. Did he think I was different from other girls? I didn't go out and about; I just went to school with my friends, and even when I met their brothers I didn't stop to talk. And all of a sudden this stranger bobs up. Strange in every possible way— his demeanor, his clothes, his whole appearance.

My brother tried to think whether he hadn't met him somewhere before. Where was he from? Perhaps not from Vitebsk at all? Where did he live? Who were his parents?

Something told him he was out of the ordinary. That curly hair. Perhaps he was a painter. My brother remembered seeing some young men like him strolling through the streets with their paint boxes.

My brother looked at me as if he were seeing me for the first time. What had I to do with a painter? He was beginning to get angry. I'd deceived him.

All my brothers thought of themselves as three times as old as me. I was the youngest, and therefore always a little girl who'd forgotten to grow up. For them I was a kind of doll, to be played with and teased. They were a bit envious of me too. Every year I won a prize at high school and graduated to the next class. They'd had a religious education and would never be able to go to a secular college. So in their eyes I was rather a prodigy.

And here I was grown up all of a sudden, and like all the girls they met in town. And worse still, my boyfriend looked like some wild creature out of the forest, with eyes that shone in the dark.

I stood guiltily between the two of them, not knowing which to turn to first. My mouth was too dry to speak.

Say something, I implored silently, so my brother knows you're human!

I could feel Mendel drawing away from me, as if I'd become

a stranger too. I was afraid he'd leave me there in the dark
street with the boy, and run home and tell everybody: "Guess
what! Bella's got a boyfriend!"

He'd wake the whole house, and everyone would come running. Even the servants would poke their noses around the
door. And the night watchman would have to know all about
it: "Was it a boy from a respectable family, or a crook?"
Speculation would run rife. My brother would keep the best
till last: "He's an artist!"

But they'd all be too sleepy to take it in. It would be better
to wait until morning and tell Mother at the same time. He
wouldn't want to upset her during the night. Let her have her
sleep. In the morning, in the bustle of the shop, she'd be able
to bear the bad news better.

How was I going to look her in the face? What should I say?
Should I tell her the whole story? That he was Thea's friend,
that I met him at her house, that I hardly said a word. It was
he who'd done all the talking. About what? Oh, nothing in
particular. He just looked . . . And I . . . And he . . . But how
could I explain? And anyway, Mother never had time to listen
to long rigmaroles.

"Be quick, I'm in a hurry. Just tell me the end."

But what sort of end was I to think up for her? I quailed. I
didn't want her to be angry with me. She had enough trouble
with my brothers, who all did just as they pleased.

What was I to do? This boy had no idea of the trouble he
was causing. Why had he turned up like this? Why was he
wandering around the town at night? Was he looking for
someone? Or had he just come for a glass of seltzer, like us?
Hadn't he seen I was with my brother? True, it was dark, but
his eyes pierced the dark as if it were day. Perhaps he didn't
even realize it was night.

I looked at him and saw that he really was different. His
face was long and thin, like a fox's. His movements were
quick, tentative, as if he were afraid of people, ready to take
off at any moment. His mouth, unable to close over all those
teeth, was mobile too, and his nose flared as it filled with night
air.

I could understand that a face like this might scare my brother.

But then the boy moved again and his face changed. "A yellow neck! Your skin's yellow!"

I nearly sank through the floor. It was as if the wind had snatched all my clothes off and I was standing in the street naked. Everyone could see my skin, my neck. Now my brother was free to think whatever he liked. A young man stood there talking about my skin and my neck. I was a lost woman.

When had he ever seen my skin and my neck? Was he laughing at me? Trying to provoke me? He was succeeding! Him and his colors! Even if his eyes were full of them, why did he have to let them spill over onto me? Where did he get his "yellow neck" from? Standing there talking about my skin and my neck in front of my brother! He must be either drunk or mad.

He did tell me once that, as a child, he was bitten by a dog!

My tears choked me. I touched my throat, the high collar of my dress. It was made of lace. I'd forgotten—the dress I was wearing had a yellow lace collar!

"This is lace, yellow lace!" I yelled at him. "Can't you see? And you call yourself an artist!"

I'd have liked to push it right under his nose, so that the "artist" could see which was yellow, the collar or my skin.

I tugged at my brother's arm. "Come on, Mendel," I said. "Let's go home."

I left the young man standing in the middle of the street, dumbfounded.

The Bridge

For us the bridge was heaven.

We escaped to it from cramped homes with low ceilings. On the bridge we could see the sky. In the narrow streets it was hidden by houses and steep-roofed churches. But by the bridge the river stretched out flat, and the air was empty between water and sky. A breeze brought the scent of flowers down from the public gardens.

The bridge joined the two halves of the town and was full of people during the day. In the streets they walked with deliberate tread. But on the bridge they felt uplifted by wind and water. Coolness rose up between the wooden planks. Everyone wanted to stay there, not to have to come back to earth and the hard pavements.

In the evening the air gathered into an ash-gray mist. The piles vanished into the water, and the wooden bridge stood out on its own, all white. The river beneath turned from blue to steel gray; its surface was furrowed like a plowed field. The water murmured as it flowed along. Sometimes one wave would chase another.

I had the feeling someone was following me, but I couldn't see anyone or hear any footsteps. Then suddenly a hat appeared in front of me.

"Good evening. Don't be frightened—it's only me." A hand was held out to me.

That boy again! How had he found me? And I was all alone!

I felt like calling for help. But to whom? And how? I was struck dumb. My legs felt strange, as if the bridge were shaking. Where had he come from? He could never keep still.

Oh! Did he think I'd come here looking for him?

I stood there guiltily, not speaking. But why wasn't I allowed to go over the bridge in peace anymore? Why did he have to follow me everywhere?

"Why are you so scared? Are you out for a walk? So am I. Let's go together."

He spoke as if he met me every day. He wasn't in the least shy. His voice was calm, his hand soft and warm and firm. And I didn't think he was laughing at me anymore.

I looked at him. His hair strayed out from under his hat, the curls blowing in the wind as if they'd like to fly away in it. His eyes gazed straight into mine. I looked down.

"Come on, let's get off the bridge and walk along the riverbank. It's beautiful. Nothing to be afraid of. I know—I live there."

I glanced at the dark bank, looking for a light, a sign of the house where he lived.

I wanted to run home but my legs wouldn't obey me. The boy led, and I followed. He wasn't as strange as I'd thought. He walked along beside me, sturdy as a peasant, steeped in the strength of the river.

We went down the steep steps from the bridge to the riverbank, straight down as if into a pit. The bridge hung there above us. The river glimmered like a snake. Not far off slumbered a row of low houses.

Was that where he lived, his home? He and his sisters didn't need to go to the bridge: the river came right up to their door. Perhaps it was because he lived here that the boy couldn't stay still. He swayed and floated with the river.

"Let's sit down on these tree trunks."

He was at home on the riverbank. He knew every log and could see in the dark. We soon came to a pile of trunks. When you sat down on them, they started to roll. You slipped.

"Don't worry, we won't roll into the water."

For him the river was just a puddle. He wasn't at all afraid of it. The water murmured. I didn't say a word. The water spoke for me. What I wanted to say was: "I'm not afraid of the dark river either. And I like to walk about at night too."

How often I'd tapped at a friend's window in the dark and peered through the closed shutters. My friend knew it was me. Who else would come and knock so late? She'd be getting ready for bed, and come to the window in her nightgown with her hair down. As we talked, she'd go on brushing it.

I wasn't afraid to go home alone through the dark streets.

Home! What would be happening there now? I'd been out a long time. The shop would have shut. My parents and my brothers would be sitting down to supper.

"Where's Bella?"

Mother looked around the table, then took another mouthful, and thought. She wouldn't dream I was sitting on a pile of logs in the dark by the river. And not even with one of my friends, but with a strange young man.

Mother couldn't swallow another bite. She'd shake her head. I could see her eyes filling with tears. I could see her scolding me.

A wave leaped at my feet. A log slipped, and I nearly fell off.

"What's the matter? Why don't you say something? Is it true they call you the Queen of Silence?"

And I thought I'd been speaking volumes!

The Birthday

Do you remember one summer evening when we were sitting on the riverbank near the bridge? There were flowers all around us.

The bench was at the top of the steep slope, and below us the river lay so still it seemed about to fall asleep. At our feet shrubs and blossoms emerged from the long grass and grew all over the slippery bank.

The bench was narrow. We had to crane forward to see the water.

We sat in silence. There was no need to speak.

We'd been watching the sun set in front of us. It had taken a long time to disappear. It had blushed, nestled against the sky, shot out red flames that lit up the crosses on the church steeples and set the whole city on fire. Then, pale and exhausted, it vanished over the horizon.

We watched from our bench as though we were sitting up above it all. It was strange how the steep bank here reached up to the sky, while on the other side the sky reached down to the flat shore.

When the sun was gone, a flock of little curly white clouds appeared and drove away any star that tried to shine. Then came a patch of dark-blue sky that drove away the clouds. We sat and watched, waiting for the moon.

When would she be allowed out?

We looked away for a moment and there she was. She had broken through the darkness and the clouds and was lighting up the sky. Then she hid herself again, frolicking like a child let out of school, playing hide-and-seek with the clouds, sporting with her reflection in the river. Perhaps she was teasing us too. She knew we were there just for her.

A little while ago it was day, and now it was night. They say everyone is born under a special star. I turned and looked at you. Your eyes were full of light.

"How old are you?" I asked. "When were you born? Do you know?"

You stared at me as if I'd just dropped out of the sky.

"Do you really want to know? I often wonder myself. My father told me that, to get my brother David out of military service, he added two years to my real age. He said we couldn't fool God, but that if it kept David out of the army, God would forgive him for fooling an official."

"So when were you really born?"

"We can work it out if you like. I'm the eldest. Nyuta is my eldest sister. Not long ago I heard my mother say to Father at supper, 'Hasha, why don't you do something about Hanka?'—that's what we call Nyuta—'Everything falls on me. How long has she got to wait? God willing, she'll soon be seventeen. Go and talk to the matchmaker—you pass right by his house.' So if Nyuta's seventeen, I can't be more than nineteen."

"What day were you born?"

"Why do you want to know everything? Curiosity killed the cat!"

"Not everything—just your birthday."

"Only my mother knows that. And she's probably forgotten, with all those children. But when we quarrel, my sisters always say, 'No wonder you're crazy—you were born in the month of Tammuz!'"

The stars laughed with us, as if they had come out just to listen.

"You'll say I'm silly, but do you know what I think? Perhaps you really did come into the world when your father said. But when you saw what the world was like, you were scared, and it took you two years to get used to it!"

"Do you really think that?"

Your face clouded over, and so did the sky. You moved away from me. I didn't feel like laughing anymore.

But although I don't know how I did it, I did somehow find out the date of your birthday.

That morning early I ran to the outskirts of the town and picked a bunch of flowers. I can still remember how I scratched my hands trying to reach some tall blue flowers through a hedge. A dog ran out and barked at me. I just managed to get away, but had to leave the lovely flowers behind. Then I went into the fields and picked some more, pulling up roots, grass, and all, so that my nosegay would smell of the earth.

When I got home I gathered together all my bright scarves and silk squares, and even took the colored quilt off the bed. From the kitchen I collected some biscuits and pieces of fried fish, the sort you like. Then I hurried into my best dress and set off for your house, laden down like an ass.

Don't imagine it was easy carrying all that. It was a hot day. The sun had been scorching down since early morning, and the cobbles in the streets gave off waves of heat. And I had to cross half the town to get to your place.

The shopkeepers stood in their doorways taking the air. All these women knew me and knew where I was going. They winked at one another.

"Hey, where's the silly girl going with all those parcels?"

"Don't say she's running away from home, God forbid, to live with her handsome young man? You never know with girls nowadays!"

It was a good thing you lived across the river. When I'd left the streets behind and crossed the bridge to the other bank, I felt free.

The windows were shut in the little houses by the water. The housewives kept out of the sun and were working in their kitchens at the back.

I breathed a sigh of relief. A cool breeze rose from the river. The water hurried along beside me. I hurried with it. Behind me the sky stooped down and propelled me along by the shoulders.

That summer you had a room of your own, remember?

It wasn't far from your parents' house, and you'd rented it from a policeman. His little white cottage with its red shutters was like his summer helmet with its red trimmings. It was on a corner, by a long wall enclosing a convent standing in a large garden.

Did you think a policeman and a convent would protect you from danger—even from yourself?

I knocked on your shutter. You often kept it half-shut even during the day. Was it to soften the light, or so that you couldn't be seen from the street?

You let me in yourself so that your landlady wouldn't see me. I came so often—and today I had all those parcels. I stood and waited for you to open the door. It wasn't easy to manipulate the bar.

"What is all this?" You hustled me in and stared. "Have you been away?"

"Do you think people only have parcels when they've just got off the train? Guess what day it is."

"Ask me another. I never know what day it is."

"No, I don't mean what day of the week. Today's your birthday!"

Your jaw dropped. You couldn't have been more astonished if I'd said the Czar had just arrived in town.

"How do you know?"

I undid my scarves and draped them over the table and over the walls. I spread my colored quilt over your bed. And you suddenly went and rummaged among your canvases and put one on the easel.

"Don't move," you said. "Stay just like that."

I was still holding the flowers. I wanted to put them in water before they died. But I soon forgot all about them. You dashed at the canvas with such energy it shook on the easel. You plunged the brushes into the paint so fast that red and blue, black and white flew through the air. They swept me with them. I suddenly felt as if I were taking off. You too were poised on one leg, as if the little room could no longer contain you.

You soared up to the ceiling. Your head turned down to mine and turned mine up to you, brushing against my ear and whispering something.

I listened as your deep, soft voice sang to me, a song echoed in your eyes. Then together we floated up above the room with all its finery, and flew. Through the window a cloud and a patch of blue sky called to us. The brightly hung walls whirled around us. We flew over fields of flowers, shuttered houses, roofs, yards, churches.

"What do you think of it?"

Suddenly you had come down to earth again, looking back and forth from your painting to me, now going near and now stepping back from the easel.

"Still quite a lot to do, eh? Can't leave it like this. Where do you think it still needs more working over?"

You were really talking to yourself, anxious about what I was going to say.

"Oh, it's very good! And the way you flew!"

"We'll call it 'The Birthday.' "

Your heart had stopped pounding now.

"Will you come again tomorrow? I'll paint another picture. And we'll fly away again."

FROM MY NOTEBOOKS

Morning

"Bashutka, get up! It's late!" Sasha was standing beside the bed and shaking me by the shoulder.

I pulled the blankets up over my head and turned my face to the wall. I kept my eyes shut and couldn't see anything.

"But it's still dark."

"What are you talking about? Your mother's been in the shop for ages. Your father's saying his prayers. Come on, get up and let me brush your hair. I won't have time later on."

"You stuck the comb in my head yesterday. I don't want you to do my hair anymore."

"Don't be silly. You can't go around all day with your hair in a mess. People will think you're not respectable."

"Let them! Who cares?"

"Come on now, Bashenka. You'll see, I won't hurt you this morning."

Sasha go hold of my tousled braid and attacked the tangles with a sharp-toothed comb.

"Ow, stop it, you're hurting!"

"Nearly finished. I'm being as careful as I can. Do you think it's easy trying to comb a sheep's head?"

She spat on her hands and tried to compose my unruly locks.

"Monster!" I yelled as I escaped at last. Two tight braids hung down my back, tied together with ribbon.

In the dining room the samovar was still on the table.

My parents both got up early. Father took advantage of the peace and quiet to read his sacred books. He had a little rest in the afternoon. Mother never thought she had the right to rest. Everything was on her shoulders—the children, the shop, the house, and the staff in both. She hardly even slept at night.

But my brothers just got up when they felt like it. Her whole life long, my mother dreamed that one day we'd be like other people and all get up early.

"If you got up earlier you'd have more time," she used to argue. "As it is, you sleep half your life away."

What difference did it make? The samovar was kept boiling from early morning. If it went off the boil, someone called Sasha to bring more hot coals. So there was always a glass of tea ready.

"Sasha, can I have a clean glass?"

"Sasha, can I have a spoon?"

None of us ever thought of moving, though the cupboard was just behind us.

"Sasha, we've run out of hot milk."

Abrashka, who was always the last to get up, didn't stop shouting until there was a jugful of milk right in front of him. Then he'd skim off the skin with his fingers and gulp it down, making a face at the others. Abrashka was the joker of the family.

"What are we having to eat today, Mendel?"

The taciturn Mendel sniffed. "Smells of cinnamon."

"Let's go and see what's on the windowsill."

My brothers all had a sweet tooth. Twice a week—Tuesdays and Fridays—Chaya would bring bring in some big black baking sheets covered with generously stuffed puff pastries and put them down on the windowsill.

"Let them cool off for a bit."

The pastries lay there steaming. Some had risen more than others. One sort leaked a filling of butter beaten up with poppyseed, like black sand. Another, stuffed with cheese, lay in a pool of cream. Others again were filled with chopped apple and had cracked open in the oven, oozing golden juice.

But before I knew what was happening, several of the pastries had vanished, and all that was left on the windowsill was poppyseeds and crumbs of cheese. Then my brothers would turn to the cupboard, where there was a big tin of cinnamon spiced-cookies stuffed with currants and dipped in icing. They stuck to your fingers and crunched under your teeth.

At this rate the morning's baking wouldn't last out the week. Chaya wrung her hands when she saw the windowsill empty.

"At least leave some for your mother and father!"

Then the boys would run out to buy sweet rolls, or send Sasha to the Polish confectioner's for some little cakes.

"Give me one," they'd threaten each other, "or else I'll tell the rebbe you've been eating nonkosher pastries."

As well as relatives, one of the shop assistants might eat with us, or a traveling salesman. The samovar stayed on the table all morning. Beggars came too, hungry and asking for alms. Through the kitchen door they could see the samovar on the table, together with the glasses and the sugar bowl. One of them would pluck up his courage and say, "Chaya, may I come in for a glass of tea? I haven't had so much as a drop of water since this morning."

His wrinkles would deepen with self-pity.

"Have as much as you like, as far as I'm concerned," Chaya would answer, adding with a wry smile: "One good-for-nothing more or less—it's all the same to me."

The beggar went to the table, rinsed out a glass, and filled it with tea.

"How many does that make this morning?" Abrashka would tease him.

The old man would peer at him over his eyeglasses, not knowing whether he was serious. He'd smile nervously, sip at his tea, and choke on a bit of sugar. Then the older boys would turn on Abrashka.

"Why can't you leave people alone?"

Some of the poor come so regularly that, before she took the samovar away, Chaya would mutter to herself: "But has So-and-so been in yet?"

Once one of them, a man as thin as a lath, had the nerve to drink the whole samovar dry. His day was divided between the synagogue and our table. He knew exactly when the samovar was put out in our house and when it was taken away, and at the right time he'd leave his prayer shawl on the bench in the synagogue and come to our place for some tea. If there was no milk left, he'd take the empty jug out to the kitchen and mumble, "Just a drop, enough for one glass."

When he finished his last glass, he used to sit there exhausted, waiting for his red nose to cool off.

The door of the dining room was suddenly pushed open, and there like a black shadow stood Reb Shlomo, our teacher. My brothers' breakfast stuck in their throats.

"Up at last, then, you rascals?" he cried. "Have you said your prayers? Not yet? But you're sitting down eating your breakfast! Did you at least say the blessing over the bread? Well, come on, now, time for lessons. You've wasted half the day already."

He himself hardly slept at all. Once he put his nose in a book, he might stay up studying all night. So his eyes were always bloodshot, as if he had a fever. Food and drink didn't interest him. His gaunt form went back and forth about the room like a pendulum. He noticed everything. The fringe of one of the boys' prayer shirts was ragged. Another had had his hair cut too short. The rebbe was consumed with anguish because he couldn't manage to get the Torah into his pupils' unwilling heads.

He stood there in the doorway, but looking as if he might flee at any moment. His shiny black coat was part of him, hanging ever more loosely about his meager frame. Only his skullcap fitted tightly, as if it were glued to his head. His face

was shadowed by his long sidelocks and tangled beard. All his clothes were black except for a bright-blue fringe on his prayer shirt. It hung out from under his jacket like a patch of sky emerging from the clouds. The long fringe stirred as if swaying in the wind, and from time to time Reb Shlomo would lift it to his lips, as if to quiet both himself and it.

He lived in our house, but hardly ever left his room. When would he have had time? All day long he was studying Torah. In the morning he studied it with Father. That must have been the best part of the day for him. Everyone else was still asleep, and the house was quiet. The two of them, the rebbe and my father, used to discuss difficult passages of Scripture or study a page or two of the Talmud. When they got tired, they'd sit down and have a glass of tea. In silence.

Sometimes the rebbe thought to himself: "Perhaps I got a bit too heated just now, arguing with Reb Shmuel Noah. It is his house, after all."

And he'd get up and vanish into his room. He took his phylacteries out of the velvet case and wound the thongs carefully around his hairy arm. Then he started to sway back and forth and from side to side, and kept on until his bones ached.

Then he'd go and look for his pupils, who'd just got up.

"What's to become of them? Do you think they try to learn anything? No, they'd rather play. Not like good Jewish children at all. Avremel, you'll soon be thirteen—you've got your bar mitzvah coming up. And have you thought what you're going to say in your speech? No, your head's just full of nonsense. Modern children—how am I ever going to get anywhere with such a crew? It's hopeless!"

Reb Shlomo lapsed into thought. Abrashka seized the opportunity to ask, "Rebbe, may I go out and play in the yard till lessons begin?"

Reb Shlomo leaped up as if his chair had caught fire.

"Shirking again, eh?" He grabbed Abrashka by the sleeve and hauled him into his room. Then he ran his finger over some lines in the Bible and found the place.

"Right. Begin!"

And he started to sway to and fro. Abrashka began to

giggle. The rows of letters danced on the page. He watched the teacher's beard wagging up and down in time with his lips. But Abrashka had lost the thread, and stood there with his mouth open as if he were trying to snap at it in midair.

"What are you jabbering about?" cried the rebbe, springing up. "I can't understand a word."

You could hear him all over the house.

"Wretched child! Make fun of everybody, would you?" There was the sound of a slap. "Perhaps that'll teach you to put your tongue out at me! I'll get the Torah into your head if I have to thump it in!"

"I didn't mean it, rebbe. My tooth hurts—I was only feeling it with my tongue."

But by now Reb Shlomo was beside himself. His hands were shaking. He took down the well-worn leather strap from its nail on the wall, rolled up his sleeves, and seized hold of Abrashka.

His eyes blazed as if this were some sacred rite. In no time at all, Abrashka's trousers were down and the strap was beating down on his behind. Abrashka howled.

"I won't do it again, rebbe! I won't do it again!"

But the teacher was beyond seeing or hearing now, and just went on thrashing him. Finally Abrashka managed to slip out of his grasp. But in doing so he fell and hit his head on the floor. This brought the rebbe back to his senses. He slumped into a chair; the strap dropped out of his hand. Abrashka rolled as far as the door, got to his feet, pulled his trousers up, and fled without a backward glance.

He immediately bumped into Father, who was standing with his face to the wall, silently praying, his eyes closed. He was wrapped in his prayer shawl as in a white cloud, and completely absorbed in his devotions. Abrashka stopped in his tracks, ashamed of himself.

Even if Father had heard what was going on, he must just have thought to himself: "The rebbe knows what he's doing. It's only natural for children to be beaten." And he'd have returned to his prayers. The phylacteries on his brow shone like a dark star beneath his prayer shawl. One arm was raised as if making a sign, the flesh constricted by the thongs bound around it. He held a prayer book in the other hand, but didn't need to look at it.

Suddenly, through all the din, came Mother's voice as she hurried from the shop into the house.

"Does anyone know where he is? Shmuel Noah, how much longer are you going to be?"

She was getting agitated. Every morning bills had to be paid for goods previously bought on credit, and she was afraid she wouldn't have enough cash when the time came. Father could have told her what to do, but clearly he was still lost in contemplation. His prayer shawl was billowing about, but on the spot; he showed no sign of moving. He was quite capable of praying all morning. Mother shrugged.

Of course he could hear her voice through the shawl. But he wasn't sure whether he was hearing it today or remembering it from yesterday. Every morning Mother went on like that. What was all the fuss about? Either there was enough money in the till, or you could go and borrow some from a neighbor. With God's help, you could always pay your debts. Why moan and groan about it?

But Mother was still anxious. It was already eleven o'clock, and she didn't have enough money. She went back into the shop and consulted the bookkeeper.

"Hershel," she asked him, "how much have we got to pay out today?"

The quiet bookkeeper, sitting half-asleep over his ledgers, woke with a start, adjusted his eyeglasses, and leafed through the pages. He ran his finger over the entries, occasionally stopping or referring back and forth. Please let him not make any mistakes!

"Today's the fifth . . . The fifth . . . Here we are . . ."

"Rivka, how much have you got in the till?" Mother asked the cashier yet again.

Rivka had been counting ever since the shop opened. The kopeks stood in front of her in little columns which she moved hither and thither, checking and rechecking. But the answer always came out the same.

"It's ten to eleven already!" cried Mother. "Why don't you say something, some of you? Here, hand me my shawl."

And she ran next door.

"Reb David, could you lend me some money?"

"How much do you want, Alta?"

"Fifty."

He smiled. "Of course. Why are you so upset? Come in."

Between neighbors, that was nothing to get worked up about. He had great respect for Mother. It was she who really ran the shop.

After a few minutes she was back home again. She called my eldest brother.

"Here, the money's in my shawl. Run to the bank—you've still got five minutes. But be careful! There are always thieves hanging around there."

Then she gave a sigh of relief and straightened up, as if a great weight had fallen from her shoulders.

It was at eleven o'clock that the day really began.

Evening

After dinner the family scattered. Dullness descended. Then, late in the evening, my brothers would straggle home.

Father would be sitting at the table drinking tea. When the door opened, he looked up.

"Where have you been?"

"Nowhere."

Father took another sip and asked again.

"Whom did you see?"

"No one."

Father began to raise his voice. "So what have you been doing?"

"Nothing."

My brothers shrugged their shoulders. My father, as if he were the one at fault, lowered his head, sipped his tea, and said no more. My brothers sauntered across the dining room, then, as soon as they'd shut the door behind them, hurtled down the stairs, pushing and shoving, to their room in the basement. There they were free, away from the shop and from our parents.

They were always squabbling.

"Where's my notebook? I've got a lesson to learn. Hey, I don't want you drawing all over it!"

"You're always leaving fingermarks over my books. You might at least wash your hands after you've been gorging buns!"

"Oh, leave me alone!"

Then they started to scrap, the book got dropped, and they chased each other around the room. Trying to get out of the way, I hit my shin on an iron bedstead. As they rushed by, one of the boys gave me a pinch.

"Hey, stop it! I didn't touch your beastly book!"

"You shouldn't get in the way!"

He batted me aside like a ball of wool. As a matter of fact, I was muffled up in wool and wadding from head to toe.

The room was freezing cold. The narrow beds were crowded together around three of the walls. An ink-stained table stood on a floor of bare boards. On the fourth wall there were two tall windows with heavy wooden frames, but all they looked out on was a deep pit into which no light ever penetrated. The room was below ground level, and the pit was covered with an iron grating to prevent passersby from falling in.

No sun ever entered the room. Even in the middle of the day, when up in the street it was warm and light, down there it was dark. If a ray of light ever did get through the grating, it was immediately cut off by the foot of some pedestrian. Children sometimes got their shoes stuck between the bars. So you never felt like climbing up on those subterranean window-sills. What was there to see? A patch of dark earth strewn with litter. Sometimes there was a smoldering cigarette butt. Sometimes people spat.

At night those blind windows looked sinister.

"Do close the shutters," I begged.

The two leaves shut together like a folding door. They were fixed in place by an iron bar laid across them like a sword and bolted at one end. Instead of blind windows, a mute wall.

"Light the lamp. Where is it?"

"Sasha took it this morning to fill it. But she forgot to bring it back."

"Let's light the stove, then."

The wood was already laid in the white-tiled oven, with strips of birch bark poking out between the crisscrossed logs. My brothers lay on the floor, and I made room for myself between their legs.

A match was struck and the bark caught fire. First came a wisp of smoke, then a spurt of flame. The bark curled up and disappeared, and the little flame crept over the logs, licking up the drops of moisture. The wood began to pop and crackle, then split and caved in, surrendering to the blaze. The kindling, consumed by the flames, withered away, and the coals above began to glow. Fiery blue tongues ran along them and were reflected in the boys' faces.

"Abrashka, go up to the kitchen and fetch a few potatoes to bake in the stove."

Abrashka jumped up.

"And ask Chaya for a herring while you're at it."

The rest of us sat around the glowing coals with glowing cheeks, occasionally wielding the poker.

"Hey, how did you get Chaya to give you such a nice fat herring?"

"You don't think I waited to ask? I pinched it out of the barrel myself."

The big potatoes were tossed among the embers. Their skins shriveled at once in the heat. The herring writhed like a little snake, turned up its tail, and started to sizzle. When it was black and dry, we blew on our fingers and gingerly picked it out of the fire.

While we were munching we suddenly felt a draft. Someone had opened the door.

"Why are you all sitting here in the dark?"

Sasha came in with a swish of skirts, carrying a lamp which gave off a smell of kerosene as well as light. The lamp itself, together with Sasha's flowered dress and flushed cheeks, brought some brightness and cheer into the room.

"Out of the way, kids. The stove's gone out. Let me shut the

draft, or all the heat that's left will go up the chimney."

She raked out the coals with the blackened shovel, then stood on a chair and shut the little iron door.

The room was plunged into gloom again.

What should we do now? Mother and Father were still in the shop.

"Here, Bashutka," said Sasha, getting hold of me, "come and have your supper before the others, and get to bed. School tomorrow."

I would rather be in the kitchen with her than in the bare room with closed shutters. In the kitchen, with its little lamp, it was cozy and light, and the copper pans shone on the walls. On the table there were eggs, bread, milk, plates, and dishes. Chaya bustled around the oven, muttering away even when her back was turned.

"What would you like for your supper, Bashenka? Sardines? A piece of fried fish?"

She didn't wait for me to answer. She'd already put a little black fish in the hot fat.

245

"Here—done to a turn!" She put the plate in front of me, then sat down opposite to make sure I ate it all. She also piled on some sour cream.

I rubbed my eyes. I was getting sleepy.

My bedroom was long and spacious, but dark. The only light came in from the dining room. I was afraid to look into the corners. I knew they held only spare beds, but their legs and pillows were invisible in the darkness. Sometimes one of my older brothers slept there, passing through on some journey. Sometimes it was a commercial traveler or our apprentice.

I was always the first in bed, the blankets pulled up over my head, scared to look out at the dark. The buzzing of the light in the dining room sang me to sleep. The rest of the family had their supper late, and as I drowsed I could hear the clatter of plates and cutlery. They'd finished the fish and were having coffee. Chaya stood in the doorway with a long list in her hand, waiting for Mother to look around.

"Well, Chaya, what is it?"

Mother was reminded that there was the house to take care of, as well as the shop.

"Let's see your list, then. How much did you spend?"

Chaya handed her a sheet of paper covered with figures, and began to complain about how expensive everything was. But all the same, she'd gotten things very cheap. Mother didn't know anything about the price of food—she never went shopping. But she too kept saying how expensive everything was. Chaya laid her hand on her heart and swore she did her best.

I fell asleep.

Suddenly I woke up in a cold sweat. I listened. But there was no sound from the dining room. They'd all gone to bed. But I thought I could see something gleaming in the dark. And it was the creaking of springs that had awakened me. I looked out from under the blankets. I could hear footsteps. Was I dreaming?

Suddenly there in front of me was a white phantom. Its legs were swallowed up in the gloom. A pair of long white arms hung down on either side of a sort of inflated bag. I dived back under the covers. But I'd recognized the ghost. It was the apprentice. But what did he want? Why was he so near my bed? I'd never seen him in his nightshirt before.

He melted back into the darkness. All I could hear was the creaking of his bed.

I couldn't get back to sleep. I kept watching to see if his blankets moved. But I was afraid to scream in case I woke everyone up. I only just lasted till morning.

"Mother, do you know what happened last night? The apprentice . . ."

"What on earth are you talking about? Really, a big girl like you! Aren't you ashamed to say things like that about anybody? Now hurry up and dress, and get off to school."

With lips compressed, I began my day.

The Staff

Whenever for any reason my parents had to take time off, they used to say, "Bashenka, go and mind the shop."

I'd climb up on Mother's high stool. The shop was full of assistants. Their heads and shoulders rose up above the counters.

Whom was I supposed to watch? Them or the customers?

As they went by, they'd give me a pinch or grab at one of my arms or legs. They all tried to tease or tickle me. I'd start to squeal, and then they'd push me around the shop, stool and all.

Mother appeared in the doorway. "Have you all taken leave of your senses? Haven't you got anything better to do than play with Bashenka? You've certainly chosen the right place! Look at all the stuff left lying about!"

Then she turned on me. "And you! Why do you lead them on? No excuses! Just let me have a bit of peace and quiet."

She went out again.

Then I sat and watched the assistants wrapping and unwrapping the stock. White tissue paper rustled as it enfolded gold rings and pins and brooches set with colored stones. They glittered in protest at being covered up.

They were always being polished and counted, and then wrapped up in thick brown paper as a precaution against theft. True, there was always a watchman outside; but you could never be sure of everyone inside.

All the staff had been with us for years. They'd learned their trade in the shop, grown up together there.

Huneh, a dark-haired bachelor, was the oldest. He was usually silent, but when he saw me his whiskered mouth would curve into a smile. His somber eyes never lit up, though; they were like stagnant pools. His clammy hands felt as if they'd just been fished out of it. I pulled my own hand away if ever he touched it.

He spoke only to the customers, and then in as few words as possible. A real clam. You couldn't even tell what he was thinking about from that low forehead, smooth as a plank. Not about anything pleasant, that was certain. But although he was too shy to utter his thoughts, everybody knew one of them: he was looking for a wife.

Every evening before he went home he'd put on a melancholy expression, take out the latest photograph the matchmaker had sent him, and ask my brother Jacob to write a letter for him. Every evening it was a different girl. If Jacob wasn't there, Huneh would sit down himself and copy out a model letter from the etiquette book.

Rosa was just the opposite. She brimmed over with words, and you could hear her penetrating voice all over the shop. Her mop of hair was held high, as if to show she wasn't afraid of anybody. It was better not to start her off: she'd launch into a long story, then burst out laughing, always trying to make an impression. If a young officer came into the shop, she'd overwhelm him with witticisms as well as wares. Her eyes shone as brightly as the rings, trying to monopolize his attention, displaying her smiles at the same time as her merchandise. He'd buy not only what he came in for but also what she'd talked him into.

Though there was always plenty to do in the shop, the assistants just trailed around, especially one fair, lanky young fellow. He never exerted himself, and spent most of his time undoing and tying up parcels. But he preferred playing with me.

"Here, Bashenka, shall I give you a seesaw?"

He stretched out his long legs and waggled his feet invitingly. When I sat on his knees, he'd bend them and stretch them alternately, rocking me back and forth. It really was like a seesaw.

But when I got close enough to catch a glimpse of his greasy locks, I'd slither off, leaving him sitting there affronted.

Avremel, the apprentice, had come to live with us as a boy. At first he was shy and fearful. But he soon showed another side, and turned into a sturdy young rascal, a bold, dark youth with a mouthful of big, strong teeth. He looked as if he could swallow me in one gulp. I was frightened of him.

Rivka, the cashier, hovered nervously over her till. She was a plain girl from a poor home, and couldn't get used to handling a box full of money. She kept looking to see if it was all there, counting the coins and checking the notes to make sure they weren't forged. She trembled whenever a customer gave her money, and quaked again as she handed him his change.

Hershel, the bookkeeper, sat in a dark corner at the back of the shop with his back to everyone. Had anyone ever seen his face? He was as silent as his account books, but while they were fat, he was lean and dried up. He had eyeglasses rather than eyes, and his legs were as thin as the pencils stuck behind his ears. Figures flowed from his pen and deployed themselves in columns over the pages of his ledgers. He was always peering at them, afraid that if he took his eyes off them they'd go astray, together with the goods they represented.

Every year before the high holy days he would surround himself with all his books, and go through the rows of prices and figures like a general inspecting his troops. He could tell exactly how many of every article had been sold in the course of the year, and how many were still left in the shop. Nothing escaped his eager glasses; he threw himself into the ledgers

body and soul. If he found one item unaccounted for, he leaped up trembling as if he'd uncovered a theft, and reported it to my parents in tones of catastrophe. The air grew dark with gloom.

The silent Huneh, after working in our shop for twenty years, finally found a bride. With her dowry he opened a shop of his own, full of stock he'd "borrowed" from my parents.

Going out with Father

Father couldn't be bothered with ordinary customers. If it wasn't someone really important, who would deal with him and with him only, he didn't even stand up when they came in. But when some merchant arrived from far away to buy jewelry, then he'd stretch a point and converse about worldly matters.

Often he'd just stand there motionless near the till, his pale face gleaming like a patch of sunlight in the darkness of the shop. His blue eyes seemed to bask in thought. What about? I didn't think it was ever about us children. Perhaps it was about a passage of the Talmud he'd been studying that morning.

His tall, thickset figure seemed set apart. I was never afraid of him. I liked being with him. He made me feel safe.

Sometimes—and it was almost as if he'd moved house—he'd sit on a chair by the door. Every passerby greeted him with respect. He answered politely, but looked dreamily up at the sky as if watching for the first star to come out. I stood by his chair like a puppy.

"Bashka, why don't we go for a little ride? Fetch your things."

I didn't need telling twice. I was back in a moment, pulling my hat on as I ran. I loved going for a ride in a droshky. Whenever one of our staff had to take a parcel to the station, I always begged him to let me hang on to the back of the droshky. Anywhere. Just for a little way. . . .

So to go for a drive with Father, right out of town—it was like being transported into another world.

We settled ourselves comfortably in the droshky, yielding to the rhythm of the wheels and not saying a word. But to me it felt as if we were singing at the tops of our voices.

Soon we'd leave the noisy cobblestones behind us, and the wheels would sink deep and silent into the sand. We'd forgotten the city, escaped from it as if forever.

"Reb Shmuel Noah, shall I turn back now? Aren't you tired?"

The coachman had turned around to speak to us, interrupting our dreams. Father didn't answer. The coachman used his own discretion about how far we ought to go, then turned homeward.

Father skipped down from the droshky, refreshed. His blue eyes had become bluer, and there was a tinge of color in his pale cheeks. I couldn't bear to get out yet, and stayed with the driver a few minutes more, as far as his stand. Then he said, "Now then, Bashenka, off you go. Home."

The Watchmaker

Whenever I got bored sitting alone in the house, I used to go into the shop. It was always full of life there, like a wedding. But where could I stand so as not to be in the way of the staff? There was so little space I got tossed from pillar to post like a ball.

"What are you hanging around for? Go home. We've got enough to do without you."

"There's nobody there. I'm afraid."

"What do you mean, nobody? What about Sasha? Go on—she'll keep you company."

I bit my lip and went. But I didn't go back into the house. I stopped by the watchmaker's bench. I could stand there out of everyone's way, and when the watchmaker was working he forgot all about me. I liked the old man. He was the younger watchmaker's father. Their benches stood by the shop's two windows.

I used to tuck myself away behind a corner of the old man's table, which had an iron vise fixed to it. The bench itself was all battered and scratched. Bits of the surface were peeling off like dead skin. Here and there lay little heaps of sawdust which got in your eyes if you blew at it. Scattered all over the table were little wheels and screws, gold cases, dials, and tiny springs. Round watch crystals like babies' eyes lurked at the back. Everything was strewn about like flotsam.

But to the watchmaker each of these items was precious, and he guarded every one like the apple of his eye.

I wasn't allowed to touch anything, much less pick it up. I just stood there as motionless as the vise fixed to the bench.

People kept coming to pester the old man. Why didn't all the clocks strike at once? Why did each one wake up at a different time? No one ever thought the watchmaker might be interested in anything else. He himself almost forgot he had a home of his own, that he was a father and the head of a family.

He'd got used to being scolded like a child, and wasn't even embarrassed at his son being there, at the other bench, to see it. I couldn't see his face. He crouched so low over his work his nose almost touched it; his little beard did brush the table. A black cylindrical loupe stuck out from beneath his wrinkled brow. It looked as if it had been screwed into his eye. In his hand—almost part of it—he held a tiny pair of pincers.

He'd take a watch out of the drawer, rub it with his beard, hold it to his ear, and then sniff at it. The watch seemed to nestle in his hand. He touched it with the pincers, and the lid flew open with a little sigh.

I bent over the naked innards with him. No matter how small a watch it was, there were the same little wheels and cogs humming and spinning in all directions. As soon as the watchmaker touched one of the wheels with his pincers, they all stopped dead. It was as if their heart had been paralyzed. They waited anxiously for the cold metal to go away, so that they could start tripping and dancing again.

If the old man heard the heart of a watch beating too slowly or too faintly, he'd bend down over it even more closely, giving a push here and a pull there, shaking it, breathing into it, warming it up. The watch sucked life and strength from him like an infant. Then he'd open his drawer again and put it away to rest.

The drawer was a sort of nursery. The watches lay there in cribs, little boxes softly lined with silk and velvet. The prettiest watches, set with diamonds, slept peacefully in the knowledge that the old man would find time to fondle them again, to stroke their little heads and caress their shiny cheeks.

On nails around the sides of the drawer hung a lot of plainer watches. Their hearts beat against the wood to remind the old man that they were alive too, and waiting patiently for the moment when he'd lift them down. The watches were like children to him. When he wound them up, it was as if he were playfully tweaking their ears. He taught them to walk, tested whether they went too fast or too slow, set the hands forward or back, and when they got tired, put them to bed. He knew them as a doctor knows his patients. Perhaps he didn't want them to be cured, so that they could stay in his drawer forever.

When a watch was very ill, he'd put a drop of oil in it and tuck it into his vest pocket. It would get better more quickly close to his heart. He really did think more about his watches than about his own family.

There was an old wife waiting for him at home who never went out anymore. The house was very small, but she had to look after it all by herself. Their only son sat working listlessly by the other window, as if forgotten. His father left the least valuable watches to him.

Every so often the young man would look up and gaze out enviously through the window at the people admiring the goods on display.

"Some people have all the luck," he'd mutter. "Nothing to do but wander around and stare in shopwindows."

His father's eye would descend on him. "What are you mumbling about, sitting there doing nothing? You'd be better off learning your trade a bit better. Keep your eyes on that watch before you ruin it!"

But before he'd finished venting his spleen on his son, Mother would interrupt.

"My God, where can I find the right time in this place? Does anyone know what the time really is?"

In burst an irate landowner. "What have you got to say to this? That watch you're supposed to have repaired still doesn't run properly. It stopped as soon as I got it home."

The old man just sat there and thought. "God Almighty! What do they expect? It's easy to grumble. Human beings are all created different. And watches are living creatures too."

But he didn't say anything. He just bent lower over his table and screwed his glass more firmly into his eye. He'd rather listen to the ticking of watches than to the shouting and bawling of men.

The watches knew people were talking about them and buzzed comfortably into his ancient ear. When anyone shouted at the old man, he crouched down as if he were trying to crawl into the dark drawer too. All you could see were his ears, open like doors to catch the sound of clockwork.

The truth was that he was glad when a watch was brought back to him. Devil take the man, what did he know about watches? He bellowed so loud himself, how could he hear whether his watch was running or not?

He snatched the watch out of the customer's hands and blew into it to dislodge the offending speck of dust. The watch, revived, began to tick sadly, telling him how lonely it was in the dark of its owner's vest pocket, how roughly he twisted its head around to wind it, not even saying good night, always wanting it to go on and on without stopping.

The watchmaker put it away in his table drawer for a good rest, consoling it with the promise that he wouldn't give it back again in a hurry. He'd think of some excuse. The customer would just have to wait.

"Sorry, sir. It'll be a long job."

But Mother overheard. "Why? What's the matter with it? Why can't it be put right immediately? What is all this?"

"Don't get excited, Alta. Whose fault is it, anyway? The gentleman broke the watch himself. I'll lend him another so that he'll know what the time is. Here, this one's not so fragile."

He kept a number of these watches by him—cart horses, which gave the golden thoroughbreds a rest.

Unlike everyone else, I always believed our old man was the only person who really knew how to mend watches. I still won't take mine to anyone else to be repaired. So they lie unmended and lifeless in my own drawer.

The Boat

Every day Abrashka and I went to the bridge to see what was happening on the river. There was always plenty to look at: ferries crossing from one bank to the other, boats passing up and down. Even the waves gave the river no rest, everlastingly tumbling over themselves and dragging its waters far away.

If only I could have gone with them. Just once.

"Bashka, what are you dreaming about now?"

My brother gave me a dig in the ribs.

"Look, do you see that boat just starting off for the other side, full of people? . . . That's him—the one in the glasses. Look, you can see them flashing."

"Who? Where?"

"Are you blind or something? It's Uncle Beril. He goes home on the ferry every evening. Quick, if we hurry we can ride across with him."

"Can a boat fall apart, like a raft?"

We raced down the rickety wooden steps to the riverbank, the damp sand glittering below. The river was so close it was as if we were already on the water.

"Uncle! Uncle Beril!" we shouted.

His heavy boots made the sand spurt up as he walked along toward the ferry.

"Well, well, look who's here! How did you come? Swim with the fishes?"

"Are you on your way home?" Abrashka asked.

"You must be a mind reader. And what if I am?"

His eyes twinkled behind his eyeglasses.

"I can see by the look on your faces that you want to come with me. Well, I can understand Abrashka. But Bashenka— aren't you scared?"

He pinched my cheek. Of course I was scared. But I didn't say so. Abrashka would have made fun of me.

We all went and climbed into the boat waiting patiently in the water. It rocked as we got in. The other passengers moved up to make room for us, but the old boatman didn't so much as glance at us. His suntanned face and his beard made him look more like a peasant than a Jew. He was rolling a cigarette in his stubby fingers. Then he spat into the water and moistened the cigarette paper with his tongue. It was harder for those rough hands to roll a cigarette than to row the boat across the river.

He didn't speak; just spat. As if there weren't enough water in the river already.

We sat down on either side of the boat, trailing our fingers in the water and touching the long oars resting alongside. They looked like extensions of the boatman's own gnarled arms.

"How much longer are you going to wait, Reb Yid?" asked my uncle. "Do you expect the whole town to come aboard?"

The old man just sat and waited. No one spoke. I looked at the river and was silent too. Suddenly the boatman looked up, glanced around, and muttered into his beard, "All right, that's plenty. Move up closer together."

Then he turned, spat on his hands, seized one oar, and pushed the boat off from the bank. There was water all around us now, and a cool breeze, as if we were at sea. The boat moved up and down through the waves, cutting through one

and riding another. The water churned and eddied in the sun, sometimes lit up and sometimes in shadow. I thought I could see fish with scales of silver.

We all sat huddled together, heads down, gazing at the water as if to help the boat on its way. I held on tight to Uncle Beril's sleeve. We seemed to be floating along in another world. The distant earth reached up to the sky.

There was no sound to be heard, no voice. Even Abrashka was silent. No one moved. Only the boatman bent forward, leaned back. The oars skimmed the surface, then dipped in. The other bank beckoned noiselessly. Had I gone deaf?

I longed to get to the shore, to feel the sand under my feet, to run again over the solid earth.

The String of Pearls

Whenever Father went into the shop, he just stood there thinking. Was he pondering the passage from the Torah that he'd been studying that morning? Or brooding over the new woes he imagined lurking on all sides?

The hustle and bustle of the shop didn't interest him at all. As for spending hours persuading someone to buy a bowl or a watch for a wedding present—he left all that to Mother.

Yet it was with him, my pious, silent father, that the gentlewomen of the town liked to deal. Especially one, the wife of the rich director of an insurance company, who'd brought her to our town from God knows where, probably to parade her in front of his friends.

He was a short, lively man with a ready smile and a joke for everyone. His eyes shone behind his glasses. His head shone too, no matter how carefully he brushed his few remaining wisps of hair over it.

He liked company. And admiration. A swarm of young men with nothing better to do all day—in the evening they could at least play cards—hung around him. As soon as he appeared in the street, they'd all rush up to greet him.

"Good morning, sir," said one. "Did you sleep well?"

"What a question," said the next, pushing him aside. "You showed them all a thing or two last night, eh, sir? What a hand! They were all left openmouthed!"

"Yes, it's no easy matter to get the better of our friend the director!"

You could hear them laughing all the way along the street. The director's gold-rimmed glasses, borne aloft by their flattery, danced along delightedly.

When he brought his new wife home, the young men couldn't contain themselves.

"A nice trick to play on us! Not a word did you let slip! Perhaps you were afraid of the evil eye."

"Well, sir, you certainly have all the luck."

"Worth waiting for, sir. Such beauty! Such charm! This place has never seen the like!"

And they transferred their enthusiasm to the frail young woman who'd fallen like an angel from heaven among that gang of idlers.

At first she didn't know where she was, and smiled on everyone. And she did bring her husband luck. He even seemed to grow taller. But he had no time to spare for his wife. He merely lavished gifts on her. And so she acquired a taste for the glitter of gold and jewels, and came to our shop nearly every day.

When her shining black carriage drew up outside on its silent rubber wheels, the assistants all peered out of the windows, whispering excitedly.

"Here comes Mrs. Bishowskaya. Where's the boss? Call him, quickly!"

The burly coachman pulled up opposite our windows, and the lady disappeared for a moment behind his mountainous form. She scarcely touched the cushions as she rode along. She seemed to float, ready at any moment to float completely away. Even when she'd alighted from the carriage, her slender figure swayed as if she were still riding along inside.

Her face was always white as alabaster, but though it never had a tinge of color, it was radiant. Her eyes were almond-shaped, her glance at once laughing and gentle. She wore a tiny hat on top of her piled-up golden-brown hair. Passersby stopped to look at her as soon as she started to walk along the street. The men stared, the girls whispered.

"Look at her dress! You can see it must have come from abroad."

"I call that really smart."

"And the trimmings! She always chooses lace to go with her complexion."

"It does your eyes good to look at her. All silk and satin!"

Mrs. Bishowskaya made her way shyly to the door of the shop and pushed it open with a white-gloved hand. She seemed to bring a flower-scented breeze in with her. As soon as she saw Father standing in his usual place by the big iron safe, she glided over to him. Father, always a model of politeness, greeted her warmly. "How are you, Mrs. Bishowskaya? Have you had a pleasant summer?"

"Splendid, thank you. More people than ever, from all over the world. And the countryside . . . Do you know the Austrian spas?"

"Yes, I've been once or twice. Very beautiful."

"If you'd been there this year, you wouldn't have recognized the place."

No matter how noisy it was in the shop, she never raised her voice, but cooed softly as a dove. Her rare laughter was like a fountain.

Father looked at her and thought: "So rich, so pretty, yet there she stands timorous as a little bird." But his own serenity soothed her, and soon she spoke more freely.

"Yes, I had plenty of company this summer. It was even more cheerful and amusing than usual—and yet rather sad too, sometimes. One of the local officials didn't want me to come back home. Look at the necklace he gave me. I've brought it to show you."

She took out of her bag a slender blue velvet case. When

she opened it, there lay a diamond necklace. Father picked up his loupe and bent over it.

"Well, he certainly wasn't joking! These large stones are quite rare. I only wish I could get some like it for my customers. Would you like to have a look?"

He handed her the glass.

"See—absolutely flawless. The first water! But as for the smaller stones—well, they'll do, but between you and me . . ."

"Exactly. That's why I brought them. There are too many small stones. It makes the necklace too heavy. Like the gentleman himself!"

Father couldn't help laughing with her. But then her eyes grew sad.

"As you know, I'm quite good-tempered, I don't make a fuss. But this time it was too much! Those foreign doctors make a fortune out of me." She laughed again.

Father pretended not to hear. Why did she have to tell him all this? She'd only be embarrassed afterward. He changed the subject.

"So what would you like me to do with the necklace? Keep just the larger stones? Good, that'll make it more beautiful as well as more valuable. More of a piece.

"And now . . . Do you remember, before you went away you asked me to find something for you? Well, I didn't forget. I kept on looking, and finally I found what I was looking for."

He smiled. "A real treasure!"

"Truly?"

Her face lit up too, as if a full moon were suddenly shining down on it.

"You're wonderful! A true gentleman! I've always said so."

Father was now even more embarrassed. He blushed, turned around, and started fumbling for the keys of the safe. It was fireproof, made of cast iron, and, standing in its corner by the wall covered with shining silverware, it looked even blacker than it really was.

There were two safes in the shop. One stood near Mother's high stool and was full of gold watches, chains, brooches, bracelets, and rings. The other—Father's—tall and enigmatic,

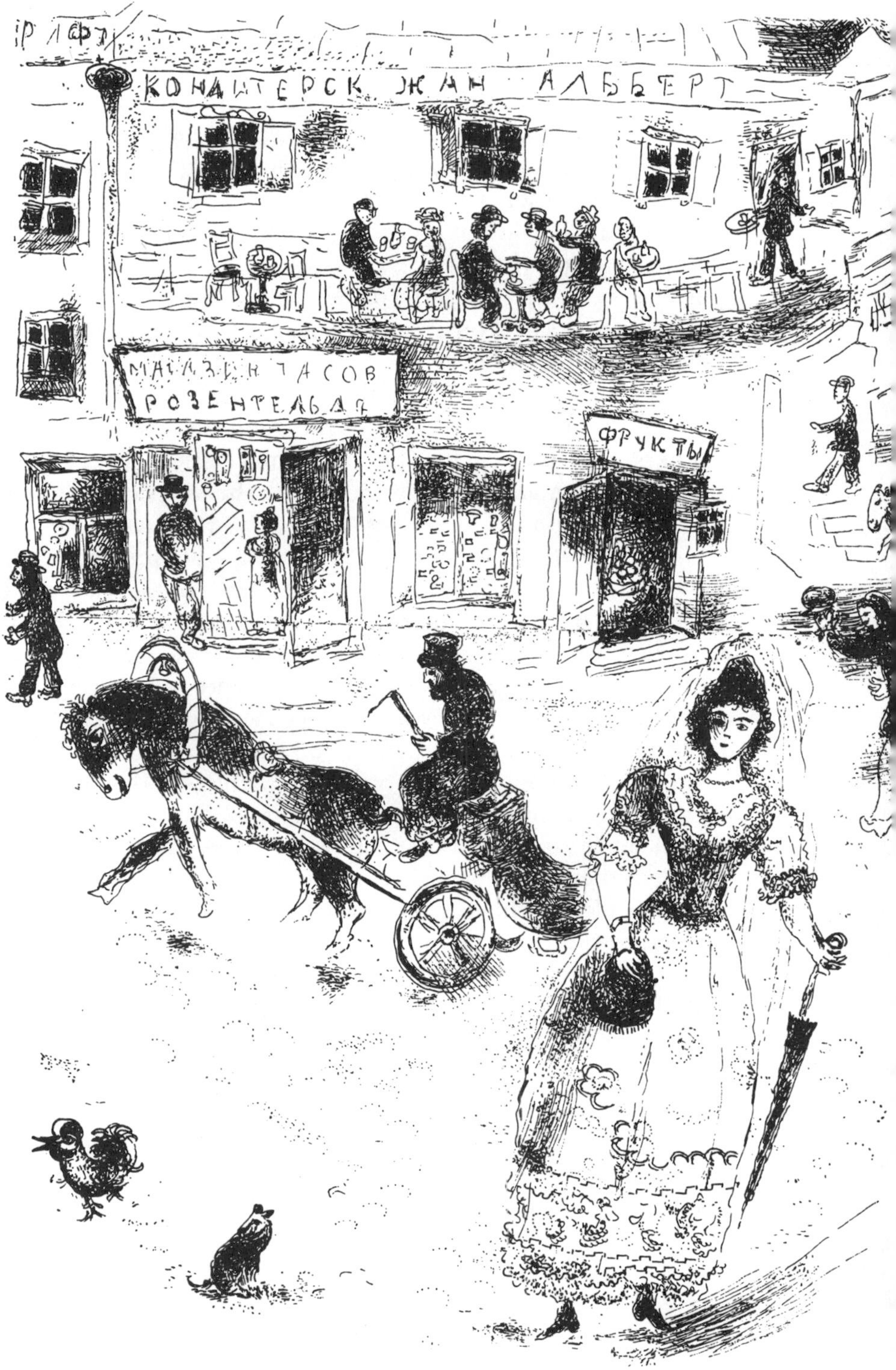
ФРУКТЫ

was covered with mysterious symbols and seemed to hold the secrets of the ages.

Only Father had the keys to this one. And it wasn't easy to open. Each of the ornate and jealously guarded keys seemed endowed with some magic power. But Father inserted them one after the other with the assurance of a sleepwalker. Clicks were heard deep in the lock, and the heavy door swung open, emitting a draft of cool air.

Inside were shelves and drawers full of boxes and packages wrapped in thick brown paper, perhaps to protect their contents from the evil eye.

Father was always worried about the evil eye.

"Why do you put so much in the window?" he'd say to my brothers. "It only excites people's imagination. Every good-for-nothing can gawk in, and they think the shop's stuffed with gold and diamonds."

Only Father ever touched the really valuable pieces; only he knew what was inside every parcel. He could tell just by touching it, as if his fingers could see. And he touched each packet differently, his eyes changing color according to the color of the stones. Now they kindled with sun-gorged fiery rubies; now they cooled with the ocean green of emeralds, or deepened with the heavenly blue of sapphires.

And the diamonds—their brilliance pierced both the eye and the tissue paper in which they were wrapped. They were kept in a special set of drawers in the inmost recesses of the safe.

Above them, in a bag of their own, were the pearls.

Father picked the bag up carefully, feeling it all around to make sure the pearls were all there. They were subdivided up into smaller pouches, according to color, from iridiscent white to dull yellow, a whole spectrum. Some were pale pink, like a baby's cheek. Some were black, but lustrous as dark eyes.

"Show me everything," said Mrs. Bishowskaya. "I haven't seen any uncut gems for a long time. I've been longing for them."

Father, whose head had been deep in the safe, turned around with his hands full of packages.

Mrs. Bishowskaya's eyebrows went up and her eyes poised, ready to plunge into each jewel as into a refreshing spring.

"You know how it is—you want something different every day. And even in one day you don't feel like wearing the same jewel morning and evening."

Father nodded. "What would you like to see first?"

He unrolled a square of velvet, spread it over the glass-topped counter, and unwrapped the first packet. Shining rubies were released from their tissue paper.

Both heads craned forward. A rosy reflection glinted on Father's brow. A faint gleam lit up Mrs. Bishowskaya's eyes; her pale cheeks grew warmer.

"How they burn! Only a little stone, but how it blazes!" She shaded her eyes with her white hands. "No, they're not for today. Today I'm a little sad."

Father looked at her. Sad, when she was looking at precious stones? What was the matter with her?

He opened a bag of sky-blue turquoises. She touched them lightly, like someone stroking the head of a little child. Then she pushed another packet—amethysts this time—aside.

"They don't cheer me up. They don't say anything."

Father put them back in their crumpled tissue paper and opened a packet of diamonds. A firmament of stars poured onto the counter. The polished facets of the stones sent out rainbow shafts that jabbed at one another like splinters of broken glass and made Father's fingers look transparent. One by one, they slowly came to rest on the square of velvet. Then they lay still, sparkling as if fanned by some invisible bellows.

"They can drive people mad. They pierce right through me. I'm not sure I like them." She looked down and was lost in thought. "When you go into a room wearing a diamond neck-lace, and their light clashes with the light of the chandeliers— it's intoxicating!"

She saw herself in a low-cut, lace-trimmed, white silk dress, standing at the door of a ballroom, dazzled by the lights and the mirrors. All eyes were turned toward her. She hid her face with her fan. Suddenly there was an arm around her waist. She let herself be drawn into the dance, was conscious of an ardent gaze, felt her breath mingle with that of another. . . .

She sighed and looked up at Father, busy with his packets.

He stole a glance at her, then rustled the wrappings more loudly. The sound helped her shake off her reverie. One look at his emeralds and she was wide awake.

"Oh, they're full of promise. They lure me like the sea. But you have to feel sure of yourself to wear them. . . . No, not today."

"Perhaps that's enough for now?" suggested Father gently.

"Oh, no!"

He picked up another packet. "I promised you something, and I've kept my word," he said.

He unwrapped the paper, and out came a shower of pearls. Large and small, they rolled onto the velvet cloth as onto a sandy beach, thirsty for light, redolent of their ocean home. It was as if they were suddenly coming to life again. Even those that time had tarnished were cleansed by contact with the air. Wrenched long ago from the shells where their existence had begun, they seemed to seek living skin—a hand, a finger—to cling to now instead.

Mrs. Bishowskaya held her breath. Her eyes filled with other pearls. Her whole face was a pearl.

"Oh!" she whispered. "Thank you! Just what I wanted!"

Father picked out the larger pearls one by one with a pair of tweezers and held them up to the light, as if to see whether they'd grown while hidden away in the dark. The smaller ones he set gently aside.

"You're not big enough yet," he seemed to say, "but with God's help you'll grow."

In next to no time a long row of pearls took shape on the velvet square.

"Do you know," murmured Mrs. Bishowskaya, "now that I've seen this one, I don't care at all for the necklace that man gave me. But I don't want to seem ungrateful."

"Well, wear that one in public and keep this one for yourself."

"Thank you!"

"Would you like to know how much the pearls weigh? Almost nothing, really. It's the light that makes them look larger than they are. Here, I'll show you. . . ."

From a small box he took two slender cords which resolved themselves into a tiny pair of scales with two minute pans. It looked like a toy. In one pan he put an almost invisible weight, and in the other a pearl. Its luster tipped the scale.

"And they're all alike," said Father. "All light and pure. But you know yourself—it's the play of light we judge them by. You don't often find a set like this. I know they'll give you a lot of pleasure."

She stretched out her neck as if the pearls were already strung and she was wearing them. Then she tossed her head and straightened up.

"You don't know how much good you've done me. You've brought me back to life. . . . There's a secret I must tell you. My mother used to have a string of pearls. Oh, not like these! Hers were old and yellow. They'd belonged to my grandmother, and must have got dull against the old woman's wrinkled neck. My mother was left an orphan very young. But someone put the string of pearls around her neck at her wedding. It was the only thing that had come down to her from her own mother.

" 'I nearly cried my eyes out,' my mother used to say. 'Those pearls must have been made of iron not to dissolve completely away.'

"My mother brought nine children into the world," Mrs. Bishowskaya went on, "and for each birth she wore the pearls. She believed it would bring her mother to her bedside to bless her and the newborn infant.

" 'The pearls shine brightly,' said my mother, 'and they'll make my children bright and beautiful too. Aren't you as lovely as a pearl?' she used to say to me."

A bashful smile passed over Mrs. Bishowskaya's face, then vanished. She sighed, and her voice grew sadder too.

"Once my mother had a child that was stillborn. She didn't know it was dead. But she asked the people looking after her to see what was the matter, because she felt as if ants were swarming all over her.

"They found the pearls scattered in the bed. The string had

broken. She couldn't take her eyes off them. She was bathed in sweat, and they looked to her like tears.

" 'The baby's dead, isn't it?' she said.

"She lost her youth at the same time as the necklace. She didn't have any more children. . . . You see the power pearls have?"

Mrs. Bishowskaya looked up.

"And now I shall have my own string of pearls. I'll wear them always. Perhaps I'll bring something beautiful into the world too. I'm still young.

"So now you understand why the pearls mean so much to me. You'll string them for me, won't you? . . ."

And having unburdened her heart, she flew out of the shop as if on wings.

Winter

The room was hot. Logs popped and crackled in the stove. They'd just been brought in from the pile in the yard and were angry at being tossed straight from the cold into the heat. It was snowing. On the other side of the tightly sealed windows, the flakes floated down over everything, slowly, ceaselessly, as in a dream.

"What are we sitting in here for? Come on, let's go out in the yard."

Abrashka grabbed his coat and shot out. Before Sasha had finished muffling me up in wool from head to foot, he'd already rolled over and over in the snow.

It was cheerful out in the courtyard. We made a snowman. Soon our woolen gloves were soaked. But how could you really have fun with the snow in that tiny little yard? It was like a well, enclosed on all sides. And the walls were full of windows and doors. As soon as you threw a snowball, it hit a pane of glass.

A fanlight would open and a man yell at us as raucously as if the snowball had hit him in the throat.

"Clear out, you little devils! I'll teach you to throw snowballs at people's windows. . . . There they go again! Just let me get hold of you both—I'll twist your ears off!"

Then another voice from a second fanlight. "There he goes, yelling at the kids again. Do you want to deafen us all, you old fool? Leave them alone! Let them play!"

"Is it your window they hit? Mind your own business!"

The yells were exchanged back and forth between the two fanlights, which clicked open and shut like the clashing of sabers. Then came the sound of someone rushing down the stairs.

"He's after us! Come on, we'll show him who can run fastest!"

And Abrashka dragged me with him to the gate leading into the street. There I paused in astonishment.

The street was full of people, but instead of walking along they were slipping and sliding, falling down, getting up again, and trying to hurry on. Sleighs glided silently by, the horses stepping as if in velvet shoes over a carpet of white.

The sun shone down. The snow glittered as if the whole town were spangled with silver. We heard a burst of laughter and hurried toward it. At the top of the street, a flight of steps led down to the street below. The snow on the steps was always quickly trodden to ice, and all day long idlers hung about there to make fun of the people trying to negotiate them.

"Do you think he'll make it?"

"Careful, or you'll fall! Why don't you turn back and go around the other way?"

"Leave him alone. He's going to fall down anyway."

A slip, a crash, and the crowd split their sides.

Then a smart young man arrived at the top of the steps. The crowd stopped laughing and began to heckle him.

"Come on! You're tough! You show us how!"

"Look at him—legs like a horse!"

The young man squared his shoulders, took a deep breath as if about to clear the descent in one stride, stepped forward—and fell headlong.

Then, to the delighted yells of the spectators, he gathered his scattered limbs together and slunk away.

"Black and blue, eh? Your long legs weren't much use to you after all!"

Whenever any women came along, the crowd started to laugh in anticipation. Even before the women got to the steps, they'd slip, totter, fall, and be unable to get up again.

"What are you sniggering about, you idiots? I might have killed myself! A town full of people, and no one thinks to put some sand or ashes down. And I suppose you're going to let me lie here forever?"

And indeed the crowd had deserted her.

Some way off, people were shouting and yelling, and congregating as if a house were on fire.

"Stop!"

"Help!"

"Pull up, you devil—can't you see there's a child caught under your sleigh?"

"Oh, God! A child! He's being dragged along!"

A young woman ran past us, her arms flung up in the air.

"What are they shouting about? Abrashka, let's go and see." But when I turned around, Abrashka wasn't there. "Abrashka, where are you?"

Then I was swallowed up in the crush and the cries of the crowd.

"Is he still alive?"

"Who knows? Young bones break so easily."

"My God, it's a Jewish boy!"

"God can perform miracles if He wants to."

"Whose boy is it? Did you see?"

"Yes, recognized him right away. Alta's son."

"Abrashka!"

My heart stood still.

How was it possible? He'd been standing right beside me. How had he gotten under the sleigh?

My God, what would Mother say? She'd never let us out of the house again.

Hardly able to breathe, I went along with the crowd.

Someone had managed to stop the horse.

"Lift the sleigh up! Lift the sleigh off him!" Everyone yelled at the driver, crowding around him. The horse stood hanging its head guiltily. The peasant jumped off his sleigh, crossing himself and swearing it wasn't his fault.

"What did he want to get under the horse's hooves for? You can't expect a brute beast to understand. . . . All these kids . . . you need eyes in the back of your head. . . . Holy Mother of God!"

"Never mind about the Mother of God. Help us lift up the sleigh!"

It was a long sleigh, quite empty except for a little heap of straw. On the snow, between the runners, lay something black, and a patch of red.

I shut my eyes. God, could it really be Abrashka? And was he . . . ?

The crowd got hold of the sleigh and heaved it up.

They couldn't believe their eyes. Out crawled Abrashka. He stood up. His nose was bleeding a little. And he was laughing!

By some miracle he was still alive. We'd still be able to go out and slide on the ice. I wanted to run up and throw my arms around him. But the crowd shoved me back angrily. They were now more worked up than before, furious with Abrashka for having survived. They went for him as if they'd have liked to tear him to pieces.

"Don't think you're going to get away with it, you little devil. First you frighten us out of our wits, and then you stand there grinning!"

"Little bastard—we ought to have left him lying there."

"You spend the best years of your life bringing them up, and then all they can do is roam the streets."

"But how can you keep them at home when it snows?"

"That's enough talk. We'd better take him home to his parents. His rebbe will soon teach him to go crawling under sleighs!"

They looked around for some sort of stretcher to carry him home on.

"But look! Who says there isn't a providence! He isn't hurt. Not even a scratch."

They were silent for a moment, pondering.

Abrashka took the opportunity to give them the slip and scamper home. When he reached our gate, he turned around and thumbed his nose.

"Come on, Bashka, let's go ice skating!"

The Ice Rink

The winter settled in, with white, snow-filled days and nights. The snow froze, the river was still. From the bridge we could see men fencing off a skating rink on the ice with little fir trees.

To skate on real ice skates was our dream. Abrashka had just one skate; even then the blade was rusty. He'd tie the skate onto one foot and push off with the other. The first foot made a narrow groove through the ice; the second just waved about in thin air. I tried to follow suit in my rubber boots, but I could only slide. I couldn't skate on one foot.

Every winter I kept imploring my mother, "Please, please . . ."

"Are you mad, God forbid?" she'd answer with a glare. "Ice skates? Why must you keep on? Respectable girls don't go slithering about on skates."

My eyes filled with tears. I tried to blink them away. Mother gave me another look.

"I wouldn't have thought it of you, Bashutka. You're a big girl now. You go to school. What would your teacher say?"

"Abrashka goes to school, and he skates all day!"

"What's that got to do with it? Abrashka's a boy, and a good-for-nothing into the bargain. Don't take him as an example! You shouldn't even think about such things. You'd be better employed doing your homework."

"I've already done it. I know it by heart." Resentfully, I turned away.

The following year I'd try again.

"What, still going on about ice skates? I'll give you ice skates! Once and for all, put the idea out of your head, do you understand?"

"But all my friends have got skates this year!"

"So what? Don't be so obstinate. You fall over often enough as it is. With skates you'd go and break your neck in the middle of the street."

"But, Mother, there's a real skating rink now."

"Whatever will these children think of next? Don't talk to me about it! How could you even think about going skating with all that rabble?"

But I got my own way in the end. Mother, worn down by my entreaties, finally gave in, and I was bought a shiny, brand-new pair of ice skates. I couldn't take my eyes off them. They were called "Sniergurishki," which is Russian for "fairy princess." Their steel blades gave off a sort of chill. Just to touch them made your hand go cold. They were so shiny you could see your own reflection in them.

Abrashka was jealous.

"You'll break your ankles. Look, the points are all crooked."

He was tired of his one rusty old skate and was trying to scare me. And I was rather worried. Would I be able to keep my balance?

I hurried to the shoemaker's.

"Reb Laizer, I've got some new skates. Would you fix them onto my shoes, please?"

The old man looked up from his bench, tossed his shaggy head, spat some wooden pegs out from between his lips, and peered at me over his glasses.

"Does your mother know about this? It'll ruin the soles, you know."

"Yes, she knows."

He shrugged. "Hand them over, then."

And my little shoe found itself perched on the last, in the place of a large boot.

The shoemaker punched holes in the soles of my shoes, fixed bits of metal in the holes, then screwed the skates on.

"The things children think up these days!"

Abrashka kept on teasing me. He hoped I'd get so nervous I'd hand my skates over to him.

"Anyway, Abrashka, your feet are too big. My skates wouldn't fit you. But if you'll go and ask Mother for five kopeks to get into the rink, I'll let you borrow them."

"Why should I be the one to ask? You're the favorite—it's you they bought the skates for."

"Oh, you are a beast!" I flounced off into the shop.

Mother was busy. Would those wretched customers never go? But when they finally did, she started wrapping things up and putting them away. She was still on edge from the bargaining and haggling. Did I dare approach her now? But another customer might come in at any moment.

I hung about Mother's high stool.

"What are you dawdling around here for? You can see I'm busy."

"Mother..." I stammered. "Can I...it's only five kopeks...just this once?"

I couldn't bring myself to say "skating rink." Perhaps the phrase would slide into her ear all on its own.

"Now that I've got my skates...they'll get spoiled in the yard...."

Mother whirled around on her stool as though I'd fired a gun.

"Ice skates! Ice skates! More nonsense? Haven't I got other things to think about? *They*'ll get spoiled! It's your feet that'll get spoiled!"

I seized the opportunity. "Not at the rink, Mother. At the skating rink I'll just skim along!"

"Well, it's enough to drive a person mad! Yesterday skates, today an ice rink. What will it be tomorrow?"

I couldn't think of anything else to say to persuade her, so I just stood there behind her stool. What was she afraid of? The shoemaker had fixed the skates to my shoes; the ice was flat and smooth, not like in the yard. How was I to explain?

But then another customer came in.

Well, that was that. No skating rink today. As soon as Mother saw the new customer, she pushed me away. "Now stop pestering me. I haven't got time."

She turned to the cashier. "Give her the five kopeks, and let that be the end of it!"

I grabbed my skates—I'd left them at the back of the shop—and rushed off to the river before Mother could change her mind. I flew along. My feet didn't touch the ground. The houses and streets flew along with me. When I got to the river I was red in the face from exertion and cold.

A great sheet of white stretched from one bank to the other, and through it went a path of snow, trampled into a road by the carriages, sleighs, and horses crossing over. People on foot streamed across like a column of ants.

I took a cautious step toward the skating rink. There was a sudden burst of music.

"Boom, boom! Come, come!" The drums called to me. I hurried toward the rink.

It was hidden on all four sides by its fence of little fir trees. They stood there dreaming with their feet in the snow, scarcely able to hold up their icy branches. They were linked by strings of paper lanterns, red and green and blue, swinging in the wind. The band was playing, and couples danced around as in a ballroom.

I approached the entrance, spellbound.

Some street urchins were larking about among the trees, quacking like ducks and jeering enviously at everyone who went in. When they saw me they started to whistle.

"Look at her! Got her own skates and can't even stand up on them!"

Could they tell by just looking at me? I felt like going straight home, but running the gauntlet of those boys was more daunting than the ice itself.

The manager of the rink came to my rescue. "Clear off!" he bawled to the urchins.

The ice squeaked underfoot, shining like a mirror. Boys and girls swept by, laughing, their skates carving figures in the ice. To me it looked like magic. Their laughter was infectious. I put on my skates as fast as I could.

As I tottered along the wooden walkway that led to the rink, my feet felt as though they were tied together with string. I could see the ice sparkling between the planks.

Suddenly a boy skated up. Did he feel sorry for me? He swerved to a halt—it was a sort of bow—and pushed a chair mounted on runners toward me.

"Jump in and I'll take you for a ride."

Before I had time to think, I found myself sitting in the chair. The boy dug the point of one skate in the ice, then took off, pushing the chair in front of him. In what seemed no time at all, we were on the other side of the rink. The boy flew over the ice. The chair bumped along, and I with it. Was he trying to hurl us both over the trees and into the water?

"Hey, stop it, you lunatic! I've had enough!"

He braked, stopped the chair, and tilted me out.

"Right—so now skate!"

He laughed, and swooped away.

Boys and girls swirled around me, laughing and flashing their white teeth. It was like being pelted with snowballs. I went along with them, and was soon as hot as if the ice were burning under my feet. The fir trees seemed to give off a haze of heat. They swayed to and fro, now larger, now smaller, lowering their branches and shooting snow and barbs of ice into my face.

I raced across the rink as though fiends were after me. Suddenly my path was barred by a chain of boys. One of them got hold of me and linked me into the chain, which sometimes contracted and sometimes sprayed out all over the ice. Suddenly the leader halted and swung the whole file around and around like a snake. The last one in the chain shot up into the air, then came down with a crash.

I staggered drunkenly home, my skates slung over my shoulder. My bones ached; my feet felt like logs. The river and the streets all merged into one: my head was full of a dream of white.

Spring

Winter was over. The cold and the snow were gone. There wasn't a cloud in the sky, and the breeze was gentle and full of promise.

"Spring is on the way!" it sang like a shofar.

Everything woke up and stretched after its long sleep. Here a crack could be heard, there the sound of tearing, as the sap rose in the branches. Elsewhere an animal would rise onto its feet or up into the air.

It was a holiday. Everything was cheerful and bright and warm again. The air was fresh; the sun was high and young. Everything flourished in its kindling rays. The past had died, rotted away during the long months of snow. Now everything was reborn.

Every day there was something new. The day itself grew longer, and the wind blew high in the sky, bringing scents, hummings, whispers, rustlings.

There wasn't any grass yet, but the bare earth was stirring down to the last grain of soil. Its hard crust was softening. At the first touch of sun it would start to buckle, and all would be covered in a blue mist.

In the daytime the earth melted, letting out the breath it had been holding all winter. The soil seemed to move about in search of nourishment. It stuck to your feet. And how good it felt to have the good old familiar earth there instead of the snow.

The whole universe seemed in sympathy with Mother Earth. The sky opened its arms to embrace her, and the sun blessed her as with a million lighted candles. Its rays got into every nook and cranny of the soil, warming it, drying it out.

And then the first blade of grass appeared, the first bird. The sun healed the baldness of the boughs, covering them with quivering green leaves.

The birds arrived in droves, fluttering and chirping. Bees and flies hummed merrily. Everything returned. And the tender earth decked itself out and drank in sun and strength, just as an old house fills with happiness when its scattered children come home.

The river roared blissfully as the ice floes melted; the water churned like a millrace. There was so much of it that the banks scarcely held. It was as if winter, before it was banished for good, was venting all its wrath into the river.

The current chased the ice, shoving and harrying it. The river blustered and roared as if the winds had burrowed down to its depths.

The sky couldn't touch bottom, though, however deep it dived.

Right in the middle of a fine day it would suddenly darken. A black cloud, riding in the wake of the wind, arrived. There was a flash of lightning, a clap of thunder. And the cloud, transfixed, dissolved into torrents of rain, so deafening one thought the whole sky was emptying.

The streets were inundated. Water streamed down from the hills, filling ditches and gutters, dislodging pebbles and dragging them noisily along with it. The rain pounded the roofs, then gushed from the eaves down onto the deserted streets.

The drivers had jumped down from their carts, thrown sacks over their horses, and run for shelter. The horses stood alone in the rain, streaming, heads bowed, ashamed at being forsaken. Lashed by the downpour, they sidled closer together.

Suddenly a dog darted along the street, snuffing at the rain. The horses brightened up. They were no longer alone. The people sheltering in doorways laughed and whistled.

"Come in out of the wet, you stupid hound!"

The dog, shivering with cold, his coat soaked and gleaming, slid about in the mud. His tail hung like a bedraggled string. But he stayed out in the rain just to spite everybody.

We children envied him, frolicking about in the wet.

Everyone stood around waiting for the cloudburst to end.

"What a flood, eh?"

"A few more like this, and we won't need to go down to the river—we'll have one flowing right down the middle of the street."

"What *about* the Dvina? How high is it today?"

"The Dvina?" answered someone, snapping his fingers. "A regular ocean."

"Are the rafts coming down yet?"

"What a question! Haven't you seen them? Bringing down whole forests of logs."

I nudged my friend.

"Zlatka, did you hear that? Whole forests floating down the river! Let's go and see! Abrashka's there already. Look, everyone's going."

The rain had stopped. The air was cool, the grimy gutters were washed clean, and the sky wore a rainbow coronet. The crowd had melted away.

We ran along with the others to have a look at the river. When we got to the big bridge we stopped.

There was a roar above and below—the people on the bridge, the water underneath. The river sprawled and writhed like a giant trying to elude its captors.

It groaned and bellowed and flung itself from side to side as if it would have liked to flood the whole city. Waves, gray and green and black, flung themselves against the stone piles of the bridge, withdrew to challenge them, then attacked again. Suddenly the water surged against the lower bank and washed over the little houses. The sand at the river's edge was swept ashore with it as it rose, then carried away downstream as it fell.

We stood on the bridge and watched with bated breath. Wherever you looked there was water.

Below us it foamed and seethed. Overhead the sky was saturated. Our heads swam.

The people on the bridge began to jostle and shove, and my friend and I were pushed against the parapet. We could feel the spray on our faces.

The church on the higher bank had collapsed into the water. The cross from the top of the steeple was being swept along on a giant wave. Trees from the public gardens floated after it, upside down, their leaves tossing like small bells. I thought I could see some park benches too. How many times had I sat on them!

The clouds, hazy in the sky, seemed to have fallen into the water and there become solid and motionless, huge white bears. It was as if the whole city, with its houses, roofs, and windows, had been torn up from the earth and tipped into the river.

Suddenly the crowd was crushing us worse than before.

Help! They were nearly pushing us into the water! Where was Abrashka? Where was Zlatka? The crowd pressed against us as if we ourselves were the parapet.

Then a cry went up.

"The rafts! Here come the rafts!"

The noise was deafening. The bridge shook.

The rafts appeared in the distance as if they'd just dropped out of the sky. They were moving so slowly they seemed to be standing still. The crowd fell silent. Everyone stared. The rafts drifted slowly nearer.

At each end of the first raft stood a sturdy peasant leaning on a long pole, so still and silent he might have been fast asleep. Slowly they drew closer to the bridge. You could hear the ripple made by the poles.

As soon as they were within hailing distance, the people on the bridge started to shout.

"Hey! Mind what you're doing! You'll crack your skulls! More to the left! To the left!"

"No! More to the right! To the right! . . ."

Everyone thought he knew best.

The men on the raft looked vaguely upward, then spat into the water in disgust. They'd floated along quite peacefully day after day, night after night, but as soon as they came to a town the people drove them mad with unwanted advice. As if it wasn't enough just trying to get past the bridges in one piece! Even the waves didn't manage it. And there was the crowd, actually hoping the raft would break up.

The men on the raft shook their heads. Even if they got past the bridge safely, there were still the people to contend with.

The water seethed; the stone piles snarled like angry beasts.

Now all the rafts were quite near. God, what was going to happen? I clung to the parapet and shut my eyes, afraid to look down.

"Zlatka, where's Abrashka?"

Abrashka wasn't afraid of anything. But Zlatka was trembling worse than I was. She pinched my arm with fright.

I pushed her away. "Stop it!"

Then there was a terrific crash. I opened my eyes. Where were the rafts?

The river was covered with a confused mass of logs, some long, some short. The first raft had broken up and the logs were scattered like a spilled box of matches, all going their separate ways. Each of the raftsmen perched on one log, all that remained of their raft. They still held on to their long poles.

The crowd on the bridge roared with laughter. It amused them to see the rafts break up. No one felt sorry for the raftsmen, furiously plying their poles like anglers, and trying to stop the logs from escaping. But the waves washed over them, and the logs were carried away.

Some boats put out from the shore to help collect them. It was pandemonium. The raftsmen, tossed still more by the wash from the boats, cursed and swore. The boatmen cursed back.

"Hell, can't you look where you're going?"

"And you—watch out with that pole or I'll bash your brains out!"

"Just try! . . . Hey, what are you wriggling about for?"

"Go to blazes! Who do you think you are? . . ."

Boats collided, poles clashed, the people on the bridge ran from side to side to watch. The raftsmen scratched their heads and spat in the water while the boatmen rounded up the logs.

I dragged myself sadly home. My bones ached as if I'd been split apart like the rafts. I couldn't stop thinking about them. When would they get safely past the bridge? Perhaps at night, when the town was asleep and the water drowsy, and there was no one watching.

Then, one after the other, they'd slip silent and unseen through the slumbering arches.

The Pastry Shop

From early in the morning the house was in a whirl. Everything was being washed and scrubbed. The Passover dishes were got out. Knives and forks and spoons were polished. The samovar was so bright it seemed to stab you.

"Sasha, come and look," I said. "You can see your face twice in the samovar."

"Oh, leave me alone with your nonsense. I've got to give Chaya a hand. Tonight is the Seder."

As if I didn't know! I had a list of all the things I had to buy for it. Mother was always busy in the shop, so she left it to me. Perhaps because I was so interested in food . . .

Whenever we had visitors, Mother always said, "Bashenka, you're the real housekeeper—you find us something nice."

But I knew that however much I bought or Chaya baked, it still wouldn't last out the whole holiday week. Everyone came to see us, bringing swarms of children who seemed determined to wolf down all I offered them. We always ran short, even though it looked to me as if I'd bought the whole pastry shop. Yet when it was delivered, Mother always said, "Why did you get so much?"

However busy she was, Chaya never forgot to make cakes, nor to sing the praises of her prunes with honeyed nuts. But buying and serving the pastries was my job.

I could have found my way to the pastry shop blindfolded. Even when the weather was cold, a delicious warm smell seeped from under the door and made my nostrils tingle. It was the Jewish pastry shop, where they made the best cakes and confectionery in the whole town.

My list in my hand, I stood in front of the door. It was black and charred-looking, as if it had been baked in the oven with the rest. The wood, and even the metal door handle, were always warm to the touch. I sniffed the lovely smell, put my ear against the door, and listened. It sounded as if everybody was out. All that could be heard was the crackling of the wood in the oven.

The baker, his elderly wife, and their tall, plain, unmarried daughter didn't talk much. But they always smiled as sweetly as if someone had poured a jug of syrup over their pasty faces. *Their* place never smelled of onions.

They were always dressed in black, like three burned sticks. All day long, in their worn slippers, they went back and forth from the kitchen to the parlor and back again. Why did they call it the parlor? Perhaps because of the black-framed picture on the wall, a portrait of the baker and his wife on their wedding day. It was flyblown and a bit crooked. There were a few shabby chairs, now losing their stuffing. The room was full of tables, and had come to be used as a shop.

What should I buy?

I'd been leaning so hard on the door that it opened all by itself. The dark hall was stifling. Through the open door I could see the baker's wife prodding the glowing coals in the oven with a long shovel.

"Good morning," I called through the gloom.

Still holding the shovel, she turned briefly toward me, then back to the oven.

298

"Good morning, Bashenka. How are you? Haven't seen you for a long time." She spoke to the coals rather than to me.

"Come in, Bashenka." The baker himself had appeared beside me. I hadn't heard him come into the room. "I was just wondering why Alta's daughter hasn't been in. All the doughnuts will soon be gone. Would you like some fruit jellies? They're very good today."

Now the daughter was there too. She'd stopped halfway between the kitchen and the parlor. The air was so sweet it set your teeth on edge.

What should I buy?

The tables were laden to overflowing. It was like a wedding. One table full of shiny caramel cookies resembled a cobbled street. Another was covered with white cakes light as air. Still another held golden pies with almond-cream filling. There were sweet rolls and gingerbread Stars of David. A bowl of poppy-seed filling was cooling off near a glowing dish of steaming jam.

"So what shall we send you?" asked the baker. "What did your mother ask you to get?"

I pointed at every plate on every table.

"Some of those . . . and some of those . . . and some of those. . . . Everyone in our house has got a sweet tooth."

But I was in a hurry to get out of the heat.

"Good day, then, Bashenka. We'll send the things around right away. A happy holiday to you all."

I took a deep breath of fresh air. But I had to hurry back home. I didn't want the bags from the baker's to get there before I did.

I was panting when I arrived, but the boys had already poked holes in the bags.

"Hey, stop it—those are for the visitors! What will Mother say?"

And I tried to rescue the Passover pastries.

Visiting

"Bashutka, would you like a cracker with cottage cheese, or some pancakes?" It was Chaya's gruff voice waking me up.

"What else is there?" I asked sleepily.

"What else? Just listen to the child! . . . I don't know—there may be some poppy-seed rolls."

What else could I do to put off getting up? I wasn't at all hungry. In fact I couldn't bear the thought of food. Later on we'd be having pancakes filled with jam. My stomach felt like a stuffed pancake already.

Then Sasha came in and coaxed me.

"Come and let me brush your hair. There'll be visitors this evening. And this afternoon there'll be games."

I slid slowly out of bed. "Do you think I'll win?"

As soon as Father went for his afternoon nap, my brothers and I took over the parlor. We sat on the floor, and the boys took handfuls of nuts out of their pockets.

"Odds or evens?"

They brandished their closed fists under my nose, the nuts inside tinkling like little bells. I was afraid they'd trick me—

they were always teasing. I squeezed their hands as hard as I could. I meant to win in spite of them.

The nuts shot over the floor in all directions and we rushed after them. I crawled under the tables and reached behind the cupboard; the nuts rolled into every nook and cranny. The boys whistled and shoved one another aside. We picked up one nut after another and cracked them with our teeth or under our heels.

"They taste nice dipped in wine," said my quiet brother Aaron, spitting out bits of shell.

The floor was soon covered with shells.

Sasha came in and let out a shriek.

"Look what you've done to my nice clean floor! I've only just swept it!"

We just went on chewing. She chased us out with her broom.

"Clear off—your mother will be in at any minute!"

"Here's some for you!" jeered Abrashka, stuffing some nuts down the neck of Sasha's dress.

"Idiot!" yelled Sasha, trying to shake them out of her skirts.

We laughed, and scattered through the house.

I went into the dining room. The table was covered with a bright floral cloth. It had been resting since Passover, and now it seemed to be waiting for me to do something. Very well! I went to the cupboard and got out the things I'd bought at the pastry shop.

I arranged the fruit jellies, cakes, cookies, and almonds on the pretty new dishes. I put out knives and forks and spoons. I filled the compote jar right to the brim with cherry preserves, making sure there was plenty of juice. Father liked his tea sweetened with jam. And Aunt Rachel would rather have a glass of tea with cherry jam in it than anything else on the table.

But how many people were coming? What else ought I to get out?

"Got you!" said Abrashka, flying through the dining room and grabbing a handful of teacakes as he went by. I started to complain. Now I'd have to find something to fill the gap. I was glad to hear Mother moving about in the bedroom after her nap.

"Good girl! You've got everything ready."

Mother appeared in the doorway, smiling and rested. She was holding her wig. She went over to the mirror to put it on. First she brushed out the tangles in the curls, then she set it on her head, soft and shining. I helped her collect the scattered hairpins. As she fastened one in her wig, she whispered to me as if it were a secret: "After we've seen all our visitors, we're going over to Uncle Beril's."

"Ooh!" I cried happily. I was the only one of the children my parents took visiting with them.

"There's the doorbell already!"

I rushed out into the hall.

"Happy holiday, Uncle! Happy holiday, Auntie!"

I danced around them.

Uncle Chaim Leib was smiling as usual. His ruddy countenance shone even redder in honor of the holiday, but today there was no cigar sticking out of his mouth like a chimney. His mustache twitched: one joke after another would soon pop out from behind it. Aunt Rachel, though, was quiet and reserved.

"How are you, Bashenka?" Her kind eyes beamed at me. I felt closer to her than to any of the other aunts. I used to spend the summer with her, and go to her house during the week to hear the latest news. But today I hardly recognized her.

The black silk cape which enveloped her wizened form was decked with spangles. The cape itself was too big for her, and looked as if it were still on a hanger. As I helped her off with her outdoor clothes I made the spangles tinkle.

"Mind you don't break them, Bashka. What would I wear next year, God willing?"

"Don't you want to take your hat off?"

Her hat was a bit lopsided, as if she had difficulty holding it upright. It was weighed down with flowers and ribbons. Every year she added another one.

"We're coming to see you soon, Auntie. After we've been to Uncle Beril's."

"That's right! I've got lots of nice things ready for you."

"Leave your aunt alone, Bashenka," called Mother from the dining room. "Why don't you let them come in?"

"Happy holiday, Alta. Happy holiday, Shmuel Noah."

My uncle went in at last, greeting my parents as if he hadn't seen them for years. He even shook hands; usually he just smiled.

"Happy holiday," said Father, already on his third glass of tea. "How are you, Rachel? Sit down."

Everyone found a seat.

"Well, what's new?" said Father to my uncle. "You're the one who takes an interest in public affairs."

His tone was slightly sarcastic, though he rather resented being so much out of things.

"Well, they say . . ." And my uncle launched into an account of the latest happenings. We listened with interest. Even for my father, the news was new. In fact, if it hadn't been for Uncle Chaim Leib, he wouldn't have known anything about what was going on in the town.

My uncle went on and on, encouraged by his audience. He got quite carried away. Only a joke brought a welcome interruption.

I couldn't bear all my delicious things to be neglected.

"Here, Uncle, have a tart."

He gave me a wink, and inserted a piece of pie through his mustache.

"That's what I call a tart," he said as he munched. "Did you choose it yourself, Bashenka? Well, you're a real expert! We can rely on you from now on." I went as red as a beet and retreated behind my aunt's chair.

"A preserved prune, Aunt Rachel?" I'd have liked to get her drunk on sweets. The prunes dripped honey, but, strange to say, all she wanted to do was look at them.

I went from one person to another offering fruit jellies and almonds, but they all seemed to be getting tired either of the stories or of the sweets.

One by one they got up to go. As I handed Aunt Rachel her cape, I shook it to straighten out the spangles.

"You've always liked my bits of finery, haven't you, Bashenka?" She smiled, pleased that I at least appreciated her old cloak. Shyly she started to put on her hat, so battered by the passing years it scarcely fitted her anymore.

"Happy holiday, Alta. Come and see us soon, God willing. Thank you for your hospitality, Bashenka," she said as she and my uncle left.

We went with them to the door.

As it closed behind them, Mother shook her head. "I don't like the look of Rachel," she said. "She looks quite ill."

No one answered.

The party broke up. The table hadn't been cleared. But as we went by, my brothers and I made sure that all the plates were left clean.

Next morning Mother called to me from her bedroom. "Bashenka, get dressed! We're going to Uncle Beril's."

"What shall I wear?"

"Anything you like."

I rushed out to the kitchen. "Sasha, where's my blue dress?"

"Couldn't very well get lost, could it? Here it is, take it." Then she called to Mother, "Shall I bring you your black dress, ma'am?"

She helped us both to dress. I couldn't manage the hooks and eyes on my own.

"You know, Bashenka," she said, twirling around, "you've grown out of this dress since last year. Here, I'll let your hair down—that'll make the skirt look a bit less skimpy."

She undid my long braids and brushed them out. Then, when I was ready, I watched her attend to my mother, arranging the black lace she'd ironed so beautifully over the bodice of my mother's black silk dress.

Suddenly something was twinkling on Mother's bosom. She'd pinned a diamond brooch among the black lace. Two more tiny diamonds sparkled in her little white ears. She shone like the stars on a dark night.

I wished she would stay like that, but she raised her arms and started to fasten a long pin into her hat. Two black feathers hung down behind it, waving one on either side. I was sorry I'd never tried it on; it would have swung to and fro like a bird on a branch.

Father came rushing in. "Have you seen my top hat anywhere?" He was already exhausted from struggling with his collar and cuffs. He'd much rather have stayed at home.

The top hat jumped out of its case like a jack-in-the-box. Mother breathed on the nap and smoothed it to bring up the sheen. And Father put it on.

I stared. He'd grown taller. He looked like a wall with a chimney pot on top.

Finally both my parents left the house. The top hat didn't stir. Mother's feathers began to curve around her diamond earrings.

"Look after the house, children. Don't all go out at once."

Mother was still hanging back. Even though she was all dressed up, she didn't forget the burglars of every day. I pulled at her sleeve.

"Oh, do come on, Mother! Father's a long way ahead!"

The street was full of people going visiting. The women were all in holiday finery—green, black, brown, and gold. Their large hats greeted one another, Mother's feathers bowing to confections of ribbons and flowers. Everyone in town knew my mother.

But where had Father gone to? I looked around for a top hat.

The men all walked along by themselves, their hands clasped pensively behind their backs. Every so often they would absently shake their heads. The women walked slowly, as if burdened by their best clothes and those hats decorated like the booths at the Feast of Tabernacles. Probably their new shoes pinched as well.

The sidewalk was narrow, and when I tried to elbow my way forward I got my face scratched by the beads on someone's cloak. I stepped down into the street. The cobbles were uncomfortable to walk on, but at least I didn't get bumped into.

While I waited for Mother to catch up to me, I leaned

against a telegraph pole. I could hear a buzzing inside the wood, and was afraid I might be carried away along with the telegram.

"Mother, where's Father? I can't see him anywhere."

"There's nothing to worry about, silly. He's probably at your uncle's already."

I was afraid that with the street so cluttered up with women, we might miss my uncle's house and walk right by it. I clutched at Mother again. "Well, let's hurry up, then. He must be waiting for us."

Mother stopped by an open archway. "Here we are."

I ran across the yard to my uncle's window and looked in. Yes, Father was there already. He was even sitting down drinking a glass of tea.

Aunt Mira came out to meet us. She was tall and stout, like a pine tree, and smelled as sweet as a linden. Her face was suntanned and covered with freckles. Her little eyes glowed like embers.

"Happy holiday, Altinka. I'm glad to see you in good health, thank God. Take your coat off, Bashenka."

She smiled, showing lots of teeth. As she helped us off with our outdoor things, she seemed to half-embrace us in her long arms. Before we went in to join the men, she whispered something into my mother's ear.

A hoarse voice addressed another whisper to me. "Got any nuts?"

"Hurry up and let's have a game!"

First one cousin and then another burst in. Bomke and Ziamke were round and red like two little drums, and their pockets were bulging with nuts; they yelled so loud they might have been bombarding my ears with them.

"Hush! Let them get their breath back, children," scolded Aunt Mira. "You make so much noise we can't hear ourselves speak."

Bomke and Ziamke made signs to me behind her back. My aunt spun around like a felled tree and got hold of me.

"You two go out and play in the yard," she said to the boys. "Bashenka, you come with me. I've made lots of nice things and it would be a pity for you not to taste them. Here, have some marzipan. Or have you already eaten too many sweets at home?"

She laughed. Everyone knew I was fond of sweet things. I blushed as I nibbled at my marzipan, beginning to feel depressed.

Aunt Mira's place was so small that everybody had to sit squashed together between the walls and the windows, their heads nearly touching the ceiling. You could scarcely move. People dared only whisper to the person next to them.

Uncle Beril was the quietest of all. Although he was the youngest, he seemed much older than Uncle Chaim Leib, and older, too, than his wife. His hair was so white he looked as though his head were wrapped in a clean towel. His shy smile took refuge in his dark eyes. He had a long, reddish nose and a gentle mouth. Only his eyebrows bristled fiercely. He shrank from speech, probably because he thought everyone else was cleverer than he. So he just sat there like a bashful girl. If anyone asked him a question, his pale cheeks flushed. So there wasn't much conversation around the table. Only Aunt Mira bubbled away like a kettle.

"Alta, your tea's getting cold. Have some jam, Reb Shmuel Noah—you always like my jam. Altinka, taste these cookies— I'm really pleased with them this year. Bashenka, haven't you finished your marzipan? How about a piece of cake?"

"No thank you, Auntie, I don't want any more."

"Why not? Don't you feel well, God forbid? What's the matter?"

She spun me around like a top. Everyone was looking. I sat there quietly. Too quietly. Outside, my cousins were rushing about throwing nuts at one another.

"Mother, let's go home." I clung to her skirts in embarrassment.

"Whatever for?"

Then she looked at me thoughtfully. "Well, perhaps we ought . . ."

"What's the hurry, Altinka? It's not as if you had to open the shop."

"It's getting late. And by the time we're home . . ."

She stood up. The party began to scatter. But Uncle Beril chose that moment to wake up, and started to tell Father some long story.

I was already out in the yard.

"Why didn't you come out to play, silly?" shouted my cousins, pelting me with nutshells. "Couldn't you tear yourself away from the cakes?"

I felt as if they were throwing red-hot coals.

Summer in the Country

When my parents didn't go away themselves in the summer, they used to send me to stay with my Aunt Rachel in the country.

She was thin and delicate, and always rather sad. She didn't have much to be cheerful about.

Uncle Chaim Leib, on the other hand, with his fine, shaggy beard, was always full of life, and liked to laugh and joke. He used to be out all day; you hardly ever saw him at home.

As Father didn't take him very seriously, we children didn't treat him with much respect either. We weren't afraid of him: under those bushy eyebrows his little eyes twinkled merrily. He puffed contentedly away at the big cigar forever stuck between his yellow teeth. He was always ready to play with us or tell us a story, and he let us pull his beard and play with the ivory knob on his walking stick.

He and Aunt Rachel ran a branch of my parents' shop, on the other side of the river. Every morning he came to our place to collect some stock and turn over the previous day's receipts. My father didn't have much confidence in him, even though he was my mother's brother.

But Uncle Chaim Leib knew everything that went on in the town. He dropped in everywhere: in the morning at the synagogue; later on, in the streets or in the shops or in people's homes; in the evening at the rabbi's. And everywhere he'd stay for a while to listen, to tell a joke or a story, or just to sit and watch.

And so the hours flew by, and Uncle Chaim Leib didn't have time to put in an appearance at the shop, much less at home. He'd call in for a hasty lunch and a quick glass of tea, and that was all Aunt Rachel would see of him the whole day. The rest of the time she was alone.

She pottered about in the shop on her own. The watchmaker gave her a hand whenever there was more than one customer at a time. In her effort to persuade people to buy something, she repeated the same arguments over and over again, so that by the time a customer left, with or without a purchase, she was quite hoarse and her glasses had almost slipped off her perspiring nose. Then, exhausted, she would go and sit silently, guiltily, on her high stool behind the counter. Sometimes, when there were no customers at all, she'd leave the watchmaker and his loupe in charge and retire to her apartment. In those small rooms behind the shop, she would sit and indulge in a glass or two of sweet tea.

There was no question of her lying down for a little rest. So all year she was tired, and it was only in the summer, in the country, that she was able to take care of herself. Then my uncle had no choice but to look after the shop himself.

"If Aunt Rachel's decided to go to the country," my mother said to me, "she might as well take you with her."

So we set off for a long journey. Perhaps it wasn't such a very long way, but we were going by train. And we'd have to change from one line to another, and after that jolt the rest of the way in some sort of wagon.

The last part of the journey really did take a long time, because at every village we came to, the people wanted to

know who we were—especially the little girl in the white jacket.

I looked at them through the chinks in the side of the wagon. Their swarthy faces, shrouded in dark kerchiefs and shawls, looked anxious and worried. Yet they had time to stop in the marketplace and question my aunt and our driver. Aunt Rachel answered all their queries as if she'd always known them, and when we drove on again they looked relieved, as if they'd plumbed some great mystery. They smiled and wished us a good journey.

The wheels clattered over the planks laid over the potholes in the road. When the village women were no more than dots in the distance, I stretched out on some hay.

How deliciously comfortable! The road was sandy and soft. The young trees that lined it nodded to us as we bowled along. I could feel a cool breeze on my face. Dusk fell. When we finally arrived and the driver lifted me down, I was more asleep than awake.

In our little room two narrow white beds awaited us. But we spent most of the time on the veranda, protected by an awning from the sun and the rain.

My aunt cooked us delicious meals. A pot of roasted meat and potatoes would give off a sweet smell of onions, sweet as Aunt Rachel's own dreams.

While she had her nap after lunch, I used to run out into the fields, where the sun gilded the yellow slopes of wheat. I picked blue cornflowers and red poppies, collecting them in my red skirt and making it look redder than before. Then I laid them down in the grass and pulled off the petals to see what age I'd live to. Then I blew on them, and the lighter ones blew away.

I arranged jars of flowers all over the veranda and waited for my aunt to wake up so that we could go down to the river to swim.

We undressed on the bank, which was sandy and steep. I ran straight into the water, making waves. My aunt stayed quietly on the edge, splashing herself. She bent down and

straightened up again, her arms whirling like a windmill. But she'd soon had enough, and went back out of the water.

I lay down on the sand with my eyes half shut, looking up at the sky. Then I got up, ran down into the river, and started to swim. My aunt shouted and waved to me to come back—the tea would get cold; everyone else had gone home—but I stayed in the water until I was tired.

Meanwhile, in the distance, I could see my aunt had clambered up to the top of the bank. She called to me again to come out; the samovar was getting cold. I struck out for the shore, threw on my clothes, and ran across the sand and the grass to our veranda. Aunt Rachel had already had a glass or two of tea, and was waiting for me before she cut the cheese-cake smothered in sour cream.

Often I went out rowing with some cousins of mine, a cheerful lot of boys and girls staying not far off in the village. I rowed until I got blisters on my hands. The cousins used to call for me early in the morning, too, to go picking berries in the woods. The little fruits nestled coyly among the green leaves. I gathered them with both hands, and put them to my lips intending to kiss them. But somehow they went right into my mouth, and my basket remained empty. Not until the berries no longer left any taste in my blue-stained mouth did my blue-stained hands start to put them into my basket. I bent down like a little old woman, searching every inch of ground. When I straightened up again, I didn't know whether my cousins were somewhere nearby or whether I was all alone in the woods.

Every leaf trembled, the trees sighed, dry twigs snapped off and fell to the ground. A startled bird flapped to another branch. I could hear a nightingale in the distance; for a moment it was the only sound. I called to the others.

Was that them answering? Or was it a magpie?

I didn't know where I was, or whether I was going in a straight line or around in a circle. The sun shone through the branches, hanging them with sequins of light.

A big black beetle crossed my path. Where was he going? When I disturbed an anthill with my foot, I was more frightened than the ants. They rushed madly around in all directions. Some of them climbed onto my feet. I shook my dress, starting to feel hot and panic-stricken.

Then by chance I came to the road. We all joined up again and looked in one another's baskets to see who'd picked the most berries. Then we walked home singing.

One day after it had been raining, the boys came and asked me to go mushrooming. Everything was drenched. Wet leaves lay stuck to the ground; drops from the trees fell onto our hair and down our necks. I kept treading in pools of mud. I didn't like that—I thought I could see frogs looking up at me, and whenever I heard frogs croaking my stomach turned over.

But there were the mushrooms, just freshly sprouted.

As soon as I picked them, though, their heads drooped. They were slimy and made me feel sick. Some were moldy and covered with green moss. I couldn't understand how my aunt, with the aid of a bit of butter, could turn them into such a treat.

So, between playing and walking and eating, I didn't notice the summer going by. And when it was time to go home I was twice as fat as when I came.

It was quite different when my parents rented a country cottage of their own for the summer.

Two or three wagons full of furniture, bedding, and provisions went first. Our red cow trailed along behind at the end of a rope, which chafed her neck and made her moo to high heaven.

Sasha climbed up on top of the mattresses and perched beside the driver. My brothers and I followed a few days later by train.

The cottage was built of thick logs and smelled of resin, sweet and syrupy. The walls and floors shone.

My parents came out only for the Sabbath. My brothers couldn't bear to spend the whole week in the country. So I stayed there by myself—alone and free.

I ran about the woods like a little animal.

The tall pines were fragrant under the vault of the sky. The path stood out clearly in the sunlight filtering through the treetops. Sometimes I'd glimpse the eyes of a bird. Long shadows stretched from under my feet, fleeing before me as I went along.

I went deeper and deeper into the forest, losing myself among the trees. My shoes crunched on dry twigs, swelling the woodland chorus as if I were another bird pecking among the branches.

I looked for a flat place to lie down and stretched out with my head on my arms, gazing up at the dancing patterns of sunlight and listening to the sounds of the forest: whistling, chirping, groaning, sighing, and sometimes what was rather like a baby crying.

Then, not far off, I heard the clang of metal on wood. I sat up, and there were two tall woodcutters with long black hair and beards, and shoulders like tree trunks. Each one swung an axe and had a bottle sticking out of his pocket. Two pairs of green eyes stared at me as if I were the devil incarnate. I hid my own fright and walked away as if I hadn't seen them. But I listened with bated breath for signs of what was going on behind me. Without looking around, I could tell that they had relaxed. They spat on their hands and started chopping again.

I came to the bank of the quiet river. I'd have liked to let it take me in its arms and carry me away.

Suddenly it grew dark. Black clouds had gathered and obscured the blue of the sky. White flames shot out, forked blades flashing through the air. I bent like a sapling before the storm. It started to pour with rain. There was nowhere for me to shelter.

But I loved swimming in a thunderstorm. The bank was screened from the outside world by a thick curtain of foliage. The water was warm. The lightning flickered along the far shore. I was all alone with the young trees, shivering and laughing at the thunder and the rain.

The clothes I'd left on the bank were soaked. They clung to my body as I ran home.

It was Friday evening. All the fathers and mothers were sitting on their verandas drinking tea with jam. When they saw me run by in my sopping clothes, they banged their glasses down on the table in amazement.

Early in the morning I got quietly out bed, carefully opened the door of my room, and settled down on the long bench on the veranda, my chin on my knees. In the distance I could hear the voices of the maids, who'd just got up. I stayed there reading for an hour.

Our cottage was surrounded by others, and in all of them the children were there without their parents during the week. We all used to play croquet together.

After supper we'd gather on someone's veranda, younger and older children alike. We played games, crawled under the table, crowed like roosters. We'd have gone on chatting and laughing till all hours if some grownup hadn't always opened a window and shouted at us. Then we'd go and wander through the woods singing, though the trees looked sleepy to me too.

When we were tired of games, we went to watch the trains coming and going. The station consisted of a long bench with a wooden awning over it. We used to walk along the rails, putting one foot in front of the other like tightrope walkers.

Then we'd hear the whistle of the engine, and the train would puff its way nearer and nearer. The stationmaster would totter drowsily out of his little house opposite the station and try to pacify the engine with his green flag, as if it were a runaway bull. It wheezed and panted, then began to move off slowly, then faster and faster, until all that was left was a thin trail of smoke in the sky.

One Friday when everyone was already asleep, we were suddenly awakened by shouting and laughter. I stayed in bed and looked out through the slits in the shutters. It was my elder sister, who'd come down by boat from the city with some friends. She'd woken up Chaya the cook, and there, set out on the table on the veranda, was all the food that had been prepared for the next day. Laughing and yelling, my sister and her friends devoured the fish and the chicken, oblivious to all the people asleep in the neighboring cottages.

Our rebbe wasn't going to put up with this. He rushed out barefoot, in his long white nightshirt, his gray hair and beard streaming.

"Be off, you shameless wretches!" he bawled, waving his arms.

And although my sister and her grown-up companions were all militant socialists used to confronting the police, they were still scared of the rebbe and scattered like naughty children. We could hear them singing as they made their way down through the trees to the waiting boats.

As I watched through the shutters, I couldn't help feeling hurt. Why hadn't my sister come in to say hello to me?

The summer disappeared even faster than it had come. The days grew shorter. The evenings were cool and melancholy. Everyone was busy loading up the wagons for the return to the city.

I was the last person to leave. Once more I walked among the other cottages. The windows were shuttered. From the empty verandas I looked out at the trees. They stood there sadly, bored and listless. The grass was worn and dried up. I walked slowly along the sandy path to the station, where the snorting train would soon snatch me up and bear me back to the city.

Wedding Presents

"Good evening."

"Good evening. A good year!"

The shop was being invaded by an army of fathers-in-law, mothers-in-law, and near and distant relatives.

They'd come to choose presents for the engaged couple. They shoved at the big glass door as if they were afraid there wouldn't be room for them all, God forbid. As a matter of fact, the shop was a bit small for them. Once they were all in, they could hardly move. The light from the oil lamp got in their eyes and made them screw up their faces.

"What sort of a place is this, then? It's like visiting the gentry."

They pulled out big red handkerchiefs, wiped their glasses, and inspected their surroundings.

"Well," they seemed to be thinking, "we must show we know how to behave in such fine company."

The men smoothed their beards and sidelocks, and cleared their throats. The younger and more bold blew their noses.

Until they were actually at the counter, they weren't yet really in the shop.

"All this ticking! Enough to drive you crazy!"

The older ones put their hands over their ears and moved nearer the display cases to keep themselves in countenance.

"Father-in-law, where are you? You should be the first to choose a present, please God."

A thin old man with a straggly beard was elbowed forward, followed by the much more imposing mother-in-law.

"Stop shoving, can't you. Let the bride through."

"Don't be shy, Shimka. You're engaged, aren't you, thank God! Here, hold on to me."

The tiny bride clung to her mother as to a crutch.

The bridegroom, young and dark, was lost among the older men's beards.

As soon as our assistants saw the crowd, they made themselves scarce. It would take four or five hours to deal with this lot!

They called Mother: "A bridal party. Can you come?"

Mother loomed up from behind the safe, sat down on her high stool, and looked around calmly at the crowd. Her white lace collar set off the radiance of her face, and the general effect seemed to have a soothing influence on the excited family. Without saying a word, she drew them all around her.

"How are you, Alta?"

"Not too bad, thank God. Mustn't complain. But how is it with you?"

"If only we keep our health, God willing."

"Why, has someone been ill, God forbid?"

"Oh, no, heaven protect us! But the years go by, and we make them go faster. We don't get any younger, do we? And now I'm marrying Shimka, the last of my daughters. She's my youngest, good health to her!"

"And happiness and good fortune!"

Mother's gentle smile reassured the bride's mother. She was the one who ruled the roost. Her husband, a quiet man, was older than she was and let her do the talking. She was so excited the flowers pinned to her cap kept bobbing about. And she'd only just started.

"When you think, Alta! What does it all mean? What can we do? You struggle, and where does it get you? Soon we'll be old and all alone. And then what?"

She stopped, as if driven into a corner. Some of the relatives scowled. But she soon got her breath back and went on.

"My Shimka really was born under a lucky star, though. The house was always full of suitors. But we made the right choice with this one, thank God. It doesn't matter that he's so young—scarcely out of the nest. He's such a scholar! And from such good people—the best!"

The relatives wagged their beards in agreement.

"And our David has nothing to be ashamed of. We've given a lot of thought to the marriage contract, I and my husband, may he have good health."

Someone gave her a dig in the ribs.

"What's the matter? Don't interrupt. Let me finish. . . . Alta, have you heard of Rabbi Mendele? Well, that was the groom's great-grandfather! A truly pious Jew! A prophet! If only everybody were like him. May his soul watch over his great-grandson."

All eyes were raised to the ceiling, as if the dead worthy might appear there.

"Come on, mother-in-law, get to the point," someone ventured.

The bride's mother rounded on him. "Who asked you for your opinion? You're enough to give anyone a headache."

The interrupter collapsed. But others tried to put their oar in too.

Mother knew them all. They'd already married off a number of their children, and they'd always come to her for the wedding presents.

"What's that you're telling me? So-and-so's dead? But she always looked so pretty, so strong!"

Mother couldn't bring herself to believe that one of the family was no more.

"But you were buying presents for her only the other day. I can see her now. God protect us from such unhappiness."

An elderly aunt was almost in tears. "And the poor little orphans. So young still!"

"We musn't complain, Deborah. Ingratitude's a sin. And Shlomel earns a living, thank God."

She shook her head when Mother asked where the bridegroom came from.

"No, not from Vitebsk. But Vitebsk or not, Alta, I'm telling you . . ."

There was no stopping her. It was as if the precious bridegroom might vanish if she didn't go on talking about him.

"Well, we've been lucky," said another aunt, unable to contain herself.

"Let me finish what I'm saying. Why must you butt in?"

"Who? Me? You always pick on me. What have I said? I didn't say anything."

"Quiet! This isn't the place to quarrel."

Mother came to the aunt's rescue. "How's your elder sister? Still having trouble with her legs? If heaven wants to punish someone, there's nothing we can do."

Mother sighed. The whole family sighed.

But now the time for talking was over. The bride couldn't wait to see what present they'd choose for her. She was dumpy, and still no more than a girl. While the older women talked, she gazed down at the floor. If anyone looked at her, she blushed to the roots of her hair and tried to hide behind her mother.

As for her fiancé, she didn't dare look at him. This was practically the first time she'd seen him. He stood aloof, like a complete stranger.

But suddenly the crowd remembered what they were there for. What should they buy? What did they really want? For the bride, a watch and chain and a ring. So much for that! For the groom, a good solid pocket watch was appropriate.

It took them hours to make up their minds. The mother and father and all the aunts had to feel and listen to each watch, and weigh every chain in the palm of their hand. They were buying gold, after all!

The female cousins had to try on all the rings. One day, God willing, they would be brides too. It went to their heads. Everyone set up as an expert and wanted to give an opinion or express a preference.

But with each new parcel that was opened, they changed all their former ideas.

"Why are you so set on that particular watch?" cried one cousin, a spinster. "You must compare!" She forgot her enthusiasm for a previous candidate. She was determined to get her own way. "You can rely on me—I come from the big city. I've lived right in Vitebsk all my life and made a study of the jewelers' windows."

The older relatives were more interested in weight than in looks. "What matters is the amount of gold. The other family mustn't think we're stingy, God forbid."

Although they were exhausted by now, they couldn't tear their eyes away from the shining metal. They didn't get this chance every day of the week.

Mother, rather tired too now, sat on her high stool and smiled. What you had to go through before anyone shelled out a kopek. Still, you had to make a sale. Otherwise they'd go elsewhere, God forbid.

She began to get worried and asked for some other packages, which she opened with renewed energy. Suddenly she brightened. She held out a gleaming gold watch. Her eyes shone as if she'd won the lottery. She knew she'd got them. No one uttered a word, even the elderly cousin.

Mother tried to master the pounding of her heart. She looked around quickly and sensed that someone was going to raise an objection.

"So how is your brother?" she asked. "Is he making out?"

The great thing was not to lose her hold over them. She could see the bride was on her side: she trembled whenever she looked at the little watch in Mother's hand.

But the rest of the family wasn't won over so easily. The

critical moment was approaching. All eyes turned toward the engaged couple's parents. It was for them to say.

Suddenly a new voice was heard. The bridegroom's father.

"For heaven's sake, what difference does it make? Let's settle the thing now. If the bride likes it, we'll take it, and may she wear it in good health and happiness!"

He took a pinch of snuff and relapsed into silence.

His wife couldn't let this pass. "That's all very well," she said. "But how much does it cost?"

Then the bargaining began.

Mother threw herself into the battle. She called for the ledger in which was recorded, in code, the price of every article in the shop. The book was thick and heavy. Everyone tried to get a look as the pages were turned. But how could they make it out? How could they tell which of all the thousands of black signs represented the glittering gold watch?

"It's much more complicated than you'd think!"

They all watched Mother's finger running through the entries.

"Ah, here we are!" The number in the book corresponded to the number on the tag. And there was the price. The elderly relatives gazed at Mother in awe.

"Alta, you must have a brain like a rabbi's!"

But of course they had to fight back.

"Alta, you know we trust you as we'd trust the Almighty. May we get as much joy from our children as we've got from the things we've bought from you. But . . . you know . . . we're not made of money. . . . It would be a good deed if you'd bring the price down a bit. . . . What do you say?"

Mother, looking as if she'd been wrongfully accused of some crime, laid her hand on her heart as if to say, "Well, if you don't trust the ledger . . ."

What she did say was: "You know my prices are fair."

"Right!" came the answer. "Well, to the listed price we have to add eight percent for overhead and tax . . ."

Someone handed Mother an abacus of black and white beads. Mother's fingers flew over them as if they were the keyboard of a piano.

The family grew uneasy. "Won't those beads ever stop? It's our money they're doing away with!"

The calculation was finished. Nearly all the beads had had to be used.

Mother looked at the abacus and said gravely, "That's my last word. And believe me, it's a bargain. I wouldn't wish the profit I'll get out of it on my worst enemy."

The family knew Mother never cheated them. But how could they agree without haggling, even over practically nothing? People would laugh at them.

They crowded around my mother. They weren't smiling anymore. Good manners were forgotten. Suddenly they were all angry.

Mother's mouth went dry, her voice broke, she longed for a glass of tea. But she stood her ground and smiled at her adversaries with her last remaining strength.

The crowd started to whisper among themselves. This was always their last card. Some made as if to sidle toward the door. Mother felt faint. Three hours' effort for nothing.

Some of them hesitated, uncertain what to do. Haggling was unpleasant—but think of all the reproaches they'd have to face later on. They too began to move toward the door.

Mother's face went ashen. Her smile was strained. In her mind's eye she could see them gone for good.

"All right! I give in—God help me!"

The crowd all came to life again, beaming. Back they surged to the counter, the bride's mother smiling triumphantly. She could teach them all how to save a kopek or two!

The shop was filled with light and merriment again. Once the presents were bought, it was as if part of the wedding were over. The blushing bride gazed at her gifts, laid out in a case lined with red velvet.

The bridegroom, still far away, was looking absently at some showcases of cutlery.

"Do you know how to wind a watch?" asked Mother, trying to bring him down to earth.

She looped the string of the parcel over the bride's finger.

"Wear it in good health!"

The girl was as overcome as if it had been her wedding ring.

"Thank you," her mother answered for her.

"May we meet again next year on an equally happy occasion."

"Amen!" said the old father, stroking his beard.

The bride's mother looked at the clocks on the wall.

"Good gracious, it's late! Time to be getting along. Good evening, Alta."

"A good year! Good health! And may your children bring you joy."

One head after another nodded amen. Everyone went toward the door.

"All right, you go first! After all, you're a year older than I am!"

"So who counts? Until a hundred and twenty we've both got plenty of time, please God!"

They left the shop happier than they came, pleased at having driven a good bargain. The girls played about and giggled as they went through the door.

"Phew! Let me out of here," cried Mother, clutching her head. She hurried back into the house for a rest.

I brought her a glass of sweet tea.

Aaron's Wedding

The only one of my brothers who used to make toys for me was Aaron.

He had a sensitive, serene, even sleepy face, as if he had some inner dream which might be destroyed if he awoke. His long, slender fingers were always in motion. He could knead all sorts of animals and birds out of bread, and turn silver paper into little bottles and cups and glasses. He coaxed tunes out of a comb wrapped in tissue paper.

One Friday evening Aaron told Mother he was engaged. There was an uproar. Even Mother was taken aback.

Busy all day in the shop, she didn't have time to remember that in the house her children were growing up, turning into adults. It didn't occur to her that they might have separate lives of their own. Her whole life was in the shop, and she assumed it must be the same for her sons and daughters.

Aaron was the only son who'd stayed at home to work in the shop. He was capable of standing in for Father, and he also went traveling to buy new stock. But Father still treated him like a little boy. When Aaron came home tired after a long journey in search of the best new items of jewelry, Father would greet him only with reproaches.

"A fat lot of use you are! What did you have to go to Moscow for? A new hat?"

But on the Friday evening when Aaron announced that he was going to get married, everything changed.

Father realized this was no longer a child, to be scolded and told what to do. He meant what he said.

Father sat and thought for a while, and then began to ask questions.

"So who is she? What sort of family does she come from?"

When he heard that she came from Dvinsk and that her parents had a small business selling silverware, he wasn't too pleased. He saw all the other shops, however small, as competition.

Nor did he know anything about the origins of the bride's family. They didn't belong, as his own family did, to the Lubavitch Hasidim. It was only after the rabbi of Bobruysk had given his consent to the marriage that preparations were allowed to go ahead.

The ceremony was to take place at the home of the bride's parents. We set about ordering new clothes.

Mother always dressed very well. For Aaron's wedding she planned a new dress for herself and another one for me. We went to the best dressmaker in town—a Polish lady, a general's widow. It took weeks for our dresses to be finished.

In the dressmaker's triple mirror Mother looked a picture. Her dress was a splendid affair of wine-colored taffeta that rustled like a zephyr every time she breathed. Both the bodice and the skirt were trimmed with old-gold lace. The skirt was so long and full you couldn't see Mother's shoes. There was a narrow train at the back, which Mother could manage by means of a mauve velvet ribbon attached to her wrist. In her hand she held a handkerchief of silver lace.

Although our safes and showcases were overflowing with gold and jewels, only two little diamonds shone in Mother's ears. A small diamond brooch in the shape of a twig rose and fell on her bosom.

My own new dress was buttercup yellow. It left my arms and neck bare, but as my skin tones blended with the hues of the material, this didn't appear too improper. At the waist there was a broad silk sash, the color of the setting sun. The skirt fell in soft folds almost to the floor, but showed my black patent-leather shoes and even an inch or two of light stocking. I wore my hair loose to the shoulders, held in place by a wide band of the same silk as my dress.

When our wedding outfits were delivered, the big wicker hamper was already packed and waiting. The dresses were laid carefully on top of the layers of dark suits belonging to my father and brothers, including Aaron.

This was my first long journey.

On the day of the wedding I went, wearing my new dress, to have a look at the bride before she made her ceremonial appearance.

She was a strapping, healthy young woman whose silk dress fitted tight over her ample bosom. She had one brown eye and one light gray. Father considered this a serious defect.

When I entered the room where she was being dressed, I was surprised that she didn't seem to mind standing there in front of everyone in her underclothes. I watched her attendants help her on with the white wedding gown. When they pinned the airy, transparent veil onto her hair, she looked even plumper than before.

Then I went and stood with all the rest near the bride's chair, waiting for her to appear. When would she come? The girls all held lighted candles to illuminate her path.

When she had taken her place on her throne, surrounded by her sisters and other relations, I looked toward the other door. Through it, slowly and unobtrusively, came my brother Aaron, escorted by Father, the bride's father, and a group of about ten other men.

I didn't look at the bride any more after that. I was too shocked by my brother's face. His naturally pale countenance was quite ashen, and after a few steps he stood stock-still. The bride's head fell heavily against the back of her throne. She'd fainted. Her attendants tried to revive her. My heart stood still.

Fortunately, she came around.

Later, under the canopy, Aaron lifted her veil with trembling hands.

"Good luck! Good luck! In a blessed hour!" everyone shouted.

I ran over to Father, threw my arms around him, and mingled my tears with his. Everyone wept.

"God knows what he's in for when the bride faints *before* the ceremony," muttered Father.

As if nothing had happened, the bride's family, with one accord, started to smile and greet the guests. The musicians struck up the first dance.

The Train

I'd always thought our town was at the extreme limit of the world. At the railway station, all the trains that came in at one platform were coming to Vitebsk, and all the trains that went out at the other platform were leaving from Vitebsk. It was the same with the river traffic on the Dvina. Even the sun appeared at one side of our horizon and disappeared over the other.

But was Vitebsk at the beginning or the end of the world?

The station always worried me. Which destination would the train leave for today?

The waiting room was full of agitation too. All the people there were waiting anxiously for their train. But they might hear the warning bell ring three times and still have to watch the train disappear without them: their destination had not been announced. So they'd start waiting all over again, as if for the Messiah.

When a window rattled and there was a flicker of flame outside, accompanied by a smell and a wisp of smoke, the whole room started up. But it was only a solitary locomotive sauntering aimlessly by, as if it were just practicing.

"For pity's sake, go and see what train that is," said one old woman to her husband.

"What train?" He gave his suitcase a kick. "It's no use asking me about it."

"Let's get out of here. Why do they keep us shut in like this?"

"Ssh! We won't hear the bell."

As they sat crushed uncomfortably together, everyone strained to hear through the din. Bundles and parcels, even the air, were jolted around almost as much as if they were already on the train.

The stationmaster was tall and portly, as was fitting in a town where the world began. The waiting room too had a high ceiling and tall, broad windows with curtains right down to the floor. One section of it was a resplendent restaurant; the tables were covered with white cloths and shining glass and cutlery as bright as the mirrors on the walls. But all the brightness was swallowed up in the passengers' dingy clothes.

The room was so crowded I was afraid the whole population of Vitebsk was leaving, bag and baggage. What would it be like, a city without people? Perhaps the houses too had been packed up and sent off somewhere.

"A trip like this is no joke," grumbled a fat woman, perspiring under numerous layers of clothing and surrounded by luggage. She had to speak or burst. "What if I were to be taken ill on the way?"

Her whole family had come to see her off. They stared at her guiltily, not knowing what to say. She was on the watch for every movement. Her eyes filled with tears.

"And what am I going to do about eating and sleeping? Sometimes people get off the train with their faces all swollen up from the draft."

They went on staring at her. She patted her cheek, then tucked a wisp of hair back under her kerchief. Her head was in a whirl. She'd lived so long with her husband, and all the time in the same place, and now suddenly the wheel of fate had turned. First death had carried off her husband, and now she too had to go away.

"Leave my luggage alone, you children, you'll break something." She turned to her eldest son. "Have I forgotten anything, Mottel? . . . Oh, where's my handbag? . . . I knew I'd lose something!"

She cracked her knuckles nervously, as if they were responsible.

"Don't stand there staring at me, children—look for it! Stations are always teeming with pickpockets. Look at the lout over there. He pretends he's a porter, thinks he can fool people with his red cap. But you can see by the look on his face that he's a thief!"

"But, Auntie, there's your bag, under the seat."

She pinched her niece's cheek. "Bless you, my dear. See what a clever girl she is?"

Everyone now stared at the little girl.

"But how can anyone keep track of all these bundles? And I don't like even to say it, but I've heard there are some thieves who'll actually cut your purse out of your pocket!"

An older man interrupted impatiently.

"Stop imaging things, Sheyne Gitel, for goodness' sake! Thousands of people travel every day, and with God's help they all get there and back safely."

But Sheyne Gitel was still like a cat on hot bricks. What did an elderly uncle know about trains? All he knew was the way to the synagogue and back. She took no notice of him.

Someone sneezed. She gave a start.

"Oh, the whistle! Go out and see if it's here! It could arrive at any moment, and I'll need time to check my bundles . . ."

Suddenly the stationmaster appeared in the doorway. His coat came down to his ankles, like a big red flag. Silver buttons shone on his chest. He coughed, and everyone jumped to attention. He lifted one hand and seemed to grow even taller. He was holding a little brass bell. Even before he rang it, the crowd surged forward.

"First call! Smolensk, Bryansk, and Orel! First call!"

He shouted and swung the bell so that it and his voice reached every corner of the waiting room. Anyone who was asleep was rudely awakened.

"Where? Where to?"

"You heard him, didn't you?"

"It wouldn't hurt him to repeat it. You can't expect people to catch everything the first time."

"Don't argue, just get your ticket out and count your bundles."

"Where are you rushing off to, you idiot? Here, carry the child, or they'll be asking us for another ticket."

"Don't just stand there! Hurry up and get us a seat."

Everyone pushed toward the door.

"Stop!" The stationmaster stood there like a wall. "Tickets, please. Show your tickets."

He started to let people through at random.

"Hey, where do you think you're going? Your ticket says Dvinsk. This train goes to Smolensk." He barred the way, and punched tickets as if he were piercing hearts.

"Second call! Smolensk, Bryansk, and Orel! Second call!"

He drew the words out. Now there was no one left sitting down. The waiters were rushing around among the tables, cursing.

"What a nerve, sitting down and expecting a whole meal with the train just waiting to go."

"Third call!"

I didn't know which faces to concentrate on. Suddenly all of these people seemed near and dear to me. And they were going away and leaving me all alone. Would they ever come back? What would happen to the town?

The engine roared, breathed out flames, and swallowed up carriage after carriage of passengers.

Through the window of a first-class compartment shone the cold stare of a successful gentleman. Traveling didn't bother him. But perhaps he didn't much care for traveling alone. You could see the unoccupied seats, with their plush upholstery and their lace antimacassars waiting for a head to rest on them.

Framed in another window, like a painting, was an elegant young woman. She smiled at me. Or was she only smiling at herself? Perhaps she was using the glass as a mirror.

Both the gentleman and the lady posed there as coolly as

china dolls. But in third class the people were all crushed together.

The train gave a groan. The passengers began to tremble. Those who were staying behind jumped off hastily.

"Sit down or you'll lose your seat!"

"Have a good trip!"

"Here, take this seat by the window. But mind you don't catch cold. Turn your collar up."

The shouts pierced through windows and doors, and hung in the air with the fluttering white handkerchiefs.

The train was taking leave of our city in a cloud of smoke. Sparks flew, flames spurted. The engine wheezed, set its wheels in motion, started to pull the carriages one after the other along behind it. The stoker's naked back gleamed as if he were roasting in hell.

I felt as if I were going home from a funeral.

The train was on its way, and I was going back to the town as to a deserted house. Would the trees still be there? Yes, they spread out like uplifted hands.

Everything is silent, I thought. Is Vitebsk still there?

Afterword

Bella wanted to work in the theater, and did work in the theater successfully. Then I came back from Paris and married her. We left for France, and that was the end of her dreams of the stage.

For years her love influenced my painting. Yet I felt there was something within her held back, unexpressed; that she had treasures buried away in her heart, like her "String of Pearls" misted over with love. Her lips had the scent of the first kiss, a kiss like a thirst for justice.

Why was she so reserved with friends, with me? Why that need to stay in the background?

Then came the day when she relived the exile of recent years; the time when the Jewish soul echoed in her once more and her tongue became the tongue of her parents again.

Her style in *Burning Lights* and *First Encounter* was the style of a Jewish bride in Jewish literature.

She wrote as she lived, as she loved, as she greeted her friends. Her words and phrases were a wash of color over a canvas.

To whom compare her? She was like no other. She was the Bashenka–Belloshka of Vitebsk on the hill, mirrored in the Dvina with its clouds and trees and houses.

Things, people, landscapes, Jewish holidays, flowers—that was her world, they were her subject.

Her sentences, long or short, written out or sketched, were now developed fully, now left indistinct like marks or lines in a drawing which must be divined rather than seen.

Toward the end I would often find her sitting up in bed late into the night, reading books in Yiddish by the light of a little lamp.

"So late! You should be asleep!"

I can see her now, a few weeks before her eternal sleep, fresh and beautiful as always, in our bedroom in the country. She was arranging her manuscripts—finished works, drafts, copies.

I tried to hide my fear.

"Why this sudden tidiness?"

She answered with a wan smile, "So you'll know where everything is . . ."

All calm and deep presentiment.

I can see her again from our hotel window, sitting by the lake before going into the water. Waiting for me. Her whole being was waiting, listening to something, just as she had listened to the forest when she was a little girl.

I can still see her back and her delicate profile. She does not move. She waits, and thinks, and perhaps already sees other worlds.

Will the busy men and women of today be able to enter into her work and her world?

Perhaps, later on, others will come who can scent the perfume of her flowers and of her art.

Her last words were: "My notebooks . . ."

The thunder rolled, the clouds opened at six o'clock on the evening of September 2, 1944, when Bella left this world.

Everything went dark.

MARC CHAGALL
New York, 1947

Glossary

Afikoman Popularly, a piece of matzah "stolen" by children during the Passover celebration and "redeemed" by the leader of the Seder.

Ark of the Covenant; Ark of the Torah A shrine in the synagogue which contains the scrolls of the Torah.

Bar mitzvah A boy's celebration of his thirteenth birthday, on which he becomes a "son of the commandment."

Day of Atonement see *Yom Kippur.*

Days of Awe see *Ten Penitential Days.*

Etrog A special citron; see *Lulav.*

Feast of Esther see *Megillah.*

Feast of Tabernacles see *Sukkah.*

Five Books of Moses see *Scrolls of the Law.*

Haggadah Story of the exodus from Egypt, read at the Seder.

Hallah White bread, eaten on the Sabbath and holy days.

Hametz Leavened bread, distinguished from matzah; see *Matzah.*

Hanukkah Eight-day feast commemorating the dedication of the Temple after the victory of the Maccabees in the second century B.C.E.

Hasidism Pietist Jewish sect, founded in the eighteenth century in Eastern Europe. Followers are called Hasidim.

Havdalah Ceremony at the conclusion of the Sabbath (or a holy day).

Kiddush Sanctification ceremony at the inception of the Sabbath and the holy days.

Kosher Fit for consumption according to the ritual laws.

Latke Potato pancake, of East European origin, eaten mainly on Hanukkah.

Lulav   Palm branch, part of a festival arrangement of plants, used during the service at Sukkot.

Matzah   Unleavened bread eaten at Passover.

Megillah   Scroll telling the story of Esther and Mordecai, read in the synagogue at Purim, the Feast of Esther.

Messiah   Anointed redeemer expected to bring about the divine kingdom of peace and justice.

Mezuzah   Doorpost to which a parchment biblical text is affixed.

Passover   Eight-day feast celebrating the exodus of Israel from Egypt.

Phylacteries   Leather capsules containing biblical texts, affixed to the forehead and the left arm during weekday prayers.

Prayer of Benedictions   Central prayer, consisting of a varied number of "benedictions." On weekdays the number is 18, actually 19.

Purim   The Feast of Esther; see *Megillah*.

Reb, Rebbe   Rabbi, teacher.

Rejoicing of the Torah   see *Simhat Torah*.

Rosh ha-Shanah   New Year's day; a solemn celebration; see also *Shofar*.

Scrolls of the Law   Parchment handwritten scrolls, containing the Five Books of Moses, the first five books of the Bible.

Seder   Evening ceremony on Passover, celebrating the exodus of Israel from Egypt.

Shofar   Ram's horn blown in the synagogue at Rosh ha-Shanah.

Simhat Torah   Yearly festival, celebrating the conclusion of the public reading of the Torah.

Sukkah   Eight-day festival commemorating the dwelling of the Israelites in huts (sukkot) in the desert.

Talmud   Record of the mostly legal and ritual discussions of the sages in the talmudic academies (third to fifth centuries).

Tashlich   A symbolic throwing of the sins into a river on Rosh ha-Shanah.

Ten Penitential Days   Period of special prayers between Rosh ha-Shanah and Yom Kippur.

Tisha be-Av   The ninth of the Hebrew month Av, commemorating the destruction of the Temple in Jerusalem.

Torah   Book of the Law; the Bible, especially the Five Books of Moses.

Yom Kippur   The Day of Atonement—a day of solemn prayer, confession of sins, fasting, and forgiveness—brings to a close the Ten Penitential Days.